HINDUISM
PAST AND PRESENT

HINDUISM
PAST AND PRESENT

WITH AN ACCOUNT OF

RECENT HINDU REFORMERS AND A BRIEF COMPARISON BETWEEN HINDUISM AND CHRISTIANITY

J. MURRAY MITCHELL

GYAN

Published by

GYAN

Gyan Publishing House
5, Ansari Road
Daryaganj, New Delhi-110002
Phone: 011-47034999, 9811692060
E-mail: books@gyanbooks.com

Distribution Network
gyanbooks.com
India, USA, Canada, UK, Australia, France

ISBN : 978-81-212-3483-2 (PB)
First Published, London, 1885

2nd Impression 2020

Printed at: Gyan Press, Delhi.

Hinduism Past and Present
Author: J. Murray Mitchell

HINDUISM PAST AND PRESENT

WITH AN ACCOUNT OF

RECENT HINDU REFORMERS AND A BRIEF COMPARISON BETWEEN HINDUISM AND CHRISTIANITY

BY

J. MURRAY MITCHELL, M.A., LL.D.

London

THE RELIGIOUS TRACT SOCIETY

56, PATERNOSTER ROW; 65, ST. PAUL'S CHURCHYARD; AND 164, PICCADILLY

1885

INTRODUCTORY NOTE.

THE title of this little work is 'Hinduism Past and Present.' Hinduism is so exceedingly vast and complex that a full discussion of the subject would require a large volume, or rather many volumes.

My desire has been to produce, if possible, a book which should be sufficiently correct to satisfy the Orientalist, and yet short and simple enough to attract the ordinary reader.

The main difficulty has been in the compression into a small space of superabundant materials. It would have been easier to present a larger work; but brevity was imperative. Still, leading facts and principles have been dwelt upon, I trust, at sufficient length to enable the reader to consult with intelligence the Indian writings contained in such a collection as the *Sacred Books of the East*. At all events, the work will form a sufficient introduction to the writings on Indian religion of such

Continental scholars as Lassen, Roth, Weber, Haug, Barth, and others—H. H. Wilson, Max Müller, Monier Williams, Muir, Cowell, etc., in this country—and Professor Whitney in America. Among investigations carried on in India, those of Colebrooke stand pre-eminent. A Marāthī work, *Hindu dharmatsen swarup*, by the Rev. Baba Padmanji, contains much valuable information on Hinduism.

Indian names often repel readers by their multiplied diacritical marks. With some hesitation it has been resolved to omit the whole of these in the body of the work; but they are given in the Index, with an explanation of their meaning. If the reader is at a loss as to the proper pronunciation of any name, the Index will be a sufficient guide.

CONTENTS.

CHAP.		PAGE
	INTRODUCTION	9
I.	THE VEDAS AND VEDIC PERIOD . . .	16
II.	THE VEDIC RITUAL	35
III.	SECTION I.—THE UPANISHADS. RISE OF PHILOSOPHY	44
	SECTION II.—THE SIX DARSANAS. METHODIZED PHILOSOPHY	55
IV.	DEVELOPMENT OF BRAHMANISM. SOCIAL LIFE. CASTE	84
V.	STRUGGLE BETWEEN BRAHMANISM AND BUDDHISM	97
VI.	RECONSTRUCTION OF HINDUISM. THE AVATARAS	106
VII.	THE EPIC POEMS	123
VIII.	THE PURANAS	132
IX.	THE TANTRAS. THE SAKTI WORSHIP . .	141

CHAP.		PAGE
X.	THE HINDU SECTS	147
XI.	MODERN HINDUISM	174
XII.	RECAPITULATION	210
XIII.	RECENT HINDU REFORMERS	222
XIV.	SUMMARY AND CONCLUSION	247
XV.	HINDUISM COMPARED WITH CHRISTIANITY	254

NOTES—

HYMNS OF THE VEDA	280
THE GAYATRI	282
THE ATHARVA VEDA	282
THE UPANISHADS	283
THE CODES OF LAW	284
VIRODHA BHAKTI	284
MODERN BRAHMANICAL WORSHIP	285
THE BRAHMO SOMAJ	287

INDEX 288

INTRODUCTION.

I.

VERY earnest efforts are made in the present day to investigate the early history of nations; and these have been attended with no inconsiderable success. No part of a nation's history is more important than that of its religion; and much valuable light has been thrown of late on many systems of faith, both of ancient and modern days.

Of the religions of antiquity, several that were once flourishing and influential have become entirely extinct. Thus, the faiths of Greece, Italy, and Egypt, so celebrated in ancient days, have completely passed away. So have the religions of the Celtic, Teutonic, and Slavonic races, as well as those of Syria and Asia Minor. But, in the Farther East, we come on systems of belief which, for reasons which it would be well to inquire into, have been possessed of much more stability, and which are to be ranked among both ancient and modern creeds. The most remarkable of these are

Hinduism and Buddhism. Both of these systems deserve the careful study of educated men.

In this little work we are to be occupied with the consideration of Hinduism—the more ancient of the two.

In this remarkable system we see the oldest surviving form of the faith that was once common to all the branches of the great Aryan, or Indo-European, family, to which we ourselves belong. The Vedas of India exhibit that faith in a form which is decidedly more ancient than that presented in the Homeric poems; and many points in classical mythology which would otherwise have remained obscure, receive elucidation from the contents of the Hindu books. Just as a critical acquaintance with Greek and Latin etymology cannot be obtained without a knowledge of Sanskrit, so we may assert that the religions of Greece and Italy cannot be satisfactorily studied without frequent reference to the faith of ancient India.

For these reasons, then, as well as on account of its great antiquity and long-continued existence, Hinduism presents a most interesting subject of investigation. Nor is the interest lessened by the circumstance that the influx of Christian, and Western ideas generally, is telling at the present moment with great power on the faith of India, and threatening not merely to modify, but to destroy it. It has clung tenaciously to life for more than three thousand years; but the end seems now approaching. A stupendous revolution is going on in India which has many striking points of resemblance to the change which took place over the Roman Empire when the ancient Paganism was slowly expiring.

One word as to the spirit in which the study of Hinduism should be carried on. We trust that neither our readers nor we can enter on it with our feelings as little moved as if we were preparing to examine merely some philosophical or scientific problem. For we are about to deal with *religion*—with a subject bearing directly on the honour of God and the welfare of human beings. Hinduism is, at this moment, the creed of a hundred and ninety millions of our brethren. What, during its protracted reign of more than three thousand years, has it told them of God and man, and sin and salvation, and heaven and hell? How far has it proved a faithful guide amidst the perplexities of life? What comfort has it supplied to the sorrowful? We have to think of human hearts with all their trembling sensibilities—not of abstract principles and passionless laws. And if, as our inquiry proceeds, we should find that Hinduism has often spoken erringly and ill on matters pertaining to the Divine glory and human weal, how should it affect us? The Roman poet could boast of the pleasure of being able, from the 'serene temples reared by the teaching of sages,'[1] to look down on the crowds of men wandering far and wide in the vain quest of truth and joy. Very different from

[1] 'Edita doctrina sapientum templa serena.'—*Lucretius.*

such cynical scorn will be the feeling of him who truly loves his kind. His emotion will resemble that which filled the breast of Him 'whose name is above every name,' when 'He beheld the multitudes, and was moved with compassion towards them, because they fainted, and were scattered abroad, as sheep having no shepherd.'

We must further explain that we by no means desire to deal with our subject as if there were a lawsuit between Hinduism and Christianity, in which we held a brief for the latter and intended to press to its farthest consequences every point that is adverse to the opposing party. On the contrary, we feel ourselves in duty bound to do the utmost justice to Hinduism, and to point out its merits as faithfully as its demerits. Time was when non-Christian systems of religion were regarded by Christian writers as simply masses of unrelieved falsehood; but such was not the belief either of the Apostles or the early Christian authors. The declaration of St. Paul is that 'God has never left Himself without witness,' and that 'the Gentiles, which have not the Law, are a law unto themselves.' Conscience is not wholly extinguished in the human breast; it speaks, indeed, often in feeble and faltering accents; but we shall welcome even its faintest whispers when it testifies on behalf of God and goodness.

We shall begin at the beginning, and try to study Hinduism chronologically. It is very true that every winding of the great stream has not yet been explored; nor can we fix the precise point where it was joined by such or such a tributary: still, we are tolerably well acquainted both with its fountains and with the course which it has hitherto pursued.

II.

When a Hindu is asked what his religion is, he at once replies that it is contained in the Sastras, or sacred writings;—he does not speak of unwritten tradition as authoritative.[1] What, then, are the accredited sacred writings? The Hindu will generally reply that they are 'the four Vedas, the six Darsanas or philosophical systems, and the eighteen Puranas.' This sacred literature is exceedingly voluminous. The Vedas contain at least thirty thousand long verses. The philosophical writings, with their commentaries, are also very extensive. The Puranas comprise probably a million and a half of lines, without including supplementary treatises, called Upa-Puranas. It follows that very few Hindus are well acquainted with their own Sastras. Even the most learned Brahman can hardly have read more than a fiftieth part of them.

The Hindus make a distinction between direct and indirect revelation. Certain portions of their

[1] The number of Sanskrit works, as brought to light by the investigations of the Government of India, is not less than ten thousand. Rajendra Lal Mitra holds that the entire number of Sanskrit books (Hindu, Buddhist, and Jaina) is not under twenty thousand. The writers he estimates at four thousand.

literature are classed under the head of *Sruti*-literally, 'that which has been heard.' An eternal, Divine voice is supposed to have uttered these portions; and the favoured few who heard them treasured them up and repeated them for the good of others. They are also said to have been 'seen' by holy men.[1] These writings constitute a direct revelation, and are fully authoritative. Other books are classified under the head of *Smriti*—literally, 'that which is remembered.' No eternal existence is claimed for these; their authority is derived from their being a faithful representation of the sense of the *Sruti*.

There is some resemblance between the distinction thus drawn between the two classes of authoritative books, and that which Roman Catholics have stated as existing between the Bible and the Fathers.

In addition to the two kinds of works now mentioned, the Sanskrit language contains multitudes of writings for which inspiration is not claimed; for example, the extensive dramatic literature. Some important works—particularly the great heroic poems, the Ramayana and the Mahabharata—occupy a sort of middle ground between the fully inspired and uninspired.

Again, there is an important class of writings, of comparatively late origin, known by the name of Tantras. Some writers have claimed an authority for these equal to that of the Puranas.

[1] 'The words of Amos . . . which he saw' (Amos i. 1).

In some cases the philosophical writings have been excluded from the list of inspired books.

It will thus be perceived that there is much uncertainty as to the extent of the Hindu Canon. No Council has ever been called to consider the subject; and the conception of a Church or Pope—one infallible authority in matters of faith—is foreign to the Hindu mind.

The Sruti comprises the books known under the name of the Veda, or Vedas. These are universally admitted to be fully authoritative.

CHAPTER I.

THE VEDAS AND VEDIC PERIOD.

THE term 'Veda' means *knowledge*.[1] Generally four Vedas are mentioned; but sometimes they are spoken of as if they constituted one book. They are written in an ancient form of Sanskrit, as the Avesta is in a cognate language usually termed Zend. Originally a Veda was understood to consist only of two parts; but, at a later period, a third was added. The first is called Sanhita, or Mantra, and consists of praises and prayers composed in verse. The second part, the Brahmana, is chiefly in prose; it explains how the Mantras are to be used, the origin and meaning of the rites, and the proper mode of performing them. The Brahmanas are thus commentaries on the hymns. The third part of the Veda is contained in the Aranyakas, or 'forest treatises'—so called because they were studied by ascetics in the forests.

[1] From the root *vid*, 'to know' or 'see'; which is etymologically the same as εἴδω and *video*.

The parts of these which discuss philosophical and religious questions regarding God, the soul, the destiny of man, etc., are termed Upanishads. These are written chiefly in prose, partly in verse. It is important to note that the three parts of a Veda are not only very diverse in character, but for the most part different in age. As a rule, the Upanishads are the latest, and much more recent than the Hymns. They are not parts of the Veda proper, but appended disquisitions, which, however, are now deemed the most holy portion of the Veda; and on this account they should not be kept in a dwelling-house, but in the temple. All this implies a sad confounding of things that differ; and it could have been assented to only when the sense of the most ancient part of the Veda had been in a great degree forgotten.

When we speak of the Veda and the Vedic religion, we must exclude the Upanishads from consideration. We must also distinguish between the Hymns and the Ritualistic writings, or Brahmanas. The Brahmanas of each Veda are later than the Hymns of the same Veda; and they generally contain a somewhat different theology. When we use the term Veda, then, we shall include only the Hymns. The four divisions of the Veda are called respectively the Rich, or Rig V.; the Saman, or Sama V.; the Yajush, or Yajur V.; and the Atharvana, or Atharva V. We need not pay much attention to the second and third. The Sama V. contains only verses extracted from the Rig V., and arranged for the use of certain priests[1] at the chief sacrifices. The Yajur V. appears in two forms, called the Black and the White (or Taittiriya and Vajasaneyi). It is properly a liturgical work in prose, with hymns, or extracts from hymns, interspersed. It also borrows very largely from the Rig V., and contains texts arranged for another class of priests.[2] The Atharvana comes next to the Rig V. in importance, from which about a sixth part of it is taken.

The Rig V. means the *Veda of praise.* It contains 11,000 verses and 1017 complete hymns—or, according to another recension, 1028. We must speak with great caution as to the time when these hymns were composed, and with still more caution as to the date when they were collected and committed to writing.[3] The oldest hymns may take us as far back as the year 2000 or 1800 B.C.—say, about the age of Abraham.

There is no small diversity of character among the hymns. Some of them are tolerably simple; and these may be regarded as the spontaneous utterance of religious sentiment; but there is a larger number that are involved, laboured, and unnatural.[4] We cannot assert that even the oldest are all simple

[1] The Udgatris. [2] The Adhvaryus.

[3] The art of writing does not seem to have come into use long before the Greek invasion of India in the fourth century B.C. The collection of the hymns may have been from about 1000 B.C.

[4] 'Whole hymns must remain to us a dead letter,' says Max Müller. Why? The conviction is growing among scholars that many of them are intentionally obscure.

and childlike. From the first we see the sacerdotal stamp deeply impressed on these compositions. The Rig Veda itself must have been mainly written, and wholly arranged, by priests; and both the selection and arrangement must have been made with a view to liturgical purposes. Even in the days when the first hymns were composed, religion had begun to petrify; forms and rites were coming to be deemed more important than thoughts, feelings, or deeds. The early period of Hinduism thus reveals a tendency—which is only too clearly exhibited throughout the history of religion—to substitute the external for the internal.

It is probable that the Indian branch of the great Aryan race came into India about two thousand years B.C. They were civilized to a very considerable degree. They depended for subsistence chiefly, but by no means solely, on their herds and flocks. The hymns speak of powerful kings and their great wealth. Commerce and many of the arts of civilized life were well known. They had even made some progress in astronomy. Cities, or at least towns, must have been pretty numerous. They had probably come into India in several successive bands. They were confined for a time to 'the country of the seven rivers,' as they called it[1]—or, as we now name it, the Panjâb (five rivers). They did not find the land unoccupied. They had been preceded by the great

[1] So called when the Indus and Sarasvati are included along with the five rivers of the Panjâb.

Dravidian race—which was of Turanian, not Aryan, origin, and which is now nearly confined to India south of the Krishna river. Other races, now generally termed Kolarian—which are likewise probably of Turanian extraction—may also have entered India about the same time as the Aryas. The Kolarian tribes were doubtless then, as they remain to this day, scarcely civilized; but certainly the Dravidian races were so to a very considerable degree. The intrusive Aryas met with opposition, as they pushed on from the North-west of India: and although in the nature of things there must occasionally have been friendly intercourse between the two great races, yet hostility evidently was the rule, and at times it must have been intensely bitter. The language in which the Vedic poets speak of these enemies is uniformly that of unmingled, vehement hatred. They are also reviled as 'noseless,' 'speechless,' 'godless;' because, forsooth, their nasal organ was less prominent than that of their rivals, their speech was not allied to Sanskrit, and their deities were different from the gods and goddesses of the Aryas. That, morally, the one race at all surpassed the other, does not appear. The earlier occupants of the soil gradually retreated before their gifted, energetic enemies; we may say they did so as the Britons slowly gave way before the Saxons and kindred tribes who came swarming over the German Ocean. What deeds of valour they may have performed, and what sufferings they may have endured, it is impossible for us to say; but, at all events, the invader was proud and pitiless; and his desire was the extermination of all that opposed him. His prayers to the gods in regard to his enemies were the most tremendous of imprecations. Here is a specimen: 'Indra and Soma, up together against the cursing demon! May he burn and hiss like an oblation in the fire! Put your eternal hatred on the villain who hates the Brahman, who eats [raw] flesh, and whose look is abominable!'

We may describe the religious belief which appears in the Veda as nature-worship. It is a great mistake to call it monotheism.[1] Max Müller justly says, 'If we must employ technical terms, the religion of the Veda is polytheism, not monotheism.' At best there are momentary glimpses of what seems almost monotheism.[2] At the same time, as nature is throughout divine, there is often an under-tone of pantheism, which, in one or two of the latest hymns, becomes distinctly audible. It is thus difficult to designate or classify the Vedic faith. It abounds in contradictions.[3]

[1] It is matter of regret that a writer of weight like Mountstuart Elphinstone, in his *History of India*, should have so designated it. His learned editor, Professor Cowell, has, however, corrected the mistake.

[2] As in R. V. i. 164.

[3] As Dr. John Muir states it, the faith has three leading characteristics:—1. Everything connected with religious rites is thought to have a spiritual as well as physical potency. 2. Every part of nature is held to be separately invested with divine power; 3. Yet all the parts are held to form one grand whole.—*Sanskrit Texts*, v. p. 411.

But we must glance for a moment at the faith that preceded the Vedic. As the striking resemblances among the Aryan languages allow no doubt to remain that they have all sprung from one source, so the religions of the various branches of the Aryan race prove that these must have had, at one time, a common faith. This is especially clear regarding the chief divinity acknowledged by the Greeks, the Romans, the Iranians (ancient Persians), and the Hindus. This divinity was understood to be wise, powerful, and good; he was not, in the strict sense of the word, a creator, but an organizer of the world. In every case this divinity was the god of heaven. This fact cuts up by the roots a vast growth of speculation respecting the origin of religious faith being, as Mr. Herbert Spencer would say, in ghost-worship; and it certainly gives no countenance to another frequently expressed hypothesis—that polytheism preceded monotheism. It is easy to trace in the Aryan religions the continuous advance of polytheism; and when the crowd of deities wearied the worshipper, or philosophic thought began to call these beings in question, it was to pantheism that recourse was had, rather than to monotheism.

In ancient pre-Vedic times a place of undisputed pre-eminence must have been held by the deity Varuna. This name is etymologically connected with *'Ουρανός, heaven.* Its original signification was 'the encompasser,'[1] and it was especially the

[1] It is derived from *vri*, to encompass, surround.

extreme vault of heaven to which the term was applied in Vedic times. But we may affirm that in the pre-Vedic period it was not the visible heaven, but the deity presiding over it, that was the object of worship.

In the Vedas the word designating *God* is *deva*, which etymologically means *brilliant, shining.* The deities, then, were *the bright ones.* Castren, a high authority especially on Turanian religion, maintains that throughout all Asia it has been pre-eminently to heaven that adoration has been paid. He says that, among all uncivilized people, heaven, considered as living (*der beseelte Himmel*), is the supreme divinity. But at the point to which we can trace back Aryan thought and life—that is, the time when the great Indo-European race was still undivided—we cannot call them uncivilized; and we can bring no evidence of their ancestors having been so. We believe that to worship heaven as living was a descent—a falling away from higher and truer conceptions of divinity.[1]

In Vedic days Varuna—the god of heaven—does not retain his unapproached superiority. But very lofty attributes are still ascribed to him, and

[1] It has sometimes been maintained that, during the Vedic period, there was a gradual elevation of the religious consciousness. On the contrary, we assert a gradual degradation. From Varuna to Indra was a great descent; from Indra to the deities of the Atharva V. was one still greater. Farther, it seems in a high degree improbable that the conception of heaven as a physical object was gradually exalted until the God of heaven had such high moral

ethically he stands by far the highest among the divinities. It is he that upholds the order, both physical and moral, of the universe. He rewards the good and punishes the evil. A power approaching omnipotence, and a knowledge approaching omniscience, are both ascribed to him. Although by no means implacable, yet to the impenitent wicked he is severe and stern; and it is a most instructive, and by no means unintelligible, circumstance that, in certain hymns, there begins to be manifested not only a dread, but a strong dislike, of a being so awfully pure and just.

An acute critic[1] has said that there are two great deities, Varuna and Indra, 'between whom the religious consciousness of the Vedic Aryans seems to oscillate.' The conception of Indra was undoubtedly the later in origin; it does not take us back to pre-Vedic times; the idea seems of purely Indian origin. The return of the rains, after the long drought of the cold and dry seasons, was hailed in Northern India with unspeakable rejoicing; it was like light dispelling darkness, or life succeeding death. When the sky, which had for eight months been painfully bright and stainless, began to be veiled with clouds floating north-

attributes ascribed to Him as belong to Varuna. This theory assumes a gradual elevation of religion of which there is no evidence; and it denies a degradation of which the evidence is overwhelming. Indra undoubtedly superseded Varuna; that is, low ideas built on physical phenomena came in place of high moral conceptions of divinity which are almost worthy of being ranked with those of the Old Testament.

[1] Bergaigne.

ward from the ocean, and when the higher summits were wrapped in mists, every man felt his heart expand with hope ; for relief from the intolerable blaze of light, the stifling heat, and the suffocating dust, was now at hand. When the clouds were light and floated overhead without dropping down their watery treasure, it was held that some demon was carrying captive 'the cows of the sky,' to confine them in the caves of the mountains. The sight was most tantalizing, for the people stood in the midst of burnt-up plains and dry watercourses, and often of dying cattle. But when the lightning flashed, and the thunderbolt pierced the dark enswathing vapour, it was regarded as the work of a friendly deity warring against the demon (Vritra), and compelling him to set the precious liquid free, so as to let it fall, to the refreshment and joy of all the inhabitants of earth. That friendly deity was Indra. He thus corresponds pretty nearly to the Jupiter Pluvius of the Romans. Indra soon came to be described as a mighty warrior, striding victoriously to battle. He never forsakes his friends. If they supply him abundantly with offerings, he asks no questions about their character ; he will to the uttermost support his supporters—those who give him his favourite nourishment. Indra has no high attributes. Next to his joy in battle, his main characteristic is his delight in the intoxicating Soma juice. He rushes 'impetuous as a bull' to the place where it is flowing ; and he quaffs it 'like a thirsty stag.'

When it came to be said that 'the haughty Indra takes precedence of all gods,' and Varuna was overshadowed by such a rival, there was certainly a very deplorable declension in the religious belief of the Aryas. Sensuous and sensual conceptions took the place of moral ones. But the explanation is not far to seek. St. Paul supplies it: 'They did not like to retain God in their knowledge.' They were overawed by the serene majesty of Varuna; they were terrified by his awful purity. Indra, on the contrary, was both a mighty god and a boon companion; and when they liberally shared with him the beverage which they liked so well themselves, he was completely won over to their side. Deterioration has thus marked Hinduism even from the most ancient times.

Even in the days when 'Varuna the king' was supreme, he was probably not the sole divinity. Every force in nature, every great phenomenon, every striking object, came to be reverenced, worshipped.

A third divinity of a remarkable character was Agni, the Fire (*ignis*). Physically he was very wonderful; produced from the friction of two pieces of wood, he devoured his parents. His powers were extraordinary; yet, though a mighty being, he condescended to reside in their dwellings; he repelled the darkness and the enemies—wild beasts, evil men, and fiends—that lurked within it. When 'fed abundantly with butter' he rose heavenward in his brightness, and bore the prayers and offerings to the gods. He was 'approached with reverential homage, both morning and evening.' But he was not confined to the wood from which they had laboriously extracted him ; he could leap out suddenly from the hard stone when struck, or from the dark cloud. He pervaded all things ; he was therefore one of the very highest of the gods.

The early Hindu explained the phenomena of nature by his own human experience. We knew a little child in India who, on seeing a bright star hanging by the side of the moon, exclaimed, 'Oh ! look at the mother-moon with her baby.' We do not know whether the child repeated what some native servant had said, or expressed its own simple thought ; but this well exhibits the childish interpretation of nature which prevailed in Vedic days. Even as the child, or savage, attributes life to surrounding objects, so did the ancient Hindus. Hence gods were multiplied more and more.

The Sun may be the first mentioned after the three great divinities noted above.[1] He is preceded by the two Asvinas and Ushas the Dawn. The return of light, as the first streaks of morning appeared in the east, was a very wonderful and beneficent event. Lustrous and lovely were the

[1] Yet the Sun does not occupy quite so high a place as we might have expected, or as he holds among the Santals and other Aborigines. Byron, in *Manfred*, speaks thus—

'Glorious orb ! the idol
Of early nature . . .
Which gladdened, on their mountain tops, the hearts
Of the Chaldean shepherds, till they poured
Themselves in orisons.'

Asvinas—the beams that heralded the dawn; and the Dawn herself—ever young, ever fresh, ever fair—was a marvel that drew from the Hindu poets their strains of sweetest song. So, too, the Winds were gods—Vayu, and the Maruts, or Storm-winds (literally 'howlers'), were of high importance. The Earth was a goddess. The Waters were goddesses. The Moon scarcely received the notice we could have expected; and the Stars are seldom mentioned in the most ancient books.

The reader may perhaps still ask whether it was the outward, visible object, or a being supposed to preside over it, that received the homage. In the Avesta, the sacred book of ancient Persia, there is a distinction made between these two things; and the homage is unquestionably paid both to the outward object and to a spirit or genius presiding over it. But the Hindus have never made so clear a distinction between these things as the Iranians did. The Indian mind in modern days fluctuates between the two ideas—mixes them—often confounds them. In Vedic times it was more the visible, tangible object than any presiding spirit to which the homage was paid—the object being personalized.

The deities in the Veda are spoken of as being 'thrice eleven' in number. We also hear of three thousand three hundred and thirty-nine divinities—a vague amplification, to denote that the powers surrounding men were very numerous. We shall see that, in later days, even this amplification was greatly amplified. The philosopher Hegel has justly affixed the epithet 'measureless' (*maasslos*) to the Hindu imagination; it revels in vastness, vagueness, mystery—soon losing all sense of fitness, or proportion, or harmony.

In the Vedic pantheon there is no system, no fixed order. In his turn every one of the greater deities becomes supreme. The family relationships among them are utterly confused: it would not be difficult to show that any god was at once his own grandson and his own grandfather. We need not wonder at this chaos; for the connection between natural phenomena may be looked at from different points of view.

Almost each of the deities has a female counterpart, or, as she is called, a wife. But the goddesses are very indistinct both in character and function, with the notable exception of one already referred to—the Dawn. The Earth, called 'the broad one' (Prithivi), has been also mentioned; but her importance—never great—seems to have decreased as time went on. Aditi ('the boundless expanse') occupied a somewhat high place, as being the mother of gods and heroes.

The conception of triads is pretty frequent in Hinduism. In later Vedic days—the fourth century B.C.—it was stated by a leading commentator (Yaska) that the divine energies were summed up in the three gods—Fire, Air, and the Sun (Agni, Vayu, and Surya); but this is the generalization of a philosopher, and too much stress should not be laid upon it. It was in later days that the notion of a triad of gods became common.

Reference has been already made to the circumstance that the Iranian and Hindu religions were originally connected. After several branches of the great Indo-European family had successfully migrated to the West, the ancestors of the Iranians and the Hindus evidently still remained together or at least were closely allied. Hence the connection between both their religions and their languages. It has been demonstrated that Ahura, or Ahura Mazda, in the Avesta was originally the same as the Varuna Asura (the Lord Varuna) of the Veda. Mithra, who in the Avesta originally was the deity of the shining heaven, and who latterly became identified with the Sun, corresponds to Mitra (the friend), who in the Veda is almost always coupled with Varuna. Mitra became more and more associated with the light of day; while Varuna tended to be so with the awe-inspiring heavens as revealed at night.[1] Vayu, the wind, is the same both in the Avesta and the Veda.[2] Agni greatly resembles Atar, the genius presiding over fire.

But a still more striking connection exists between the Soma of the Hindus and the Homa of the Iranians. (The words are the same, with the usual dialectic change of *s* into *h*.) Soma is the

[1] In the Avesta there is also a strong bond between Mithra and Ahura Mazda. Thus, 'May Mithra and Ahura, the strong gods, come to our help.'

[2] Vayu seems to have been originally almost as important a god as Indra; but his greatness gradually decreased.

expressed juice of a milky plant growing on the mountains (*Asclepias acida*, or *Sarcostemma viminale*), which, when fermented, is intoxicating. When Paracelsus discovered alcohol, his laudations of it were abundantly hyperbolical; and perhaps we cannot feel surprise that the simple-minded Aryas were astonished and delighted when they first experienced the exhilarating effects of Soma. Still, as they seem to have drunk it to excess, the debasing results must have been well known; and it is one of the most saddening things connected with the Veda, that the glory of the Soma should be celebrated with such unbounded rapture. Bacchanalian poets have been effusive enough, at all times, in their praise of wine; but generally one sees a twinkle in the eye which shows that the bard is more than half in jest. It would be a relief if we could persuade ourselves that the Vedic singers are only playing with us when they make Soma the king of gods and men, the creator of heaven and earth, and the sovereign ruler of all beings. Most strange that the juice which they had crushed out from the milk-weed—which they drank themselves, and gave their gods to drink, and which never quite lost its physical character—should at the same time be deemed a god, and one of the very mightiest of gods.[1] In the religions of the world many things are morally worse than

[1] Dr. Haug was one of the few Europeans who have tasted the Soma as legitimately prepared. He says, 'It is a very nasty drink; and has some intoxicating effect.'

this; but nothing is more absolutely childish. We may note that, though the praise of Homa in the Avesta is extravagant enough, it never rises to the same height of folly as the laudation of Soma did in India.

The importance naturally attached to the sacrificial fire and to the libation led to the exaltation of Agni and Soma. Similarly, the prayer or invocation was invested with mighty potency, and Brahmanaspati or Brihaspati, the lord of prayer, became an important deity. He may be called prayer personalized.[1]

It is remarkable that the word *deva* (god), which is applied to the highest beings in the Veda, is in the Avesta used to designate demons.[2] Several of the Vedic deities, in fact, are in the Avesta degraded into fiends,—even the mighty Indra himself is so. It has been conjectured that there must have been collision, conflict, between the two races—the Iranian and Indian—which had been originally one; and that a violent reconstruction of the ancient faith took place, probably through the teaching of the famous Zarathustra (Zoroaster). This is possible, but by no means certain. In Iran, the supreme divinity Ahura was never dethroned, as Varuna was; monotheistic ideas were gradually strengthened; the distinction of god and devil was more strongly emphasized; and those beings who

[1] In like manner the Avesta almost personalizes prayer; and certain potent prayers are prayed to.

[2] In Zend, *daeva;* which in modern Persian becomes *div.*

were rivals, not servants, of Ahura were necessarily regarded as evil.[1] Thus, in an ethical point of view, the Avesta stands always higher than the Veda.

The worship prescribed and exemplified in the Veda was not idolatry, in the sense of image-worship. Yet, although the recognized ritual was free from this taint, it is difficult to believe that images were quite unknown. The description of certain divinities is so precise and full, that it seems to have been drawn from visible representations of them.

An important part of Hinduism consisted in the worship of the *Pitris* or Fathers (*patres*). This class of beings is not to be confounded with the gods (*devas*). Yama, the first mortal, was the offspring of the sun. He travelled the road by which none ever returns, and is now the ruler of the happy dead. He now drinks the Soma draught, 'in the innermost part of heaven,' surrounded by other Fathers.[2]

The preceding remarks have had reference to the oldest of the sacred books, the Rig V. The next in importance is the Atharva V., which contains nearly 760 hymns. Many of these are repetitions of parts

[1] The word *deva* came thus to mean *demon*. This fact reminds us that in classic Greek δαίμων denoted a superhuman being, whether good or bad. Augustine mentions that, by his time, through the spread of Christian ideas, it had come to be used only in a bad sense.

[2] In the Avesta he is Yimo the Ruler (Yimo Kshaeta); in whom the idea of a fall from original blessedness, which is discernible in the Vedic Yama, becomes unmistakable. From Yimo Kshaeta was derived the story of King Jamshid, so famous in later Persian mythology.

of the Rig V. What is original is, for the most part, greatly inferior in a moral point of view to what is contained in the older Veda. The deities are often entirely different. The Rig V. acknowledges no evil divinities; sorceries, incantations, and obscene practices are not inculcated in its hymns. But the Atharva V. manifests a great dread of malignant beings—fiends, in fact; and their wrath is earnestly deprecated. Talismans are invoked, as possessed of boundless power; and charms for the destruction of enemies abound. Altogether, with the exception of a few hymns which appear to be the relics of a former period, the Atharva V. is a wretchedly low collection; and the question at once forces itself upon us, How is this marked inferiority to the more ancient books to be explained? Two explanations suggest themselves. The Aryas mingled with the original occupants of the soil, and both their blood and their religion became contaminated. This is one way of accounting for the great falling off. Or, again, there may have existed from the beginning a higher and a lower form of religion; and the Atharvana presents the latter. But, in truth, we hold both of these suppositions to be correct; the two causes apparently combined to produce the painful result. It is in the highest degree improbable that at any time in India there existed only one form of religious thought among the Aryas. Systems which have flourished luxuriantly in later days had their roots, we may believe, even in the earliest period.

CHAPTER II.

THE VEDIC RITUAL.

THE second part of a Veda is called the Brahmana. Professedly the Brahmanas explain the modes of performing the various parts of worship; but in reality they do much more than this. They are discursive treatises that deal not only with ritual, but questions exegetical and dogmatical; along with which they give many explanatory legends. In an intellectual point of view they are decidedly inferior to the Hymns. Pedantry and puerility mark every page; literary merit they have none; their sole value is from the light they throw on the development of the sacrificial system, and religious thought generally.

The most ancient part of these treatises may date from about the sixth century B.C., or at most two centuries earlier. There thus had been a long time since the composition of the earlier Hymns, during which religion had become more and more petrified. Thought and feeling faded away in proportion as ritual was enlarged.[1]

The religious observances had been developed to a very considerable extent even before the composition of the earliest Brahmanas. 'The rites,' says Haug, 'must have existed from times immemorial.' He contends that they even preceded the Hymns. We must ascribe the commencement of sacrifice to pre-Vedic times; and it seems to be in reference to their origin in former ages that the Rig Veda itself calls the rites of sacrifice 'the first religious rites.'[2] That a complex ritual, and elaborate ideas as to its significance, should have been so early in existence, is a matter full of significance.

We cannot discover that there were any temples —buildings set apart for worship—in Vedic times. Worship was performed generally in the house. A room seems to have been set apart for the sacred fire; and when a grander ceremonial was required, a space was enclosed for the occasion, which might be either covered or open

Worship was personal, or social in the sense of domestic,—very seldom what we understand by public worship. Farther, each man dealt with the gods on his own account. When it was domestic, the husband and the wife could worship together; and if there were more wives than one, the chief

[1] One is reminded of Coleridge's words: 'An appropriate ceremony in religion is like a golden chain round the neck of faith; but you must not draw the chain too close, lest you strangle the faith.'

[2] R. V. i. 164. 43.

wife was the one associated in the act. The presence of any others, whether worshipping or not, was an interruption to the service.

The worship consisted of offerings, prayer, and praise. The chief offerings were clarified butter poured on the fire, and the expressed and fermented juice of the Soma offered in ladles. The Soma was generally mixed with water or milk. The offerings were usually thrown into the fire, which, as it blazed high, was understood to bear them or their essences up to heaven. Sometimes the gods and 'fathers' were invited to come and seat themselves on the sacred grass with which the floor was strewn, that thus they might partake of the precious beverage. The remainder of the Soma was generally drunk by the worshipper, or, in somewhat later days, by the officiating priest or priests. Hymns of praise and prayer accompanied the offerings.

It was distinctly understood that the offerings nourished and gratified the deities as corporeal beings. 'They who present to thee oblations, augment thy vast strength and thy manly vigour.'[1] As in the case of men, so in that of the gods, exhilaration was produced by drinking the fermented Soma juice; and as we have seen, Indra in particular indulged in it to excess; his love of liquor was 'intense.' Bloody sacrifices were also offered. The animals were chiefly sheep, goats, bulls, cows, and buffaloes. But the great sacrifice

[1] R. V. I. 54.

was that of the *Asvamedha*—the sacrifice of the horse; the ceremonies connected with which are detailed with disgusting minuteness in the Rig Veda itself (R. V. i. 162. 163).[1] This rite, which apparently descended from pre-Vedic times, continued for many centuries to be regarded as the greatest of all sacrifices; and in later days, when not one, but a hundred horses, were offered, the potency of the ceremony was irresistible; it made —if the worshipper desired it—the throne of the mightiest deities to totter.

The sacrifice of human beings, if not frequent, was yet in existence. Though practised, it does not seem to have been approved; and, among the higher classes, it gradually ceased. It is referred to as 'the way of the Sudras,' the tribes that had been conquered and enslaved. It doubtless continued long among the middle and lower classes; and, in truth, it has not ceased up to this day. Whether it was a practice handed from pre-Vedic times, or adopted from the aborigines, does not very clearly appear.

We cannot state with certainty the ideas at first connected with the very remarkable rite of sacrifice; nor can we fix the succession in which they arose. The conception of the gods requiring nourishment has been mentioned as very prevalent; the food of man was necessary also to

[1] From the Yajur Veda we learn that, along with the horse, 609 animals of various kinds, wild and tame, were tied to 21 *yupas*, or sacrificial posts, and offered.

deities. Again, the offerings—including animal sacrifice—were eucharistic. The important idea of sacrifice being expiatory existed in Vedic times; and we see no reason to believe that it was not pre-Vedic. Farther, the belief prevailed that the offering was a substitute for the offerer. We also hear of a divine being—Prajapati, or Vishnu—being the victim; or again, the being offered is the primeval male, Purusha—who is, however, identified with the Creator. Very remarkable indeed are such conceptions as these; and we do not seem sufficiently to account for them by ascribing their origin to a tendency in the Hindu mind to push every idea to excess; we may rather regard at least some of them as the relics of primeval revelation—fragments of patriarchal faith borne down on the stream of time. We do not assert that this is proved; but, most assuredly, it cannot be disproved. We may well study, then, with reverent curiosity, the teaching of the ancient books regarding 'the nave of the world-wheel,'—that which was believed to uphold the order of the universe—the great, mysterious, awful rite of sacrifice.

The Hymns celebrate the power, exploits, generosity, and sometimes the personal beauty, of the deity addressed. In exchange for praises and offerings presented, he is asked and expected to bestow his favour and help. Temporal blessings are mentioned and implored—such as life, food, wealth, children, cows, horses, protection against danger, success in battle, the destruction of enemies, and so on. The praises bestowed on the god were believed to increase his power.[1] The favour which he granted hardly depended on the moral state of the worshipper. The confessions of sin are very defective; so much so that Professor Weber asserts the religious sense of sin to be wanting altogether.[2] We think, however, this language is too unqualified. We require to distinguish between the Vedic writers. Some do appear to have a sense of defilement that is not merely ceremonial; we might call it a smothered sense of personal sin.[3] Other hymns do really little more than reiterate in endless forms the prayer, 'Here is butter; give us cows.'[4]

In the Brahmanas—poor as they are intellectually—there seems rather more reference to the ethical qualities of the gods generally than we find in the Hymns. But there was no real advance; for Varuna, with his sovereignty and high moral attributes, was more and more eclipsed.

It is sad to see how rapidly prayer degenerated into a kind of spell or charm. It became a magical formula, the sounds of which were irresistible, even when they were not understood; only they must

[1] 'May our praises augment thy power' (R. V. I. 10).

[2] Weber, *History of Indian Literature*, p. 38. So Goldstücker: 'Ethical considerations are foreign to these outbursts.' Similarly De Quincey says that 'the Greeks and Romans had not the faintest vestige of an idea of what in Scripture is called sin' (*Works*, vol. x. p. 240).

[3] As was to be expected, it is especially in hymns to Varuna that any right idea of sin is perceptible.

[4] So Barth. We may enlarge the expression to this: 'Here is butter; give us cows, and we will bring more butter.'

be fully and exactly pronounced, or woe to the wretch who blundered! When prayer and sacrifice were offered in due form, the gods would certainly grant the worshipper his request. We see the idea that they *will grant* passing into the idea that they *must grant*; and there gradually grows up the tremendous conception of extorting, by sacrifice or austerities, a desired boon from reluctant gods. But if this dreadful conception appears at all in the Vedas, we see it only in the germ.

The Hymns were produced in the north-west corner of India, chiefly in the Panjâb. When most of the Brahmanas were composed, the Aryas had advanced eastward, perhaps as far as the country between the Ganges and the Yamuna (Jumna). The language of the Hymns has by this time become unintelligible to the mass of the people, and obscure even to the learned. Now, therefore, the sacred texts become stereotyped. The official 'man of prayer'—the Brahman—has become absolutely necessary. He probably cannot compose hymns, or offer extempore prayers; but he can repeat them ready-made, and in fixed, proper formulæ. The worshippers are now passive; the Brahman prays and sacrifices for them. He alone possesses the requisite knowledge of the sacred texts; and of the perilous precision with which they must be uttered he alone is capable. Thus the men of prayer became an order, and steadily grew into a caste. All persons of their own class could enter into this; and, as we have heard it ex-

4

pressed in India, a horse is not more separate from a donkey than a Brahman was believed to be from a man of lower caste. This exclusiveness—inhuman though it often was—was for the purpose of guarding the purity of their blood. Mixture with the non-Aryan inhabitants of India has taken place to a very large extent in other cases; it is among the Brahmans, if anywhere, that we are to seek for the descendants of the primitive Aryan settlers. This comparative purity of blood secured a measure of intellectual superiority—the Aryans being undoubtedly a more gifted race than any of the earlier inhabitants of India. Of that intellectual superiority the Brahmans have, from the beginning, been fully conscious; and they have systematically employed it for their own exaltation. With remarkable ability, with inflexible determination, and with unrelenting selfishness, they went on, throughout many centuries, encroaching on the rights both of princes and people. The usurpations and demands of priestly power have been striking enough in other places; but the pretensions of popes and priests in Europe fade into insignificance when compared with those of the sacerdotal caste in India.

Education was necessary for the Brahman when he had become the depositary of the sacred texts—which were probably still unwritten, and handed down by oral tradition. In these schools, however, there was little importance attached to what can be called doctrine; the externals of religion had by this time become nearly all in all. This we can understand; but our Western minds can with difficulty conceive how the next step was taken. The gods were thrown into the shade, and the rites became the great divinities. The principle of association has worked with great force at all times in India; and soon everything used in worship became holy, became itself divine, and an object of worship. Thus the texts with their mysterious potency, about which the mind of the priests was so greatly exercised, absorbed the attention almost to the exclusion of the beings they were addressed to. If the incantation was right, all was right.

Meanwhile the ritual gradually became more and more elaborate and complex. The great celebration of the Soma sacrifice came to be exceedingly expensive; it required a host of priests, and lasted sometimes—in theory at least—for hundreds of years. High worship was thus an aristocratic thing, possible only for men of wealth. Animal victims were frequently offered in immense numbers; a mere hecatomb was but a paltry sacrifice.

CHAPTER III.

Section I.

THE UPANISHADS:[1] *RISE OF PHILOSOPHY.*

We have seen how a stupendous system of ritual observances gradually arose, until thought and feeling in religion were overlaid, and all but smothered, by externals ; and the rites became almost independent of the deities in whose service they had been established. A reaction from this state of things, we may say, was unavoidable. The ritual could be performed only by Brahmans ; but it is very improbable that every Brahman could find sufficient employment as a priest. Hence, among such an intellectual class, speculative thought was certain to arise : and probably, even in the discharge of their priestly

[1] The meaning of the term 'Upanishad' is not certain. Sankara Acharya explained it as meaning the 'setting to rest' (or destruction) of ignorance. Others would render it 'sessions,' *quasi* 'lectures.' Others again say it means that which 'sits beneath,' *quasi* 'mystery.'

functions, some were led to ask, What is the meaning of all this? Worship had become to many a round of mechanical ceremonies; but it could hardly be so to all. Then, the Brahmans had not secured an absolute monopoly of thinking power; princes and nobles—debarred from priestly functions—could not be kept from reflection on spiritual things. The early period of the Aryan residence in India had been a stirring one; war with the aborigines must have been very frequent; and speculation, in such circumstances, could not have flourished. But the Aryan superiority in Northern India was ere long secured; and the men of action could now begin to reflect. As the race steadily pressed down the great Gangetic valley into warmer and more fertile regions, the requirements of outward life were easily met, and there was time for rest and contemplation. We believe there is, in the higher Aryan mind, a tendency to dreaminess and quietism; and now not only outward circumstances, but the climate itself, disposed it to yield to this feeling. There are even in the Hymns—though probably not in the very earliest—attempts to penetrate into the mysteries of creation and the world. Wonder is often expressed. Bold conjectures are sometimes hazarded as to the origin and meaning of things.

India, at the distant date we speak of, was largely covered with forests; and probably there were trees in sight of every village. In northern countries a residence 'under the green-wood tree' can hardly be called attractive, save perhaps in the height of summer; the return of 'winter and rough weather' will dispel the temporary charm. But in India there is almost at every season something exceedingly attractive about forest-life. The dense shade of the trees mitigates the intolerable heat and glare of day. Then comes the quiet of the evening, and the great hush of nature sinks into the inmost soul.

> 'There, as the wild bee murmurs on the wing,
> What peaceful dreams the handmaid spirits bring!
> What viewless forms the Æolian organ play,
> And sweep the furrowed lines of anxious thought away!'

Thus men who were disposed to religious thought were almost driven to seek a forest sanctuary. By and for these recluses were composed the Aranyakas, or forest treatises; and the most important parts—or supplements rather—of these are contained in the Upanishads; of which we have said above that, although properly only treatises appended to the Vedas, they have come to be regarded as their most precious part. The Upanishads are found in various parts of the sacred writings. Some are among the Hymns; others among the Brahmanas; others among the Aranyakas; and others stand by themselves. These last are appended chiefly to the Atharva V.

The text of the Upanishads is often uncertain; sometimes evidently corrupt.

The Aranyakas were not clearly discriminated from the Brahmanas; questions of ritual and other extraneous things are discussed in them. The Upanishads generally avoid such topics, and discuss the nature of the Divine existence and its relation to the human soul.

The Upanishads are generally written in prose. They are numerous; we have lists of nearly 240 of them. Ten or twelve are of special value.[1] Very few of them date from Vedic days; possibly only six, and certainly not twelve, can do so. These we may venture to assign to the fifth or sixth century B.C.; though the form in which they exist is probably some centuries later. Many of the Upanishads are quite modern productions.

Even in Vedic days—as we have seen—the process of reflection had begun. This is proved by some of the later hymns. In a few of these there are touching confessions of ignorance; such as this —'Who truly knows, or who has told, what path leads to the gods?' In eschatology—the doctrine of the last things—the Veda is singularly wanting; but the poets turn with the deepest interest to the origin of the world. They seem to have thought that, being in existence, it might continue so; but how did it ever come into existence? Beneath and around them was the wondrous earth; over them the still more wondrous sky: how came they there? and which of them was first? They could only fall back on human

[1] *Viz.*, the Isa, Kena, Chhandogya, Katha, Prasna, Mundaka, Mandukya, Brihad-Aranyaka, Aitareya, and Taittiriya. Weber says (in 1878)—'At present I count 235 Upanishads.'

analogies: 'What was the forest, what the tree, out of which they cut the sky and earth, that abide while days and many dawns have passed and gone?'[1] Or again, 'Brahmanaspati has forged the gods as a blacksmith kindles his flame.' Or again, Indra had begotten the sun, the sky, the dawn. Or yet again, all things were made out of Purusha, who was the primeval male, and yet a mighty deity. But Hindu speculation always inclines to the mysterious; and illustrations like these now mentioned were soon too simple for it. Ere long the idea arose that, amidst the unceasing flux of things, there was a something which never changed. From this it was easy to proceed to the thought that all else was only appearance, and that this alone was real. Though these conceptions were soon conveyed with all the lavish luxuriance of Oriental hyperbole, we do not know that, in the commencement, they differ essentially from the idea expressed, or implied, in the often-quoted lines of Wordsworth:

> 'A sense sublime
> Of something far more deeply interfused—
> . . . . . .
> A motion and a spirit that impels
> All thinking things, all objects of all thought,
> And rolls through all things.'

Or perhaps the language of Shelley would still better express the Indian conception:

[1] R. V. x. 31. 7.

> 'The One remains; the Many change and pass;
> Heaven's light for ever shines; earth's shadows fly;
> Life, like a dome of many-coloured glass,
> Stains the white radiance of eternity.'

Thus then reflection, speculation, had begun even before the Hymns had been all composed. The further development of thought is presented in the Upanishads. These are by no means either systematic or homogeneous. They have well been called 'guesses at truth:' for they present no formal solution of great problems. They contradict one another; the same writer sometimes contradicts himself. They are often exceedingly obscure, and to Western minds repellent—vague, mystical, incomprehensible. A few rise to sublimity; others are nonsensical—'wild and whirling words,' and nothing more. Yet there is frequently earnestness—a groping after something felt to be needful; there is the yearning of hearts dissatisfied and empty. In this lies the value of the Upanishads; our sympathies are called forth towards those hermits who saw no meaning in the stupendous ritualism that had grown up around them, or in the ever-increasing mob of deities that were crowding in. Another characteristic is the general sadness of their tone. With them commences that great wail of sorrow which, for countless ages, has in India been rising up to heaven. The earlier Vedic hymns take a cheerful view of life; but with the Upanishads we see the beginning of that despondency which, as time goes on, will deepen into the darkness of despair. Whence comes, it may be asked, this characteristic gloom? It has sometimes been traced to the unhappiness of their environment. Warfare was almost the normal state of Indian society;—war with the aborigines; war of one Aryan tribe with another; a long struggle between princes and priests, and the steady exaltation of the latter; the Macedonian invasion; the rise and rapid progress of Buddhism; war with Scythian hordes;—in all this there was undoubtedly enough to distract and depress the Indian mind. In modern Europe the evils that still afflict both the individual and society have suggested the question—'Is life worth living?' and many, perhaps an increasing number, answer in the negative. If this be the case after all that Christ has taught and Christianity has done, we cannot wonder that those ancient hermits were overwhelmed by the deep mysteries of existence and the manifold trials of life.

The teaching of the Upanishads, amidst some varieties,[1] is, in the main, pantheistic.

It is exceedingly difficult to state the chronological order in which the various systems of Indian philosophy arose. But there is some reason to believe that the sequence was as follows:

First, a belief in the sole, self-existing being; all else being the effect of ignorance or illusion.

Secondly, the belief in an original void, out of which all things came.

[1] While doctrine closely akin to pantheism is most frequent in the Upanishads, dualism is also found. Even asceticism finds a place.

Thirdly, the belief in an original plurality of selves, and of the independent existence of the world.[1]

We should only weary our readers if we went into this question at any length. Moreover, we must touch on this subject when we discuss the formulated systems of philosophy, of which the Upanishads were only the precursors.

We must, however, note that the Upanishads are by no means purely speculative. They have a practical end in view; they profess to teach the way of salvation. They point out how the human soul, ignorant of itself, attaches itself to unworthy objects, and so is again and again dragged into the whirlpool of life.

New ideas had by this time come in. Of these none was more remarkable, none more powerful in its influence, than the doctrine of metempsychosis, or transmigration. The Vedic poets never spoke of a second birth; the good went at death to the happy abode of Yama, and as *pitris* (fathers) became quasi-divinities themselves; while there are some hints in the Rig V., and more distinct allusions in the Atharvana, to punishment in gloomy pits as the doom of the wicked. We cannot say with certainty whether the idea of Transmigration sprang up of itself in the Hindu mind, or whether it was derived from the aborigines; we incline to the former supposition. The belief is not unnatural. Plato's doctrine of pre-existence involves it; and Pytha-

[1] See Gough on the *Philosophy of the Upanishads*, p. xi.

goras distinctly asserted it. But in India the belief has assumed a wild, fantastic shape; and it sways the minds of men with tremendous power. The series of births is virtually endless; the common statement is that it rises to eighty-four lacs—that is, eight millions four hundred thousand; and this in all who cannot somehow succeed in arresting the dreadful succession. According to the merit or demerit of a human being, he is born afresh into the body of a man, or a beast, or a bird, or a fish, or a plant, or a stone. 'Ah! this fearful round of births,' said the Maratha poet Tukaram—'this weary coming and going; when will it all end?' From ancient days all things on earth seemed to the Hindu to be in a perpetual flux; there was no stability, no rest, no abiding peace. Now, to the Oriental—perhaps from climatic reasons primarily—the idea of repose is essentially that of bliss; and unrest is misery. And then the horror of tenanting the bodies of wild beasts and loathsome, venomous reptiles, such as snakes, toads, and worms! But when the soul once knows itself, it is in union with the true Self, or God. The sage, however, lives on until the stock of merit he had amassed has been exhausted. Very startling are the declarations regarding the condition of the man who has reached this point. The perfect sage, as long as he lives, may do good and evil as he chooses, and yet incur no stain. Such is the efficacy of a knowledge of the Self.' [1]

[1] So Anandagiri. See Gough, pp. 61, 67, 229.

But there is a further step to be taken. When the stock of merit is exhausted, he is not, like the multitude, driven back to another birth; when his body falls away, he is identified with the one and only Self. This Self is existence, knowledge, and bliss.[1] But the existence is an impersonal, unconscious existence. With the knowledge there is no knower, or thing known: with the bliss there is no blessed one, and no sense or cause of blessedness. We presume there is not one mind in a thousand that will profess ability to extract any meaning out of such words. But, passing from such dreams, we ask our readers to note the moral characteristics of all this. Ethical distinctions are completely overturned.[2] We are expressly told that the perfect sage, when he murders, does not murder; all appearance is an illusion, a dream, from which at last he wakes.

One cannot but look with profound sadness on those hermits in the forests, dreaming life and generations of life away in such unhappy dreams, and often torturing their bodies in the hope of thus identifying themselves—or rather, recognizing their identity—with the One and All. The chief end of man believed to be the crushing out of all feeling and all thought! No wonder that a writer, who has devoted much time to the careful study of the Upanishads, declares them to be 'the work of

[1] Instead of *existence*, it would be more precise to say *that which exists*, or *an existent thing*.

[2] 'La doctrine de l'identité absolue, par la necessité de son principe, divinise le mal.'—Caro. *L'idée de Dieu*, 5th edit. p. 291.

a rude age, a deteriorated race, and a barbarous, unprogressive community.'[1] It is true that Schopenhauer professed to admire them—attracted, no doubt, by their unrelenting pessimism; but we do not see how any one can share in that admiration who does not absolutely despair of the future of humanity. The Christian, at all events, can have no sympathy with such a feeling; for he believes in a Being who is possessed of every glorious attribute, and who is emphatically called 'the God of hope.' Therefore His true worshippers are men of hope; and if the present be in darkness, or at least in twilight, they turn their eyes to the promised age,—and, lo! the landscape is all bathed in floods of blessed sunshine.

Another remarkable conception, unknown in earlier days, that came forward in this period, was that of asceticism, passing into a morbid ecstasy. Quite possibly this too was derived from the lower races around them: for among such races religion has easily run into wild excitement, both physical and mental. The worship of the god Siva comes into prominence during this period. He is the great lord of devotees, who indulge in self-torture and extreme austerity. There is some reason to connect him with the Himalaya mountains, as if he had been the god of aboriginal tribes there dwelling; but the worship may have existed from the first among the Aryans, although not a part of the orthodox system.

[1] Gough, p. 268.

SECTION II.

THE SIX DARSANAS. METHODIZED PHILOSOPHY.

The Upanishads, then, contain the first attempts to comprehend the mysteries of existence; and their teachings cannot be gathered up into an harmonious system. But, as time went on, a desire was felt to expand, classify, and arrange these earlier utterances—to make them more definite and more consistent. Hence gradually arose what we may call the official philosophy of India, which is comprised in a number of methodical treatises. These are generally called the six *Darsanas*, or 'exhibitions.' No doubt it was only by degrees that they assumed their present elaborated shape, which cannot be much older than the Christian era. They consist of the following works: 1. The Nyaya, which was founded by Gautama or Akshapada; 2. The Vaiseshika, by Kanada or Kanabhaksha; 3. The Sankhya, by Kapila; 4. The Yoga, by Patanjali; 5. The Mimansa, by Jaimini; 6. The Vedanta, by Badarayana.

The original text-books of the various systems consist of *Sutras*. This word properly signifies 'a string'; and we may understand it to denote a string of rules, or rather aphorisms. They are expressed with extreme conciseness—doubtless for the purpose of being committed to memory; and without a commentary they are exceedingly obscure.

With the purely philosophical part of these

writings we need not much concern ourselves. Their metaphysical theories and their statement of logical processes possess no small interest, and in any history of philosophy they claim attentive study; but we must occupy ourselves mainly with their conceptions on religion.

They belong to the division of Hindu books called *Smriti.* They are therefore authoritative; but not to the same extent as the Vedas and Upanishads.[1]

It is usual to classify these systems in pairs, making three pairs in the order given above; but this arrangement is not satisfactory. The Nyaya and Vaiseshika may indeed go well enough together; and the Sankhya and Yoga may with some difficulty do the same; but the Mimansa and Vedanta have very little in common. Their conjunction has arisen from the circumstance that the Mimansa (otherwise called the Purva or earlier Mimansa) deals with the ritual portion of the Vedas as explained in the Brahmanas; while the Vedanta or Uttara (later) Mimansa seeks to unfold and apply the principles of the Upanishads: and thus, as each expounds a portion of what had come to be styled the Veda, the two systems came to be bracketed together.

[1] The only case in which we ever knew them not to be recognized as authoritative scripture was that of Raja Narayana Basu (Bose), a man of position and influence in the 'Original Brahma Samaj.' But no orthodox Hindu questions their full authority. We appealed at the time to the Pandits of Poona and Benares; who at once denounced the view now objected to.

None of the six systems professedly attack, or deny, the authority of the Vedas: on the contrary, they all profess the profoundest reverence for the sacred books. It is difficult to see how the authors of some of the systems could do this with any sincerity; unless they held that what is theologically true may be philosophically false. Yet the Hindu mind has long surpassed all other minds in the ability to hold, or believe itself to hold, at the same time, two or more opinions which appear to be wholly irreconcilable: indeed, an acknowledged note of the Hindu mind is 'eclecticism issuing in confusion;' it has been said to be 'the very method of Hindu thought.' But the contradictions among the philosophical systems were too glaring to escape the notice of men capable of reflection; and accordingly the author of one Darsana and his followers frequently attack the supporters of the others. Thus the great controversialist Sankara denounces a follower of the Nyaya philosophy as a bullock *minus* the horns and tail—implying, we suppose, that he had all a bullock's stupidity without his power of fighting. The author of the Sankhya charges the followers of the Vedanta with 'babbling like children or madmen.' The Mimansa accuses the Vedanta of being disguised Buddhism. The Padma Purana maintains that four of the six systems are simply atheism.

But while thus radically opposed to each other, the six official systems of philosophy are all held to be orthodox. In this respect Indian philosophy is unlike the Greek, which was developed in entire independence of religion. The relation of Indian philosophy to the Veda resembles that of the scholastic systems of the Middle Ages to the Church.

1. The Nyaya system deserves the praise of attending to *method—i.e.*, the mode of discovering truth. It is distinguished by over-elaboration, dryness, formality; but its philosophy is by no means despicable. Beginning with the inquiry, Which is the way to attain perfect happiness? it asserts that this is found in right apprehension, true knowledge. The Nyaya undertakes to communicate that knowledge, so that the soul may attain the goal of perfect rest. Among other kinds of evidence it brings forward a form of syllogism which, though differing somewhat from the Aristotelian (built on the celebrated dictum *de omni et nullo*), is yet virtually the same, and which, for rhetorical purposes, is perhaps a more useful form. Still, the nicety of distinctions in which the Nyaya rejoices exposes it to the reproach of encouraging wranglings and logomachies, which (rightly or wrongly) has so often been preferred against the logic of the Stagirite. In matters of physical science the Nyaya—as was of course inevitable—is often sadly astray.

Whether the more ancient form of the Nyaya was theistic, is somewhat doubtful; but in its later form it is so,[1] and it ascribes to the deity intelli-

[1] Thus the Kusumanjali (a celebrated work of this school) ex-

gence, will, and power.[1] But it says nothing of moral attributes as belonging to God; nor does it recognize His government of the world. Nor can it be said to believe in creation, inasmuch as it holds matter to be composed of eternal atoms. Confluent atoms, in themselves uncreated, composed the world.[2] To call the Nyaya philosophy theistic is therefore misleading, unless the character of its theism be explained. The Nyaya has nothing to say about worshipping God; while yet it recognizes—implicitly at least—the doctrines and forms of worship inculcated in the Veda.

Soul, or rather spirit, is represented as multitudinous, and (like atoms) eternal. It is distinct from mind.

2. The Vaiseshika system, which we have said is rightly coupled with the Nyaya, is an extension of the latter. The Vaiseshika Sutras do not mention God. They go very fully into the doctrine of atoms—which, like the Nyaya, they declare to be uncaused and eternal. They are so exceedingly small that it requires a combination of at least three of them to be perceptible.

hibits an earnest attempt to prove the Divine existence. Of the Divine attributes it says next to nothing. Professor Cowell ascribes this work to the twelfth century A.D.

[1] The name of Iswara (or Lord) occurs once in the Sutras of Gautama, the founder of the Nyaya. Later writers speak of the Supreme Spirit as moulding the universe, not (in our sense) creating it.

[2] It is interesting to see in the teaching of the Nyaya and Vaiseshika, as in that of the Greek philosopher Democritus, something like an anticipation of the atomic theory of Dalton.

Another tenet common to the Nyaya and Vaiseshika is that souls (spirits) are ubiquitous, or universally diffused through space. But the spirit is united to *mind*, which is atomic and not ubiquitous; and the perceptions of the spirit are made through the mind.[1]

3. We come now to the Sankhya system. It holds that there are two primary, eternal agencies, viz., Nature (Prakṛiti, or *that which produces*) and Souls. The system is thus essentially dualistic. There is no place for God; and accordingly it is known among the Hindus by the name of Niriswara Sankhya, or *the Sankhya without the Lord.* Yet all that the original text asserts is that His existence is 'not proved.' Kapila, then, was an agnostic rather than an atheist.

[1] A short specimen of the excessive refinement of the Hindu schools may probably suffice for our readers. Thus, as right apprehension secures emancipation from pain, the question is by what means right apprehension can be obtained. Four means of doing so are mentioned; viz., perception, inference, comparison, and testimony. Each of these is explained at great length by the commentators. Then an exceedingly important matter is the *categories.* There are seven of these, viz., Substance, Quality, Action, Generality, Particularity, Intimate Relation, and Negation. The categories are thus subdivided. *Substances* are nine in number, viz., earth, water, light, air, ether, time, space, soul, and mind. *Qualities* are twenty-four in number (we spare our readers the enumeration). *Actions* are five in number, viz., elevation, depression, contraction, expansion, motion. *Generality* is of two kinds, viz., extensive and non-extensive. And so on. These, and similar distinctions, belong to the Nyaya and Vaiseshika schools. Hindu metaphysicians not only split hairs, but, as Abraham Tucker would have said, quarter them. Thus the Sankhya tells us that there are eight kinds of error; eight kinds of illusion; ten kinds of extreme illusion; eighteen kinds of gloom; and eighteen kinds of utter darkness.

There are three elementary principles (of which, in later days, we hear continually), namely, Sattva, Rajas, Tamas; or Truth, Passion, and Darkness. These principles enter into all things; and on the relative quality of each in any object depends the quality of the object.

The root of all things except soul is Prakṛiti, which may be tolerably rendered by the word 'nature.' It is not a product. It is the producer of seven things, which are themselves producers of sixteen other things. Soul is not a product, nor a producer. Souls (Purush) are countless in number; individual, sensitive, eternal, unchangeable. All that is done by Prakriti is done on behalf of soul. In its own nature soul is without qualities, until united with Prakṛiti. The union of the two is compared to a lame man mounted on a blind man's shoulders; the pair are then both (as it were) capable of perception and movement. But how and when this important union is effected is not clearly mentioned.

The Sankhya very firmly holds that out of nothing nothing comes.[1] The universe is produced by the union of nature and soul; each individual soul producing its own universe.[2] With the Sankhya, as with the systems already mentioned, present existence is suffering; and the great object of the philosopher is to obtain emancipation. This

[1] 'Gigni
De nihilo nihil; in nihilum nil posse reverti.'—*Persius.*

[2] Compare this with Berkeley's theory.

is found only through knowledge. When through knowledge the soul is emancipated from the 'fetters which bind it in its union with nature, all suffering ceases.[1]

Although Kapila was a man of acute and patient thought, it cannot be said that his system stands intellectually high. Morally, it is still lower. Contemplation is the one right occupation of the sage; there is no place for conduct. Prayer is needless, or rather absurd. Man is thus not a religious being.

4. Along with the Sankhya is generally coupled the Yoga philosophy, which is often styled the Theistic Sankhya. It agrees in its general principles with the Sankhya proper; with the one remarkable exception of acknowledging the existence of God.

The great end of the Yoga is to obtain union with the Supreme Being.[2] But the mode of attaining this great end is very startling. It is by concentration of the mind; by calling in all wandering thoughts and fixing attention on some

[1] But what is the condition of the enlightened soul? 'So, through study of principles, the conclusive, incontrovertible, one only knowledge is attained that neither I am, nor is aught mine, nor do I exist' (Sankhya Karika, 64).

[2] 'Iswara, the supreme ruler, is a soul distinct from other souls; unaffected by the ills with which they are beset; unconcerned with good or bad deeds and their consequences, and with fancies or passing thoughts. In him is omniscience. He is infinite, unlimited by time.' So Patanjali, as quoted by Colebrooke. The language is, in several points, marvellously like the celebrated description of Deity in the *De rerum natura*, 'Omnis enim per se divôm natura necesse'st,' etc.

one object. Any object will answer, if we think of it alone; other thoughts must be suppressed. When the contemplation is carried to its full extent, it is simply contemplation without any object of contemplation.

The French philosopher Degerando and many others have spoken of the necessity of acquiring a mastery over the mind, a power of recalling it from its wanderings and forcing it to dwell steadily on some proper object. So far their idea resembles that of the Yoga; but immense differences soon appear. In the Yoga the adoption of certain bodily postures, restraining the senses, suppressing the breath, and so forth—even fixing the eyes steadily on the tip of the nose—are potent means towards the end desired. Patanjali does not speak—as the Hindu poets often do—of the soothing influence of Nature, in her shady groves and quiet murmuring streams; with him the place or environment seems of no importance; and in this omission he lost a potent influence which is fitted to steady the human mind, recalling it from foolish dreams. Wildness, extravagance, downright absurdity, became the characteristic of his system. The effects ascribed to extreme asceticism are truly marvellous. The past and the future are unveiled to the gaze of the Yogi (the man fully initiated in the Yoga). He sees things invisible to others. He hears the sounds that are in distant worlds. He becomes stronger than the elephant, bolder than the lion, swifter than the wind. He mounts at pleasure into the air or dives into the depths of the earth and the ocean. He acquires mastery over all things, whether animated or inanimate. Mysticism and magic thus very strongly mark the Yoga system.

And with what object was this system studied? Frequently, perhaps generally, for the acquisition of supernatural power, and for no moral end whatever.

The question may well arise whether all the practices of asceticism issued only in dreams and sheer delusion. Or did the Yogi sometimes come in contact with powers and principles in nature of which our accepted science as yet takes no note? We will not venture to say. Our readers will answer the question variously, according as they may deem the teachings of clairvoyance, animal magnetism, spiritualism, etc., to have in them any element of truth or not. Deception, both conscious and unconscious, there has often been in abundance; has there been nothing more? For the Hindu Yogi, at all events, we venture to urge the plea that he was often not a wilful deceiver; he told what, in his state of mental exaltation and ecstasy, he believed he had seen and done. Still, we heartily assent to the judgment which an accomplished Sanskrit scholar has passed on the doctrines of the Yoga: 'Conscientiously observed, they can issue only in madness and idiocy.' [1]

5. The fifth system is the Mimansa. It need

[1] Barth.

not occupy us long. It is not a philosophical system; it is a system of Vedic interpretation, thrown into a quasi-scientific form. To Jaimini the Veda was all in all. It was its own evidence. Its very sounds existed from all eternity. The sum of human duty was to obey its precepts.

We pass to the system which has long been the chief philosophy of India, viz.:

6. The Vedanta. This word properly means 'the end, or scope, of the Vedas.' The name, however, is misleading. The doctrines inculcated by the Vedanta are entirely distinct from those of the Veda proper; they agree with those of the Upanishads, which (as has been explained) are philosophical disquisitions *appended to* the Veda. The name, however, has had the effect of enhancing the estimation of the philosophy to which it has been —whether ignorantly or artfully—attached.

The Vedanta philosophy is said to have had its origin with the sage Vyasa. This personage, however, we may dispose of as mythical. The most distinguished champion of the system was the sage Sankara Acharya, who probably flourished after the year 700 A.D. His influence in the exaltation of Hinduism and the depression of opposing systems (such as Buddhism and Jainism) was immensely great, and equally so in the diffusion of the Vedanta philosophy. We may indeed say that his influence on the theology of India has been as great as that of Augustine on the theology of the Western Church.

A clear and brief statement of this philosophy in its developed form is found in the Vedanta Sara; and of this authority we shall now largely avail ourselves.

The Vedanta Sara distinctly states that the Vedanta philosophy is founded on 'the Upanishads and works auxiliary thereto.' It does not mention the Veda proper in this connection. It had been declared in the Chhandogya Upanishad that there was in the beginning 'only one thing without a second.'[1] So the Vedanta Sara begins by saying, 'The oneness of soul and God. This is shown by all Vedanta treatises.' It quotes approvingly the ancient text, 'The whole universe is God.' God (who is generally called Brahm[2]) consists, as has been mentioned above, of existence, knowledge, and joy.[3] He is the sole Reality. All else is only appearance; it seems, but *is* not. Its seeming existence is owing to ignorance, or illusion. Ignorance is not a mere negation; it is possessed of two powers—that of envelopment (or concealing) and that of projection. The former hides from the soul its identity with God. The latter 'projects' the appearance of an external world.[4] Brahm and Ignorance are co-eternal principles.

[1] Ekamevâdvitîyam.

[2] There is a great distinction between Brahma (or Brahman) and Brahmâ. To avoid confusion, we shall write the former thus—Brahm.

[3] Sat, chit, ananda; or (as written together) *Sachchidananda*. This is a formula continually repeated in Vedanta treatises.

[4] 'The projective power can produce any thing, even the whole external world' (V. S. sec. 39).

There are four conditions of the soul—waking, dreaming, dreamless sleep, and a 'fourth' state, which is something higher (or deeper) than even dreamless sleep. The waking man is grossly ignorant of reality; he is occupied with unreal mockeries, and believes in their existence. The sleeper is freed from a portion of such ignorance; although he dreams, and believes in his dreams. He that sleeps without dreaming is much more emancipated from delusion. But the consummation is the 'fourth' state, which it would appear can hardly be described in human language. Thus, then, according to this philosophy, although the world seen in dreams is a delusion, the world seen in our waking hours is a grosser delusion still.

The great necessity, then, is knowledge—apprehension of truth. 'He who knows what soul is gets beyond grief.' Nay, more; 'he who knows God becomes God.'

Meditation without distinction of subject and object is the highest form of thought, according to the Vedanta. But the consummation is when thought exists without an object: it must not be an object to itself.

In many of the older books a practical or conventional existence is admitted of the human soul —the Self within us—as distinguishable from the Supreme Self; and the same thing is admitted of the external world.[1] But when the philosophy

[1] Gough, however, in his *Philosophy of the Upanishads*, argues powerfully that the doctrine of Maya, or illusion, is 'a vital element

has been fully formulated, it strongly asserts the doctrine of *non-duality.*[1] The soul is one with God, although it may not know it; and the external world is a mere appearance, an illusion.

It would be vain to expect logical consistency in the statement of such transcendental thoughts. We have quoted a text about the soul *becoming* God. But if it is God already (although ignorant of its being so), how can it *become* so? The contradiction was evidently noticed, and it is met with this solution: 'Being God it becomes God,'—language which has to us no meaning. It cannot mean that the soul being God recognizes itself as God; for when the soul is emancipated it enters into unconsciousness.

We cannot be surprised if, in explaining this system, writers run into contradictory statements. They sometimes speak of transmigration and of absorption. There can, however, to the Vedantist be neither of these things. There has never been, there will never be, transmigration. The Self within us has been, is, and will be, God. *Aham Brahma*, 'I am God,' is a fundamental text of this heaven-daring philosophy. Absorption, then, is unnecessary and impossible. But even the subtlest and most logical Vedantist—not excepting the great Sankara Acharya himself—cannot

of the primitive cosmological conception,' as exhibited in the Upanishads. The duality of subject and object was thus held to be fictitious.

[1] Ekamevâdvitîyam.

formulate his theory in intelligible or consistent terms.

It is a theory which, I presume, no Western mind can acquiesce in. We hear, indeed, of pantheism, and even of a Christian pantheism, as still professed in Europe; and poets especially will use language which, logically, may involve a pantheistic view of nature; but the passionate utterance of imagination is to be distinguished from the calm dictum of philosophy. The identification of the individual with the universal soul is to all thinking men, in the words of Tennyson, 'a faith as vague as all unsweet;' or, rather, the theory is unthinkable, and those who profess to hold it befool themselves with words, and words only.

Passing from the intellectual weakness of the Vedanta to its ethical character, it is evident that moral distinctions are overturned by it. The sole existence being Brahm, or Self, sin is non-existent and impossible. It appears to exist; but that appearance is as illusive as the mirage of the desert. 'He whose intellect is not confused, even though he should kill, kills not.' In so far as this can be believed by the Hindu, it must practically exert a very evil influence; and accordingly we have clear and explicit testimony that the reception of the Vedanta theory produces a most pernicious effect on moral character.

All religion is also overthrown by the Vedanta. Humility, a sense of dependence, love to God, reverence, prayer, obedience, repentance for sin, love to our neighbour—all such things must, to a genuine Vedantist, appear absurd, and in fact impossible.

And now, glancing at the whole of these famous systems of philosophy, we may sum up our opinion in the words of Dr. John Muir: 'The only one of the six schools that seems to recognize the doctrine of Divine Providence is the Yoga. It thus seems that the consistent followers of these systems can have, in their perfected state, no religion, no action, and no moral character.'

The authors of the six Darsanas endeavoured to systematize the principles of the Upanishads, and to do so without visibly departing from Hindu orthodoxy. The result of their labour was a number of philosophical schools whose teachings were in many points irreconcilable with each other. Yet the Hindu professes to accept all the six schools as authoritative, so that if he really understands them, he believes in contradictory propositions. With regard to their theology, we have in the various schools distinct affirmations of polytheism, pantheism, and atheism, and, we may add with some hesitation, monotheism.

The points in which they agree are the following:

1. All the systems, except the Mimansa, inculcate expedients for attaining salvation; or the emancipation of the soul from the body and from desire.

2. Ignorance is the great cause of the bondage of the soul.

3. But also works, whether good or bad, bring the soul into bondage. For good works have merit, and merit necessitates enjoyment ; and bad works have demerit, and this necessitates suffering. Where enjoyment or suffering is, there is no true emancipation. The emancipated soul feels neither pain nor pleasure.

4. Emancipation is obtainable only through right apprehension. The soul must apprehend itself as distinct from the body, the senses, etc.

5. The soul is eternal, without beginning and without end.

6. Before it attains emancipation, the soul is subject to transmigration.

7. The world had a material cause—something out of which it was produced.

8. The world has always existed. It has often been reduced to its first elements and formed anew ; but, in one state or other, it has existed from eternity.

We hasten to add that although Vedantist writers very often express themselves in contradictory terms, yet, as the Vedanta, in its developed form, denies the existence of an external world, some of the principles now stated do not rightly apply to it.

The six Darsanas did not entirely supersede the the Upanishads. They are dry, and cold, and technical ; whereas, in the Upanishads, notwithstanding all their extravagance, there is a human element which appeals to the heart and awakens sympathy. Still, the recognized philosophy of the schools held a high place in India; and the contradictory utterances of the Darsanas occasioned no small perplexity. Accordingly a very earnest attempt was made to bring the discordant voices into harmony by the author of the Bhagavad Gita (Song of the Holy One). We cannot fix with any certainty the date of this remarkable composition; but it can hardly be earlier than the third century of the Christian era. By that time very considerable intercourse had taken place between India and the West. The Yavanas are spoken of in the great epic poem, the Mahabharata, with high admiration; and under that designation seem to be included the Greeks and, still more, the Greco-Bactrians.[1] It is exceedingly probable that there was some interchange of thought between East and West, especially after Alexandria had become a meeting-point between Asia and Europe. The Manicheans certainly borrowed from both Indian and Christian thought; and so probably did the Gnostics. It has also been asserted (though perhaps not fully proved) that the later Platonists show signs of acquaintance with Indian philosophy, especially with the Sankhya, Yoga, and Vedanta systems.[2] We may admit that India had 'little intellectual wealth for exportation to the Alexandrian emporium;'[3] but, beyond all question, asceticism and

[1] 'Omniscient are the Greeks, O King—heroic men surpassingly.'
[2] Lassen, *Indische Alterthumskunde*, vol. iii. p. 379-442.
[3] Gough, p. xii.

monasticism exerted, chiefly through Egypt, a powerful influence over the West. But was not the debt fully repaid? Various circumstances concur in showing that India borrowed from the West more than she ever lent. In regard to mathematical and physical science this assertion admits of no dispute; in many cases the very terminology found in Indian books is simply Greek, and one astronomical work is known by the name of Romaka Siddhanta, *i.e.*, Roman (or Grecian) treatise. In recent days Indian thinkers have been marked by exclusiveness and intellectual pride; but such was not always the case. In regard to religious ideas, India was from the beginning marvellously receptive; even the debased aboriginal faiths and rites of the land were largely absorbed and partly assimilated. Hinduism has grown to be the enormous and abnormal thing it is, both by accretion from without and by development from within.

These considerations will help us to form a tolerably correct conception of the intellectual position of the author of the Bhagavad Gita. He probably was a Brahman, and possessed of all the culture of his caste. He certainly was a man of as high intellectual endowments as any Indian sage with whom we are acquainted; at once a poet and a philosopher. Such a man would look around him, and be at first dismayed at the multiplicity of rites and the contradictions of beliefs among his people. Was it possible to bring a cosmos out of such a chaos? He would, at all events, make the attempt. And he has done so in verse at once melodious and majestic; he moves on with the stately march of a Lucretius, yet, at the same time, scattering poetic flowers around him and, like Lucretius, *contingens cuncta lepore.*

The Bhagavad Gita is inserted in the middle of the vast epic poem called the Mahabharata.[1] The interpolation was doubtless made to stamp it with authority. It consists of a dialogue between the warrior Arjuna and the deity Krishna. Arjuna was a very distinguished leader in the great war between the Pandavas and the Kauravas. The armies were drawn up in battle array; the war-shell had sounded; and the deadly strife was about to commence, when the tender-hearted Arjuna was overwhelmed with grief at the thought of imbruing his hands in the blood of men who, while opponents, were yet near relatives. His bow drops from his hand; he weeps; he cannot fight. The god Krishna, who has been acting as Arjuna's charioteer and giving him advice, here interposes with a rebuke of this faint-heartedness, and denounces his reluctance to slay the foe as 'disgraceful, despicable weakness.' And then, to prove his point, the deity plunges into the depths of metaphysical speculation, and at length reaches the conclusion—'And therefore up; on to battle, son of Bharata.' There is thus an exceeding unnaturalness in the way in which the disquisition

[1] In the Bhishma Parva, from line 830.

is introduced; but, if it was to be palmed off as a portion of quasi-authoritative Scripture, there was probably no easier or more effectual way.

Krishna, in this remarkable production, is represented as the Supreme Being himself. By the time it was composed Vishnu had attained a high place in the pantheon; he was one of the gods of the Hindu *Trimurtti* (triad); and a large body of followers regarded him as the greatest deity. Now Krishna is a manifestation, or avatara, of Vishnu. Thus, the words which he speaks are accepted as an utterance of the deity condescending to instruct men in a bodily form. And this is one great cause of the immense popularity of the Bhagavad Gita; which is not only carefully studied in Sanskrit, but has been rendered into many of the vernacular Indian languages. Thus, the greatest poem in the Marathi language is simply a commentary on the Song of the Holy One; and the whole character of the succeeding literature has been very powerfully affected by it. Several versions of it have appeared in Hindi. It is also popular in South India, and has been translated into Telugu and Canarese. The great Tamil poem, the Kural, also borrows largely from the Song.

Let us briefly glance, then, at the teachings of this important book. Its great effort is to harmonize the doctrines of the Yoga, the Sankhya, and the Vedanta. It begins by dwelling on the exceeding value of concentrating the mind, according to the first of these systems, and so attaining to union with Deity. Quiescence is essential; the sage must be absorbed in contemplation. While lauding the Yoga, the Gita steers clear of the insane asceticism and magic that are the main characteristics of the system. The metaphysics of the Sankhya as regards Purush and Prakriti, etc., are adopted. (We have explained these terms above.) But the doctrine of a Supreme Spirit as presiding over them is added—an alteration of a fundamental character. There are said to be two kinds of Prakriti; which also is an essential change. In describing the Supreme Spirit the poet seems to task his fertile imagination in heaping thought on thought and image on image, until we confess even his practised touch fails to awaken admiration or sympathy. Finally, Krishna reveals himself to Arjuna in his supreme form, as possessed of countless faces, countless mouths, countless eyes—as, in fact, all things—and blazing like a thousand suns. This passage is a striking proof of the extravagance—the *maasslosigkeit* (to use again Hegel's phrase)—of the Hindu mind,[1] which, in fact, can never discriminate between greatness and bigness, and totally lacks the taste for natural simplicity. The practical conclusion of the whole is that every man should strenuously perform the duties of his caste: and Arjuna, being a Kshatriya, or soldier, has nothing to do with whimpering; for fighting, killing, is his function. And so

[1] Another expression of Hegel's is 'The dream-state of the Hindu mind.'

the warrior is convinced, and plunges into the battle.

The book is full of contradictions. Contemplative quietism is enjoined in one place ; and in another energetic action. Farther, the attempt to harmonize the three systems of philosophy ends in total failure. Two of them must be stripped of their most distinctive features before even the semblance of unity can be secured. The Song is mainly Vedantist in its doctrine.

The incubus of caste has heavily weighed down the soul of India for ages ; and it is at this day the chief obstacle to elevation and advancement. Yet the 'Song' accepts it; glories in it ; and asserts that *varnasankara*, or the mixture of classes, is the cause of the most pernicious consequences. 'A man must not forsake the occupation to which he is born, even although it be blameworthy.' A barber's son must be a barber, whatever may be his capacities and his opportunities of raising himself. The son of a slave must be a slave. There is this compensation, however ; the very meanest—even women and slaves—may attain salvation if they place their entire trust in Krishna.

The exaltation of Krishna is one of the most notable features of the book. His earthly life was in many things most faulty, most foul ; yet the grave author of the Song regards him as an incarnation of the Supreme Divinity. Clearly there had arisen, by the time the poem was composed, a feeling of the need of believing in a Supreme

Being, who was not dim, distant, inconceivable, but who mingled in the affairs of human life. How this feeling arose is a most interesting question; but here we cannot try to discuss it, though we must do so in another place. The Supreme Being, whom, as revealed in Krishna, we have seen acting as Arjuna's charioteer, is yet declared to be not properly existent. 'I am existent and non-existent;' and again, 'The Supreme Deity is not to be declared either existent or non-existent.' Metaphysicians like W. Humboldt have believed it possible to affix a rational meaning to such language; but we need not here make the attempt. Finally, the Gita admits the existence of an external world, and makes it a part of the essence of the Supreme. This is diametrically opposed to the teaching of the Vedanta; nor is it reconcilable with what the Song itself inculcates in various passages.

One remarkable characteristic of the book has still to be noticed. Its language in many places bears a wonderful resemblance to that of the Bible. We are prepared to find in Hindu writings resemblances to thoughts and expressions in the Bible, just as we find them in Greek and Roman authors; it would be very strange if such parallelisms did not occur. But the resemblances between the Gita and the Christian Scriptures, particularly the New Testament, are so numerous that the question unavoidably arises, Could the writer of the Gita have been acquainted with the teachings of the Gospel? This point has been fully discussed by Dr. Lorinser, who has carried out a view very ably supported by Professor Weber and others, to the effect that the development of the Krishna legend has been powerfully affected by ideas borrowed from Christian sources. It is well known that various apocryphal Gospels were circulated in the East—chiefly among the Syrian Christians—from the second century downwards.[1] Translations of these were made into Greek, Latin, Coptic, and Armenian. These writings are of special importance in the history of Mohammadanism. The Arabic *Gospel of the Infancy*, which seems to have been a version from the Syriac, was ascribed to St. Peter, and had much currency in Arabia. It was the main source, in all probability, from which Mohammad drew his ideas of Christ and Christianity. We do not think it can reasonably be denied that these legends—entering probably with the Syrians of the Malabar coast—have powerfully affected Hindu mythology. It is true there is a great difference between this degraded Christianity and the lofty teaching of the Canonical writings which seems to be occasionally echoed in the Gita. Still, in Western and Southern India at least, there were Christians at the time of the probable composition of the 'Song.' Moreover, it is difficult to account for the statements of the Mahabharata regarding 'the white island' and the worshippers of one God who were

[1] See *Edinburgh Review*, July, 1868, and *Indian Antiquary*, September and October, 1873.

found there, unless by supposing that the Hindus knew a good deal about Christian countries in the West. A mind like that of our author—essentially eclectic, and laboriously gathering ideas from all quarters—would certainly have been deeply impressed by many of the Christian doctrines, provided he had become acquainted with them. If he lived in Western or Southern India, he could have had no difficulty in doing so; nor would the difficulty in any part of India have been great. So that, although we do not consider the theory of Dr. Lorinser to be proved,[1] we hold it very probable that Christian ideas were to a considerable extent early incorporated with Indian thought.

Our limits will not allow us to dwell longer on this very interesting book, in which are laboriously interwoven so many conflicting theories—in which are occasional gleams of lofty thought, but which, on the whole, is so hopelessly astray on fundamental points. Let us conclude by giving the judgment pronounced on it by M. Cousin, one of the most tolerant of philosophers, and, like the author of the Gita, essentially an eclectic thinker. 'Before this kind of theism, at once terrible and chimerical, and represented in extravagant and gigantic symbols, human nature must have trembled and denied itself. Art, in its powerless attempt to represent being in itself, necessarily

[1] Thus it is not proved that there was a version of the Scriptures in an Indian dialect. Stripped of this hypothesis, Dr. Lorinser's view is defensible.

rose without limit to colossal and irregular creations. God being all, and man nothing, a formidable theocracy pressed upon humanity, taking from it all liberty, all movement, all practical interest, and consequently all morality. Again, you will comprehend how man, despising himself, has not been able to take any thought for recalling the memory of his actions; so that there is no history of man and no chronology in India.' [1]

It would have been strange if the orthodox philosophies (which nominally acknowledged the Vedas as authoritative) had aroused no opposition. Opposition to the Vedas themselves, and to all systems connected with them, there evidently was from the first. The most famous sect of this class was that of the Charvakas —so called from a noted teacher. It inculcated

[1] Of Hindu philosophy in general, Archer Butler observes: 'The effects of such views of God and man may easily be conjectured. Upon the mild sages of the Ganges they probably produce little result beyond the occasional suggestion of elevated ideas, perhaps more than counterbalanced by the associations of a minute and profitless superstition. But, upon the enormous mass of the nation, these baseless dreams can only result in the perpetuation of ignorance and the encouragement of imposture' (*Lectures on Ancient Philosophy*, vol. i. p. 266).

Burnouf, in his elaborate preface to his edition of the Bhagavata Purana, expresses his surprise that the Hindus should have devoted all their faculties to the examination of insoluble questions and the comprehension of the incomprehensible. Other nations, he says, soon abandoned such fruitless attempts, and directed their attention to inquiries of a practical character. But the mind of India, fed on tales of the gods, disregarded the doings of men. Thus India has never cared for the history of the past, nor thought it worth while to record the events of the present.

undisguised materialism. It seems to have been marked by a light, sneering infidelity ; and it was probably in derision that the school was said to have been founded by Brihaspati, the *guru* of the gods. 'The authors of the three Vedas were buffoons, knaves, and demons'—such was the sweeping dictum of the Charvakas. Their morality seems to have amounted nearly to this : 'Let us eat and drink, for to-morrow we die.' Closely allied to these sceptics must have been the Lokayatikas, or Secularists. But it is enough to note the existence of such scoffing sects. More earnest doubters would avail themselves of the polemic of the Buddhists and Jainas against Hinduism.

We have thus reviewed at some length the philosophical speculations of India ; and, though we are saddened by the result of our inquiries, we yet cannot be much surprised. With all its patience and acuteness, the Indian mind never rose to the height of Aristotle or Plato ; and, on problems which these great thinkers failed to solve, what light could possibly be thrown by Vyasa or Badarayana ? Of the highest speculations of Greek and Alexandrian philosophy St. Paul was compelled to say : 'Hath not God made foolish the wisdom of this world ? For, after that, in the wisdom of God, the world by wisdom knew not God, it pleased God, by the foolishness of preaching, to save them that believe.' Even so is it in India.

The feeling of sadness which we confess to have experienced in the review of Hindu philosophy is so far modified by the hard dogmatism and the unbounded self-assertion of all the schools. It would be an immense relief if one word betokening distrust of their own wisdom were uttered by those teachers—such as we heard occasionally proceeding from the Vedic poets ; but there is no such word. Each theorist moves on with head erect, possessed of absolute faith in his own omniscience. It never occurs to him either that there are matters with which the human mind has no faculties to deal, or that Truth unveils her treasures only to the humble.

CHAPTER IV.

DEVELOPMENT OF BRAHMANISM. SOCIAL LIFE. CASTE.

IN order to take a combined view of the great schools of Indian philosophy we have been obliged to include the Gita, although it is of considerably more recent date than the six 'exhibitions' (*Darsanas*). But, as we desire to trace as far as possible the progress of Indian thought chronologically, we now go back to the sixth century or so, B.C.

While philosophy went on developing, sacerdotalism did so too. The cultivation of the former was not confined to Brahmans; but all religious teaching and observances were more and more monopolized by the priestly caste; and the functions which the Brahmans had once secured they tenaciously retained. It was a slow, steady process of usurpation, continued from age to age. There are clear indications of resistance on the part of other classes; and in civil matters the Brahmans were compelled to concede ample powers to the military caste, to which the rulers belonged. But their spiritual authority and claims were not for a moment relaxed. Spiritual power is of all powers the strongest, and may be the most tyrannical; and so it became in India. The system of caste was fully established by the sixth century B.C.

Codes of law had by this time begun to appear, which were to regulate civil as well as religious life. As a kind of supplement to the treatises on ritual (Brahmanas), a class of writings called Sutras had appeared. One division of these, called Grihya Sutras, treated of domestic ceremonies; another, called Dharma Sutras, referred to public right—civil and criminal law. Out of these Sutras the various treatises on jurisprudence seem to have gradually arisen.[1] The most celebrated of these books is the Code of Manu. Where, when, and by whom it was drawn up we cannot with certainty say. With some probability we may ascribe its present form to the fifth, or at latest the third, century B.C.; but it may have been only very gradually moulded into shape. Brahmanical thought pervades it all through; and nowhere does the innate pride of the Brahman appear in more repulsive forms. It would almost seem as if the very gods had been created for his special benefit.

According to Manu there are four castes or

[1] 'The so-called revealed codes [Manu, etc.] are, in most cases, but improved versions of older prose works.'—Bühler, *Sacred Books of the East*, vol. ii. p. 10.

classes that are regular: the Brahman, the Kshatriya, the Vaisya, and the Sudra. The Brahman is the priest; the Kshatriya is the warrior; the Vaisya is the husbandman or trader; the Sudra is the servant, or rather slave. There is, besides these, a multitude of impure classes, which are said to have arisen from the intermarriage of members of one pure caste with those of another. The first three classes are invested with a sacred thread, as a token that they are 'twice born'—though that name is often used to designate especially the Brahman. Unlike the Parsi religion, which gives a sacred thread as the token of initiation to men and women alike, Hinduism recognizes no 'twice-born' women. As for the Sudra, he has simply nothing to do with the statutory religious rites. Any attempt on his part to engage in them is worthy of summary punishment; and in fact Rama, the great warrior-god, when he beholds a Sudra practising rites forbidden to his caste, simply decapitates him on the spot.[1] To teach a Sudra the Veda was a grievous sin; to receive money for doing so was an unpardonable offence.

The usual word in Sanskrit to express the idea of caste is *varna*, which properly means 'colour.' The Dasyus and other aboriginal tribes who opposed the intrusive Âryas are called 'the black skin;'[2] and apparently there was—wholly apart from the natural hostility between invaders and invaded—a strong repugnance on the part of the

[1] Ramayana, vii. 74–76. [2] R. V. i. 130. 8.

fairer race to the darker. Human nature is sorrowfully consistent ; we see in all this an anticipation of the relations that have subsisted in modern times between the white and black races. Up to this day there is generally a marked distinction in colour between the highest and the lower castes. The purity of the Brahman blood has, in various places, been pretty successfully preserved.

With fixed determination, then, the Brahmans maintained for generations the struggle for supremacy, until at last the prize was won. We read of earnest opposition on the part of the Kshatriyas or warrior caste, with whom doubtless the two others, in so far as they may have been able to resist at all, must have take npart. The kingly power was a foe which it took all the skill and perseverance of the Brahmans to overcome. In individual cases, indeed, they had to give way. Thus the celebrated Visvamitra is said to have obtained the rank of Brahmanhood for himself and his family. The later legend (invented by Brahmans) represents this high distinction as having been won only by frightful austerities prolonged for thousands of years ; as if it had found it necessary to deter others from making a similar attempt. Although this was not a solitary instance of successful resistance to Brahmanical domination,[1] yet, on the whole, the priestly power continually increased. If we are to believe the Brahmans themselves, the Kshatriya race was

[1] King Janaka also is said to have opposed the Brahmans.

finally exterminated by Parasurama (Rama with the axe), the fifth incarnation of the god Vishnu. It is exceedingly probable that this legend implies a great contest between the priests and the soldiers, in which the former were completely victorious. The Brahmans seem thenceforth to have ruled all things according to their will—in other words, with a rod of iron. They now drew up the most stringent rules regarding caste. When castes multiplied, which they necessarily did as social life became more complex—each profession becoming a kind of caste—they were ready with ridiculous tales to explain their origin. Men of different castes could now not dine together. Marriages of people of different castes were detestable; above all, for a low caste man to dare to marry a Brahman wife was the horror of horrors. Some writers of respectability have almost apologized for caste; they say it has a good as well as a bad side. So has slavery, as well as many other things of the serpent's brood. They think it guarded morality, as a man would be deterred from committing offences which the law did not punish, provided expulsion from caste would be entailed by them. Yes, in that case; but what offences were so punished? Eating, drinking, and marrying—if contrary to rule; but for ages past, if not from the very beginning, the most heinous crimes could be committed without injury to a man's position in society. On the other hand, if—even under the pressure of famine—he ate food prepared by a man of lower caste, he was summarily expelled, and suffered all the frightful evils which excommunication involves in India. But as the modern development of caste will necessarily come under consideration at a later point, we shall not now discuss its moral character at greater length.

The great object of the legislation is to secure the exaltation of the Brahman; and the regulations are exceedingly detailed with a view to this. Every Brahman properly passes through four stages of life. First, he is an unmarried student; secondly, he is a married householder; thirdly, he is a hermit; and fourthly, he is a religious devotee. He enters the first stage at the age of eight, through investiture with the sacred cord. He then resides with a preceptor (guru) to learn the Veda. When his studies are completed, he returns home and marries. Marriage is a sacrament; it is generally accompanied with great rejoicings, and lasts for several days. As a married householder, he is especially bound to perform five great duties, or forms of worship: that is, he repeats the Veda; worships his ancestors; worships the gods; worships all beings (chiefly by scattering grains of rice for living creatures to eat in the open air); and shows hospitality to guests. His wife must also have certain important qualifications. She must be of his own caste, not related to him within the sixth degree; she must not have the name of a constellation, or of a tree, or of a river; she must walk like a young elephant, and must not be afflicted with red hair.

When his strength begins to fail and he has a grandchild, he must betake himself to the forest, either accompanied by his wife, or alone—after entrusting her to her sons. He must now bathe daily thrice; he must allow his beard, nails, and hair to grow; he must continually be conversant with the Veda and meditate on the Supreme. Penances are obligatory. In the hot season let him sit exposed to five fires; in the rains let him stand uncovered; in the cold season let him wear moist garments. He must live without a house, and remain wholly silent.

One does not see how the hermit could long survive under such a discipline; but if he did, he must enter on the fourth and last stage. His beard, nails, and hair are now to be clipped. He is to be provided with a dish, a staff, and an earthen waterpot. He must wander about continually, begging his food once a day. Coarse clothing, total solitude, no home, no fire to cook his food; these things are essential. Then like a tree falling into a river when the bank gives way, or like a bird pleased to quit the branch on which it has had its perch, so he cheerfully forsakes the body which is the abode of sorrow and disease. In this remarkable delineation there are a few pleasing touches: for example, the ascetic is exhorted to bear all things with equanimity, and to avoid giving pain to any sentient creature. Yet the usual note of extravagance is seldom wanting; and the ineradicable taint of error is seen in the command to suppress all love as well as hatred, as a needful preparation for union with the Supreme. But this whole style of thought is so foreign to Western minds that we can hardly apprehend it—perhaps hardly do it justice. No wonder that the Greeks were confounded to see the multitudes of men who seemed weary of life in Northern India. A happy, sensuous existence was all in all to the Greek, and death was full of gloom. To the Brahman life was misery, and the cessation of all personal existence was the supreme good. It is surely both touching and instructive to note how Greek and Indian strayed so far, in opposite directions, from the truth.

The legislation regarding women requires to be noticed, for the treatment of one-half of the population is a point of the greatest possible importance. Woman in earlier days had occupied a position of respect. We have poems in the Veda that were written by women; and in somewhat later days women often entered into religious discussions with as much zeal and intelligence as men. But as time went on, a great change took place. In the developed code women are put in the same position—at least as to religious rights and property—with Sudras or slaves. 'Women's rights' were unknown. They could have no property of their own. 'Women were created to be mothers,' says the legislator.[1] They may be married before they are eight years old. A man may have more wives than one. A

[1] Manu ix. 96.

woman is under her father in childhood, then under her husband; when her husband dies she is under her sons: 'a woman is never fit for independence.' Even if the husband be wicked, or in love with another woman, he must be revered as a god by his wife. When he dies, the widow must 'emaciate her body by living on pure flowers, roots, and fruit;' she must continue till death 'performing harsh duties.' The marriage of a widow is forbidden. Taking this law in connection with the permission—or command rather—that women be married when no more than children, one easily apprehends the deplorable consequences. Any one who has been in India, or who reflects on the results of such legislation, must be wounded in his inmost soul as he thinks of the sufferings of Indian widows.

We have still to speak of the inhuman rite of Sati (Suttee), or the burning of widows on the same funeral-pile with their dead husbands. When the British Government in India was preparing to abolish it—which it did in 1829—the Brahmans vehemently opposed all interference with the time-honoured custom; and, under their influence, almost a rebellion in Bengal seemed imminent. The Brahmans contended that Suttee was a religious institution authoritatively prescribed in the Veda. They quoted the precise passage enjoining that widows should 'consign themselves to the fire.' But when examined, the passage in question was found to inculcate the very reverse of what the Brahmans affirmed. Professor H. H.

Wilson proved that they had actually falsified the text, and not merely mistranslated it; they had changed the words of the one book which they professed to receive with awful reverence as the 'eternal' utterance of heaven. Rightly does Max Müller denounce this act as 'perhaps the most flagrant instance of what can be done by an unscrupulous priesthood.'[1] It has been calculated that, from the year 1756, when the battle of Plassey gave Britain the sovereignty of Bengal, up to 1829, when Suttee was prohibited in British territory, no fewer than 70,000 widows had thus been sacrificed. And if this estimate be even approximately correct, what pen 'dipped to the feather in human agony' can describe the horrors of the Suttee rite for the last two thousand years? The tortured and murdered women must have been millions in number. Alas for

'The fair humanities of old religion,'

of which poets vainly talk! All honour to the memory of Lord William Bentinck, who, in spite of the opposition of Brahmans leagued (*proh pudor!*) with some Europeans, dared to quench those hellish fires! The writer must be pardoned if he appear to speak too strongly; but when he went out to India the Suttee flames were still blazing in Native States; and he well remembers the thrill of horror and indignation which he felt when he read the account of the burning alive of

[1] *Chips*, vol. i. p. 35.

nine women along with the corpse of old Runjit Singh. Four wives and five slave girls who were concubines were thus murdered. But nine was only a small number; there are cases on record in which the holocaust consisted of sixty or seventy women, and even more.

The Sanskrit treatises on Hindu law are very numerous.[1] Next to Manu the Code of Yajnavalkya is held in high esteem. The latter is much shorter and more systematic than the former; but in their general character the two codes pretty much agree. Yajnavalkya's work may perhaps date from the first or second century A.D. Both of these codes are written in verse; and indeed that of Manu is sometimes truly poetical.[2]

Our limits will not allow us to dwell on the general character of Hindu legislation; but we may mention that trial by what is generally called 'ordeal' is very much more prominent in the later code than in the earlier. The forms of ordeal are as severe and unreasonable as those employed in mediæval Europe. Here again the Brahman had the easier trial. He was to be judged by weighing. If innocent, he rose upward; if guilty, the scale in which he was descended. Ordeal by fire or water,

[1] 'The total number of Dharma-Sastras, or treatises on law, is fifty-six.'—*Weber*.

[2] Manu x. 84. We must add that amidst much that is childish and not a little that is morally wrong in the great law-book, we occasionally come upon noble thoughts. Thus: 'The wicked have said in their hearts, "None sees us." But the gods see them, and so does the spirit in their own breasts.' Such a saying is like an oasis in the desert.

or the administration of poison, was reserved for the Sudra. Another point of difference between the codes is this: gambling is expressly prohibited by Manu; but the later lawgiver allows it, only insisting that a certain part of the gain shall be paid to the king and certain other persons. The Hindus had been greatly addicted to gambling even from the times of the Veda. It is probable that the earlier legislation honestly opposed it, but found its suppression impossible; and that the later was satisfied with the attempt to regulate the vice.

When the laws ascribed to Manu were drawn up, the Hindus were in Northern India near the river Sarasvati. The people seem to have lived in villages rather than large towns or scattered habitations; and we may well believe that some form of associate life was necessary to protect them against enemies and wild beasts. The country must have been much more richly wooded than it is now. The supply of water must have been ampler than at present; for the Sarasvati, which is extolled as a mighty river, now loses itself in the sands before reaching the Indus. Flocks and herds abounded. Agriculture had been originally held in high honour; but ere long 'the benevolent' objected to it, because the iron-mouthed pieces of wood wounded not only the earth but the creatures dwelling in it;[1] and hence Brahmans and Kshatriyas should have nothing to do with it. On every side of the village a space was left for pasture-

[1] Manu x. 84.

ground ; fields could be inclosed within it for cultivation ; but then, as now, the greater part of the cultivated ground must have been at some distance from the village. Rice, barley, leeks, and sugar-cane were among the most important products. Artizans of various kinds were employed ; each, as a rule, confining his labour to his own village. In fact, from the earliest days, and all through successive centuries, the village system has been indestructible—and, as an institution, complete in itself. Dynasties may come and go, but the villager clings to his inheritance, and contentedly lives and works where, and as, his fathers did before him. For women, when not engaged with household duties, the common occupations were spinning and weaving. We hear of travelling merchants ; and there was doubtless much traffic between one part of the country and another. Foreign merchants could reach Northern India by the river Indus—though the ascent was doubtless difficult then, as it is now ; and Indian products seem to have been carried to Persia, Palestine, and Egypt from an early date—although we cannot suppose that either exports or imports were on an extensive scale. Ivory seems to have been obtained from India ; and, as the African elephant had not been domesticated, war-elephants must also have been so. Indigo (the very name denotes the place of its growth) and cotton were early in use, and were also exported.

CHAPTER V.

STRUGGLE BETWEEN BRAHMANISM AND BUDDHISM.

IT has been already mentioned that ritualism and philosophy went on developing side by side. It is not conceivable that the zealous supporters of the one system aided in the development of the other. The students of philosophy, indeed, were careful to declare themselves to be orthodox believers in the Veda; but the inevitable result of their speculations was to weaken, among those who accepted their teaching, the authority of the established worship, and indirectly to undermine that of the Veda. Meantime, the ritual had assumed more and more imposing dimensions; and extravagant asceticism more and more prevailed. Sacrifice had become more protracted, more expensive, and more bloody. All religious services were conducted in Sanskrit; and the sacred texts of the Veda were in an archaic form of the language, which the priests themselves but very partially understood. Princes and people could only look on and see worship performed on their behalf. Direct approach to the deities was possible only to the holy Brahman ; and it was his inalienable birthright—the title ran in his blood. Religious instruction for the mass of the people was never thought of ; nor did the philosophers ever dream of communicating to them their daring speculations. Altogether the religious condition of India had become darker than ever—deplorably dark—by the sixth century B.C. One is disposed to think that a reaction from priestly tyranny and extreme sacerdotalism was inevitable. It has been said of the Reformation of the sixteenth century that it was certain to have taken place even had the great soul of Luther never come upon the scene ; the ever-gathering waters must have burst their way ere long. Even so in India, two thousand years before the Reformation in Europe. An immense revolt from such intolerable tyranny over the souls and bodies of men was sure to come. But the specific form which the revolt assumed was largely due to the personal qualities of the reformer. We are aware that writers of high name have doubted whether such a man as Buddha ever lived.[1] It seems to us, however, that unity is so deeply impressed on early Buddhism that we are compelled to ascribe it to one author. It is, at all events, far easier to believe that there was no Zoroaster, or no Homer, than that there was no Buddha.

[1] Such as Wassiljew, H. H. Wilson, Senart, and Kern.

It is now satisfactorily made out that the death of Buddha fell between 482 B.C. and 472 B.C.; and this, indeed, is the first certain date in Indian chronology. We cannot, in this little work, discuss either his character or his doctrines at any length.[1] There is no evidence that he was a man of high intellectual gifts; his chief characteristic was tenderness of heart. He saw overflowing sorrow all around; and with him the great question was—How shall that sorrow cease? In the portentous metaphysical speculations with which his system has been overlaid, he had no share; his aim was wholly practical. It has been asserted that he openly attacked Brahmanism; but this does not seem likely. As a mere social institution he appears to have had no quarrel even with caste, although a gentle soul like his must have mourned over its detestable tyranny; but he held that none who adopted his teachings need be fettered by it in their mutual intercourse. Men of all ranks were welcomed as disciples. Women too—although still debarred from that position which is their right—received, on entering the society, a place of comparative respect. His law, he declared, was a law of kindness, and intended for all. He preached in the vernacular language, and to masses of men. The complex ritual of Brahmanism he ignored; and sacrifice, as involving pain to sentient creatures,

[1] One of the latest books on the subject is the very instructive work of Bishop Titcomb, published by the Religious Tract Society.

was abhorrent to his whole style of thought. A prince sympathizing with the people was a sight by no means common; a prince instructing the people in their own tongue was entirely new. We cannot, then, be surprised at the effect of his public appearances. He was the man for the occasion.

A distinguished philanthropist in modern times[1] used to say: 'Disease and misery and vice exist. I have no time and less inclination to talk metaphysics about them; but my life shall be given to remedy the evil and lessen the load which is crushing down into mere animalism the beings made in God's image.' The last clause Buddha could not have uttered, for Buddha did not believe in God or God's image; but the rest of the sentiment he could heartily have adopted as his own. In respect of this tenderness of heart Buddha stands unique in the Pagan world. When we think that, without believing in God and without having the example of Christ, he was able to rise so high, we are filled with astonishment. And with regard to his atheism, it is a thing to be deplored, but hardly to be wondered at. He believed in *gods*—beings superior to men, but subject to mutation and decay; and, in the countless series of births which he had passed through, he had been himself a god, just as he had been a worm. In so far as Buddha attempted to philosophize, he seems to have agreed with the

[1] Pastor Fliedner of Kaiserswerth.

earlier Sankhya school,[1] which taught that there were souls and nature, but no Supreme Ruler. And if he turned to the orthodox Brahmanical creed, its gods were dim and distant; or, if they ever did concern themselves with the doings of men, they were unlovely and unlovable. With such divinities he had no sympathy, and it was impossible for him to honour them.[2]

It is truly remarkable that although Buddha

[1] Buddha, however, did not derive his pessimism from the Sankhya. Gradually a stupendous system of metaphysical speculation was connected with Buddhism; and, before the Christian era, this had been developed into a pure Nihilism, especially under the teaching of Nagarjuna. This asserts the existence of an original void, out of which proceeded all that is. But what *is?* Only a series of sensations. Using modern terms, we may call the philosophy of Buddhism pure sensationalism.

We have said that, in the absence of historical documents, the chronological sequence of the various philosophical systems cannot be fixed with certainty. Quite possibly the Buddhist doctrine of an original void became prominent when the high metaphysical speculations of the Vedanta had been pushed to an extreme, and the impersonal Brahm, in fact, had been reduced almost to zero. The Buddhist took only one step more than the Vedantist.

The Sankhya, as it appears in later books, is probably a polemic against the Buddhist philosophy. It strongly asserts the real existence both of mind and matter (*purush* and *prakriti*)—or soul and nature, as we may rather render the terms.

We have referred in this note to the time when the Buddhist doctrine of the void 'became prominent.' But it began in the time of the Upanishads. We read in the Chhandogya Upanishad: 'Some say that entity issued of non-entity. But how can this be?' The doctrine of an original void must therefore have been maintained by certain schools or, at least, individuals.

[2] 'Do you worship the gods?' said Bishop Heber, in Ceylon, to a Buddhist priest. 'No,' said the priest; 'the gods worship me.'

was an atheist, Buddhism speedily became almost theistic by Buddha being worshipped. It is hard to style the votaries of Krishna theists, and those of Buddha atheists; for morally Buddha stands immensely the higher of the two.

The character of Buddha was most attractive; but Buddha was a man, and he had passed into the inane; and of the gentle teacher there remained only a sweet, sad memory. This could not satisfy the cravings of the heart; and so he was turned into a quasi-divinity. But in speaking of Buddhism a clear distinction must always be drawn between the northern and southern schools. It is in the northern school that he has become a full divinity. We may say, then, that his system flourished chiefly in consequence of a reversal of his teaching on this fundamental point. Singular, surely, and at the same time most significant, that his denial of a divinity led to his own exaltation to divinity. It is a proof that man must worship.

Buddha himself believed not in a divinity, but in *Karma* (literally, *work*); which, as understood by him, we may style the principle of moral retribution. This was a higher thought than that of *Μοῖρα*, or fate; which, according to the ancient Greeks, controlled the action even of Zeus himself.

But apart from its atheism Buddha's system was greatly faulty. Salvation — all the salvation he knew—was to be obtained by people becoming monks and nuns—mendicants and ascetics. The idea of being *in* the world yet not *of* it, was far above his reach. He dealt with individuals. He could not save society; he could only destroy it. His followers could attain salvation only by abandoning all family ties.

His counsels of perfection — unless his early followers exaggerated his views — ran into an asceticism which even those who admire his unqualified pessimism will repudiate as extravagant and senseless.

We find in Buddhism much that is high and pure, much that is foolish, and much that is deplorably defective. Its vast superiority to Hinduism as a moral system is unquestionable; and yet it seems all but powerless to produce the morality it inculcates. Its best feature was its missionary spirit. It is a pathetic spectacle to witness those old Buddhist monks crossing inhospitable mountains and stormy oceans, that they might preach to barbarous races that poor gospel of theirs—the best, alas! they had to offer—declaring that all existence is misery.

In India Buddhism contended with Brahmanism for fully a thousand years; and when Asoka (who deserves the appellation of Emperor of India as much as any ruler ever did) had embraced it and given it his powerful patronage, it seemed not unlikely to prevail finally over its rival. But it was not so to be. Various causes combined to overthrow it. For one thing, the Brahmans had all along maintained their intellectual superiority, which they showed both in speech and writing.

The Buddhist style has been called 'the most detestable of all styles;' and the thought was generally as feeble as the expression. Society also rebelled against a system which aimed at its dissolution by drawing into monasticism and mendicancy every man who was in earnest about salvation. Then, Brahmanism was national; Buddhism was cosmopolitan: and this difference, which at first helped Buddhism, the astute Brahmans would turn to full account when at last the Indian princes roused themselves to repel the Northern invaders. In the end Buddhism disappeared from Indian soil. It was, however, a dear-bought victory to its opponents. They retained their power by surrendering many of their distinctive principles. Many Buddhistic ideas had so penetrated the Indian mind that they could not be uprooted. Accordingly these were skilfully interwoven with the Brahmanical system; while, at the same time, some of the deficiencies of Buddhism were carefully supplied.

For a long time there was no open conflict between Brahmanism and Buddhism. Buddha, we have said, did not inveigh against caste; though he taught his followers to rise above it by constituting a spiritual community of which any man—or woman—might become a member. Let us do justice to this lofty conception of brotherhood, so widely different from the narrow selfishness of Brahmanism. The Brahmans must undoubtedly have disliked the bold innovation; but probably open war between the rival systems did not commence until the Buddhist fraternity began to share in the gifts of which the Brahmans had hitherto had a monopoly. Although the Buddhist was professedly a mendicant, his order was often rich; and to the Brahman this was altogether intolerable.

We do not know that there ever was a persecution of Buddhists on any large scale. Local outbreaks there must have been, as there have often been between rival sectaries in India; and in all such collisions the pacific Buddhists, if true to their principles, would fare the worse. But there was no sudden fall of Buddhism; there was a long and gradual decay, until it finally disappeared from India about the end of the twelfth century A.D.

CHAPTER VI.

RECONSTRUCTION OF HINDUISM. THE AVATARAS.

BUT the Hinduism that gradually arose as Buddhism faded away was a vastly different system from that which had previously existed. We find in it especially distinct traces of Buddhistic thought; we may say that an undertone of Buddhism is audible through all later Sanskrit writings, and equally sō in the vernacular literature. Sacrifice was set aside; and great regard for animal life was inculcated. This was a stupendous revolution; a reversal, one might say, of the deepest thoughts of the early Hindus. No more even of horse-sacrifice—that rite of dazzling splendour and tremendous potency;—a sentiment, often heard in modern India, began to sway the national mind: 'Non-killing is supreme religion.'

Again, the main strength of Buddhism was Buddha; first, the living man, and after his death, his memory. Assuredly it was not its wild asceticism that gave Buddhism its influence; nor was it the stupendous and incomprehensible metaphysics that soon clustered around the system : it was the mild, loving man himself. That compelled an admiration which speedily passed in many cases into adoration. The influence of Buddhism is traceable as clearly as anywhere in the *Avataras*, or 'Descents' of divine beings to mingle in the affairs of human life. It is especially the god Vishnu who thus 'descends.' Round the naturalistic divinities of the Veda there had gathered a mass of fable which served in some degree to humanize them. Still, much of their original, physical character remained ; and they had few or none of the attractive attributes of Buddha. The latter had by this time come to be regarded as a brother-man with a heart full of sympathy with the sorrowful, and yet a kind of deity, possessed of superhuman power. The Brahmans chose two great legendary heroes, Rama and Krishna, whose names were associated with events in history as famous in India as the War of Troy was in Greece ; they represented them as divinities who had 'descended' to earth. These were as truly human as Buddha, and still more divine. Round the simple Buddha there had gradually clustered a wild mythology, the offspring of a depraved taste, so that the touching history of the man was not easily traced amidst the false ornaments so lavishly thrown around it. The Brahmans yielded to this morbid appetite for extravagant fiction, and, as far as in them lay, outdid the Buddhists in its gratification. There is much reason to believe that the tale of the warrior-god Rama was of Buddhist origin, and in general the 'descended' god retains the Buddhist attribute of gentleness; but the metamorphosis of the Buddhist into the Hindu prince reveals the wonderful fertility of the poet's imagination. Later on, the taste of the people became yet more corrupt, and still the Brahmans ministered to its cravings; so that, in the god Krishna, all the finer elements of character have disappeared, and the poet strives to appease the cravings of an imagination utterly debauched. Buddhist legends were abundantly childish; but they never were impure. Impurity, however, is an almost unfailing mark of Hindu literature; and we venture to explain this, not by attributing it to utterly corrupt taste on the part of the writers, but rather to their determination to supplant the Buddhist stories by stories still more wonderful, and at the same time more stimulating to the polluted minds of the people.

Thus, indirectly, Buddhism was to be supplanted. How could it now maintain its existence? It was beaten with its own weapons. But the Brahmans were not satisfied with assailing it indirectly. They made a direct attack upon it by representing Buddha as the ninth 'descent' of Vishnu. The gods and the daityas (the latter pretty much corresponding to the Titans of classical mythology) had warred with one another, and the gods had been defeated; whereupon they implored

Vishnu to destroy their victorious foes. The god accordingly became incarnate in the form of a naked ascetic on the banks of the Narmada river; and with glozing words overturned the religion of the Vedas, and thus effected the destruction of those whom he had so seduced. Of the many daring conceptions of the Brahmans this may be called the most horrible. Of all their divinities Vishnu is believed to be the one in whom especially resides the attribute of *truth;* yet even he is declared to have become incarnate for the purpose of disseminating a lie and plunging giants and men into perdition! We apprehend it would be difficult to find a lower depth than this even in the lowest Pagan faith.

We have spoken of three of Vishnu's avataras. These are sometimes said to have been twenty-two in all; but the great 'descents' are ten. In a celebrated passage of the Bhagavad Gita, Krishna thus explains to Arjuna the reason of the descents:

> 'When fades the true and flourishes the false,
> 'Tis then, 'tis then, that I must interpose—
> To save the holy and to crush the bad,
> To rescue right, from age to age reborn.'

A noble conception, certainly; but the avataras are, in fact, utterly unlike the idealized picture thus supplied by the poet.

It is not very easy to extract any meaning out of the first three 'descents.' In the first of all the god becomes a fish. It has been conjectured that, with their wonted spirit of accommodation in matters of faith, the Brahmans may have introduced this conception in order to win over certain tribes that worshipped the fish; or perhaps we should say that, when they could not expel the worship, they deified the fish. We are more inclined, however, to the belief that we have, in this descent of Vishnu, a tradition of the deluge which has been metamorphosed in the wild style of the Brahmans. Manu, the ancestor of the human race, faithful among the faithless, was divinely warned of the coming catastrophe. Accordingly he built a ship, and entered it along with seven holy men. When the flood came, Vishnu assumed the form of a fish; and the ship was fastened to a horn on its head, and so drawn on and attached to a lofty peak in the Himalaya mountains till the deluge abated. This is very much the sort of story which the bizarre imagination of the Hindus would invent if they had heard of the deliverance of the righteous Noah and his family of seven persons. Another statement is that a daitya named Hayagriva stole the Vedas from the god Brahma when he was asleep, and that Vishnu, in the form of a fish, plunged into the deep to rescue them. This seems to indicate the restoration of religion.

The second descent of Vishnu was in the form of a tortoise. During the deluge various precious things had been lost in the ocean. Accordingly, for the purpose of recovering these, the god, in the form of a tortoise, took up his station at the bottom of the mid-ocean. A mountain was placed by the deities on his back, and the serpent Vasuki was twisted around it. The gods and demons then took hold of the serpent, the former grasping his head and neck and the latter his tail, and, pulling against each other, churned the ocean—the mountain serving as a churning-stick. Fourteen precious things were thus churned out. It requires considerable ingenuity to discover the principle of the selection of these so-called 'jewels'—among which are a marvellous horse, an elephant, the cow of plenty, the moon, nectar, and (oddly enough) poison. To give the rationale of things irrational is beyond us; but this descent should naturally indicate the reappearance of objects which had been engulphed by the waters of the deluge.

The third descent was in the form of a boar. The daitya Hiranyaksha had carried the earth down into the abyss. Vishnu assumed the form of a boar, fought with him for a thousand years, and brought the earth up again. It looks very probable that this account refers to the reappearance of the dry land when the waters of the deluge had subsided.

The next descent was that of the man-lion. The daitya Hiranyakasipu had obtained from the god Brahma the boon that neither god nor man nor animal should be able to slay him. He conquered the three worlds, and carried off the sacrifices that belonged to the gods. His son Prahlada was a devoted worshipper of Vishnu; and the father in wrath made every effort to slay him—throwing him into the fire, plunging him in the deep, and so on. All in vain. Prahlada still called on Vishnu, and was rescued. The daitya indignantly asked, 'Where is your god?' The son answered, 'Everywhere.' 'Is he in this pillar?' shouted the daitya, striking it. Instantly the pillar opened; and Vishnu issued from it in the form of a creature that was neither god nor man nor beast, but a man-lion, and at once tore the daitya in pieces. We may, with some probability, hold this legend to refer to a struggle between the followers of some of the aboriginal faiths with advancing Hinduism, which ended in the triumph of the latter.

The fifth descent is said to have taken place in the Treta yuga, or second age of the world. Bali, a descendant of Prahlada (mentioned above), was engaged in offering sacrifices, with a view to displace Indra from his supreme dominion. To prevent him from succeeding, Vishnu became incarnate in the form of Vamana, a Brahman dwarf, and begged of Bali as much territory as he could measure in three steps. The unsuspecting king said that this was a very poor request to be made to one who was sovereign of the three worlds—heaven, earth, and hell; why not ask more? With a show of profound humility, the incarnate deity replied that he did not desire and could not accept of more. His *guru* warned the monarch to beware of this extraordinary guest and his equally extraordinary modesty; but Bali would not listen to his remonstrances. The boon was granted. Whereupon Vamana, spreading out his form to vast dimensions, strode with two steps through heaven and earth, and then putting his foot on Bali's head (or body, as it is otherwise expressed), crushed him down to hell. There can hardly be any doubt as to the historical meaning of this legend. It evidently refers to the mode in which the wily Brahmans obtained their supreme authority, by wheedling the unsuspecting rulers of the land. This explanation is confirmed by the fact that Bali is still commemorated, at least in Western India, and that the return of his happy reign is earnestly implored.[1]

The sixth descent of Vishnu was Parasu Rama (Rama with the axe). He was the son of a Brahman father and a Kshatriya mother. (In this we have a reminiscence of the time when intermarriage between people of different castes was still allowed.) The Kshatriya kings were tyrannizing over the Brahmans: for example, the father of Parasurama had his cow taken from him; whereupon Parasurama, who armed with his tremendous axe was irresistible, slew the offender. His sons retaliated by slaying Parasurama's own father. It was now internecine war; and the champion with the axe, travelling over the earth

[1] The people throw away all the dirt and sweepings of their houses, and with exuberant joy and the clash of musical instruments, exclaim in their uncultured rhymes—

'Let pain and sorrow pack,
And Bali's reign come back!'

twenty-one times, cleared it of the hated Kshatriyas, with the exception of a few children, for whom their mothers implored mercy at the Brahmans' retreats.

The meaning of this legend hardly requires explanation. That the Kshatriya race was ever annihilated, or nearly so, is utterly improbable; but it suited the purpose of the usurping Brahmans to maintain that none had henceforth a right to claim the time-honoured name of Kshatriya.

The seventh descent was in the person of Rama, or Ramachandra. His history is contained in the great heroic poem called the Ramayana. It is highly probable that the original form of the Rama legend was of Buddhist origin, and written in the interests of Buddhism. The Buddhist virtue of gentleness still adheres to Rama; but the poet Valmiki has, with no small skill, transformed the earlier legend, and made it support the claims of Brahmanism. The poem may have assumed its present form a little before the Christian era. The hero-god Rama has long been one of the most popular divinities; and this is partly owing to his own attractive character, the womanly virtues of his wife Sita, and the history, at once romantic and pathetic, of the loving pair. Moreover, Valmiki writes in melodious verse; and the version of the poem in Hindi, which is the most widely diffused of the vernacular tongues of India, is also an attractive and highly popular production.

Rama was the eldest son of Dasaratha, king of

Ayodhya (Oude). When a youth, he won his bride Sita by being able to bend a wonderful bow belonging to her father, King Janaka of Mithila.[1] His stepmother intrigued against him, and he and his attached wife were sent into banishment, in the Dandaka forest, which covered a great part of the country north of the Godavari river. Sita, in Rama's absence, is carried off to Lanka (Ceylon) by the king Ravana—a personage with ten heads and twenty arms. Rama, with the assistance of the monkey-king Sugriva, collects an army of monkeys, and advances to the straits that separate Ceylon from India. The way in which he bridged the strait is described with even more than the usual lavishness of Hindu imagination; *inter alia*, Hanuman the monkey brought mountains to cast into the sea, millions at a time, a mountain on each hair of his body. Ravana is vanquished; Sita is recovered; Rama returns in triumph to Ayodhya, and is crowned king. But as Sita had lived for some time in the house of Ravana, he dismissed her, although of her chastity there could be no question. Then Sita entered the fire; which however refused to burn her; and on this, her husband took her back. The legend altogether is full of romantic tales which delight the Hindu, but from the extravagance of which the Western mind turns with disrelish. Our readers may have a good idea of Rama's exploits if they remember those of Jack the Giant-killer, which probably charmed

[1] This account does not seem to be in the Ramayana.

them in their childhood. The Hindu imagination has never risen above the childish stage.

Still more popular than the popular Rama is Krishna, the ninth incarnation of Vishnu; but morally he is immensely inferior. Krishna was born in the third age of the world. He was the eighth son of Vasudeva and Devaki. It had been predicted that Kansa, the king of Mathura, would be killed by one of the sons of Vasudeva and Devaki. The king accordingly imprisoned Vasudeva and his wife, and killed six of their children as they were successively born. The seventh was miraculously saved. The eighth was Krishna, whose name means 'the black one.' The father fled from Mathura with the child, and confided him to the care of a herdsman called Nanda, who brought him up in Vrindavana, at some distance from Mathura. The imagination of Hindu poets luxuriates in the description of the sports of Krishna and his young companions. Even as a child he performed the most stupendous miracles. Being swallowed by a frightful winged creature which Kansa had sent to destroy him, he made it feel so uncomfortable that it vomited him up again; whereupon he tore its mouth open and killed it. At the same time he performed all sorts of naughty tricks. He delighted in stealing milk, curds, and butter. His foster-mother had to bind him with a rope to keep him out of mischief; but he made short work of the rope—he ate it up. It would have been well had matters ended there.

He delighted to sport with the female cowherds of Vrindavana; and it is especially in describing this part of his history that the prurient imagination of the Hindu poets is seen to run riot. Of course we cannot dwell on the subject at any length; a few hints must suffice. He had eight chief wives; the queen of all, Rukmini, had been betrothed to another, but on her marriage-day Krishna carried her off in a chariot and made her his own wife. The total number of his wives was sixteen thousand. The Gopis (female cowherds) went one day to bathe in the river Yamuna (Jumna); and, while they were doing so, Krishna stole their clothes and carried them up into a tree, in the branches of which he hid himself. He embarked with them at another time in a boat on the river; the boat began to leak terribly, and Krishna made the Gopis stop the leak with their clothes. Sporting with the multitude of women, he so multiplied himself that each believed she had Krishna all to herself. The god Indra (by no means a spotless character) was displeased at Krishna's intercourse with the Gopis, and poured down torrents of rain on him and them; whereupon Krishna 'lifted the chief of mountains, Govarddhana, from its stony base,' and for several days and nights held it over their heads as an umbrella, supporting it with one hand—indeed, as is generally said, on the tip of his finger. And so on. The miracles ascribed to Krishna are among the most extravagant recorded in Hindu books.

It is of importance to note that Krishna is a diviner being than Rama; that is to say, while Rama is but a partial manifestation of divinity, with only half the essence of Vishnu belonging to him, Krishna is a complete manifestation—the four-armed Vishnu in the fulness of his deity. Partly for this reason, and partly, we fear, because of the licentious stories told regarding him, he is decidedly a more popular deity than even the warlike yet gentle Rama; and the multitudinous wives, or rather mistresses, of Krishna are more familiar to the mind of India than Sita, with all her womanly grace and virtue. And yet this dreadful being is extolled by the author of the Bhagavad Gita, a man of high intellectual culture, as the god of gods; and that supreme position is vindicated for him in stately and sonorous strains throughout that striking poem. How can we explain this? It is exceedingly difficult to fix the relative dates of Sanskrit works, all except the Vedas; but we would fain believe that, when the Gita was composed—probably, as we have said, in the third century after Christ—the disgusting legends regarding Krishna had assumed no definite shape; and the author of the Gita may have ignored them, or rather, indeed, have been unacquainted with them. But farther, it is easy to suppose (as has been mentioned above, p. 80) that he had become acquainted with part of the evangelic history. Then, just as the Ramayana appears to have metamorphosed a Buddhist sage into a Hindu god, so it is probable that the author of the Gita adopted the great conceptions regarding the divinity and incarnation of Christ, and applied them to Krishna as a personage already famous in Indian story. The Gita is inserted in the vast Mahabharata ; but there is no probability of its having originally formed a part of that strangely composite work : we might compare it to a mistletoe growing on an oak. It is in the Mahabharata we first see Vishnu exalted to supreme divinity. He became incarnate in Krishna, who may have been, as some believe, originally a tribal god of the Rajputs (the great military race in Central India)—probably a hero exalted into a god. The names of Christ and Krishna are totally unlike in sense, and not very like in sound ;[1] yet the former may have suggested the latter as the personage whom the poet might represent as the supreme divinity. Still, this is a possibility only, and the slight resemblance may be accidental. Krishna, as conceived by the Hindus now, is a strangely mixed character. He is the warlike prince of Dwaraka, in Gujarat ; he is the licentious cowherd of Vrindavana ; and he is the Supreme Divinity incarnate. He almost realizes the extraordinary picture suggested in the first lines of Horace's *Ars Poetica*. Unhappily the Hindu mind delights especially in the foul tales told of him in the

[1] The word 'Krishna' is composed of *K* (not in any case *Kh*), a semi-vowel which is represented by *r* or *ri*, a third letter represented by *sh*, and a fourth by *n*.

second of these characters; and among the embellishments of Hindu dwellings may often be found pictures representing him sporting with the Gopis. The influence for evil which the story of Krishna's early life has had in debasing the Hindu mind has been immense.—We have still to add how this extraordinary being died. After the great war between the Kauravas and Pandavas, he retreated with his followers to his capital Dwaraka, in Gujarat. After effecting the destruction of the Yadavas, the race to which he belonged, he himself was killed by the arrow of a hunter, who mistook him for a deer as he was sitting under a tree; and his parents, in consequence, committed suicide.

M. Jacolliot has been capable of the stupendous blunder of maintaining that in the history of Christ we find much that has been borrowed from the history of Krishna. No Oriental scholar can tolerate such an idea. Chronology and geography are wholly against it. Had it been true, it would have been the most astonishing instance of transfiguration on record. The warrior turned into a prince of peace; and the debauched cowherd of Vrindavana into a being possessed of every moral excellence! By what process of moral alchemy could such a transformation have been wrought? But it is, alas! too easy to show how from such muddy sources as the *Gospel of the Infancy* the Hindu poets, in a time of great moral debasement, might gradually evolve the pestilential tale of which we have ventured to recite only the less disgusting portions.

Of Buddha, the ninth descent of Vishnu, we have already had occasion to speak at sufficient length when treating of Buddhism. (See p. 108.)

The tenth descent is called the Kalki avatara. It is still future. As the present, or fourth, age of the world goes on, iniquity will more and more prevail. 'Wealth and piety will decrease day by day, until the world will be utterly depraved. . . . The people, unable to bear the heavy burdens imposed by their kings, will seek refuge among the valleys of the mountains, and will live on wild honey, herbs, roots, fruits, flowers, and leaves. . . . No man's life will exceed three and twenty years.'[1] Then, to redress the awful evil, Vishnu will appear in the form of a warrior, mounted on a white horse, and holding a sword in his right hand. Associating a thousand Brahmans with himself, he will utterly destroy all scorners, all neglecters of religion, and all the enemies of the Brahmans;—'all Mlechchhas (foreigners), thieves, and all whose minds are devoted to iniquity.'[2] And so the 'Age of Truth' returns; and for a long time all is purity and peace.

But only for a time. Age follows age; each worse than the preceding. Here seems to be the suitable place to mention the doctrine of the four ages (*yugas*) of the world. The first is the *Krita* or *Satya Yuga*—the Age of Truth, which extends

[1] So the Vishnu Purana. [2] Ibid.

over the period of 1,728,000 years. The second is the *Treta*, which lasts for 1,296,000 years. The third is the *Dvapara*, of 864,000 years ; and the last is the *Kali*, lasting 432,000 years. The four ages thus endure for 4,320,000 years. A thousand such periods are a Kalpa, and constitute a day of Brahma. The life of Brahma extends to a hundred years—each comprising three hundred and sixty of his days.

CHAPTER VII.

THE EPIC POEMS.

THE descents of Vishnu are first distinctly developed in the two great heroic poems—the Ramayana and the Mahabharata. Although not equal in authority to the Vedas, Darsanas and Puranas, yet they are held in high estimation, and may be styled at least semi-sacred.

The Ramayana is generally held to be the more ancient. The name denotes *the going of Rama*—the warrior god of whom we have had occasion to speak at considerable length. The author was Valmiki, of whose real existence there seems little doubt. There is considerable unity in the plan of the poem, and perhaps it is the work of a single author. Valmiki is said to have lived at Chitrakut, a mountain not far from the modern Allahabad. Of the date when he lived we cannot speak with certainty; it was probably about the Christian era.[1]

[1] Weber finds traces of Greek influences in the poem. He believes that the rape of Helen and the siege of Troy were in the

The poem professes to consist of seven books, containing 24,000 slokas, each sloka being equal to four octo-syllabic lines of English verse. But there are two recensions of the work; one more concise in diction and more archaic in its forms than the other, and probably more like the original poem. Luxuriance, extravagance, we are of course to look for in a Hindu book; but Valmiki is a true poet,—many passages are marked by a sweet, natural pathos, and he is comparatively free from those *conceits* which characterize so many Hindu writers. But, after all, so vast a composition may have had more than one author; and certainly the whole is not of uniform merit.

We need not dwell at much length on the Ramayana, as we have already traced the career of Rama in speaking of the seventh *avatara* (p. 114). The subject of the poem, as it stands, is usually said to be the extension of Aryan civilization to Southern India and Ceylon, chiefly by means of conquest. But, again, it may refer to a struggle between the Hindus of India and the Buddhists of Ceylon.

The second epic poem, the Mahabharata, is a much larger work still, consisting of eighteen books, and 220,000 slokas—the most stupendous poem which the world has seen. It is a vast encyclopedia of matters historical, religious, and

mind of the poet when he describes Sita and the conquest of Lanka. Monier Williams also points out analogies between characters described in the Iliad with several in the Ramayana.

philosophical. It is ascribed to Vyasa, *i.e.*, the arranger — a sage of whom nothing certain is known. The different parts of the work are probably of different dates; but 'the arranger' has succeeded in giving a kind of historical unity to the grand storehouse of legends. The form, at least, in which it now stands is probably later in date than the Ramayana.

The subject of the work is the great war between the Pandavas and their cousins the Kauravas. Of the former there were five; of the latter a hundred. At first they lived together under the care of Dhritarashtra, the father of the Kauravas. Quarrels arose, for under their tutor Drona the princes were taught to guide the elephant, to drive the chariot, to launch the javelin, to hurl the battle-axe, and to whirl the mace; and in all these royal exercises the Pandavas excelled their cousins. The poet's sympathies are, from the outset, with the former; to whom he ascribes all manly virtues. The Kauravas try to destroy them, but they escape. When wandering about, they hear that Drupada, the king of Panchala, is to hold a *Svayamvara*—a contest for the hand of his daughter Draupadi. Multitudes of people go to take part, or to be witnesses of the tournament (if we may so call it). Draupadi is to be the reward of him who excels in archery. Arjuna—one of the noblest characters in Hindu story—gains the precious prize; but we are startled to read that the lady becomes the wife of all the five brothers in common.

This circumstance Brahmanical commentators are eager to explain and, as far as possible, excuse; although the fact of most of the brothers having other wives of their own makes it difficult to do so.[1]

The kingdom is then divided between the Kauravas and the Pandavas, and for a time all is prosperity. Yudhishthira, the eldest of the latter, is a model king; and his subjects rejoice in his beneficent rule. But Duryodhana, the head of the Kauravas, still plots against his rivals. He invites them to a gambling festival; and Yudhishthira feels he cannot in honour refuse the challenge. He is matched with an unfair opponent, and loses. He stakes one thing after another, and still loses. He stakes himself, and loses. He stakes Draupadi (what right had he—even according to Hindu sentiment—to stake more than one-fifth part of her?), and loses. Draupadi, with dishevelled hair and weeping bitterly, is dragged before the assembled chiefs; but after a time she and her husbands are allowed to depart in peace. Then, shortly after, another challenge is given. Another game is to be played, and the losers are to go into banishment for twelve years. Once more the loaded dice are used; the Pandavas are beaten, and go mournfully into exile, with Draupadi in bitter grief. So they remain in the woods for twelve years—feeding on roots and fruits, and the

[1] Polyandry is still practised in Southern India by the military race, the Nairs. Also in Bhotan, Kulu, etc., in the Himalayas.

animals which the brothers can slay with their arrows. Bhima, the Hercules of the party, when they are utterly exhausted with fatigue, carries the lady and his brothers on his back and under his arms, and calmly marches on. When the twelve sad years are come and gone, they act as servants to the king of Virata. The Kauravas, discovering their foes, attack and carry off 'a thousand cows' belonging to the king. Arjuna (in this too resembling Hercules) has in disguise been keeping the women's apartments, but now goes forth as charioteer to the king's son, and performs prodigies of valour. So do his brothers; and the Pandavas return in triumph home. But this is only the commencement of renewed hostilities on the part of the Kauravas. Whereupon Krishna, the prince of Dwaraka, is sent as an ambassador to try to secure peace; but his efforts are in vain. The preparations for war go on; and the two great hosts ere long meet in battle-array on the plain of Kurukshetra, near Delhi. Every chief in India takes a side. The battle continues for eighteen days. Huge elephants, war-horses and chariots, bows and arrows, iron maces, drums, war-shells, horns, and trumpets; jackals howling, vultures screaming, lightnings flashing, thunders roaring, awful omens;—all these things are lavishly thrown into the description of the great hurly-burly. The chiefs—all save one—are regardless of the omens. Just as the shells sound to the encounter, the heart of the noble Arjuna misgives him. He is struck with horror at the thought of slaughtering his kinsmen and his resistless bow, Gandiva, drops from his hand. It is at this point that the philosophical poem, the Bhagavad Gita, is interpolated (see above, p. 74). Krishna reproaches Arjuna for his weakness, and, with divine authority, commands him to rush into the fight. He does so, and his murderous arrows fly thick and fast. A series of single combats is then described, almost reminding us of the battle scenes of the Iliad. The Pandavas are finally victorious ; and three of the Kauravas are all that remain of the once mighty host of foes. The triumphant warriors go to sleep securely on the field of battle ; but the Kauravas come in the dark and slay them all except the five great brothers and their wife. Female lamentations follow. The funeral ceremonies are then performed ; and the bodies are burnt. The five brothers have now none to oppose them ; but they are not happy. Friends and kinsmen have been slaughtered ; all is desolation round them. Earth is no scene of peace ; they must seek it in the heaven of Indra. They accordingly depart with Draupadi, accompanied by a dog. Arjuna flings his mighty bow and irresistible arrows into the sea. They pass Dwaraka and proceed northward to the Himalayas ; and see at last the mighty mountain Meru. But they are sorely worn. Draupadi first falls and dies. Then brother after brother falls and dies. Still Yudhishthira, followed by the faithful dog, goes on. He reaches the entrance of Indra's heaven.

Indra tells him that he can enter heaven with his body,—all his brothers and Draupadi he will find there before him; but there is no admittance for dogs! The prince declares that he cannot possibly forsake his faithful companion. Whereupon he learns that the animal is really Yama, the king of the dead, in disguise; and that Indra had been only testing him when he refused to admit the dog. Still, one great trial remains. The prince, on entering heaven, sees the Kauravas, but not his brothers. He refuses to remain apart from them; and learning that they are in hell, he proceeds to share their sorrows there. But the scene passes; all this has been intended only as a test of his virtue: the seeming hell is changed to heaven, and thereafter the brothers, along with Draupadi, enjoy eternal felicity in the palace of Indra.

We have thus presented an outline of the history (so-called) which is embodied in the great poem; but it must be remembered that the narrative is frequently broken in upon by disquisitions on matters moral, religious, or metaphysical. Thus, besides the Bhagavad Gita, which is thrust into the heart of the sixth book, nearly the whole of books thirteen and fourteen is occupied with a discourse chiefly on the duties of rulers, which was delivered on the occasion of Yudhishthira's coronation. The worthy Bhishma who delivers it proses in a manner rather trying to the reader, although we are not told that his hearers ventured to complain of his prolixity.[1]

Whatever impression the philosophical and moral portions may have made on the Hindu mind, there is no question that the story contained in the Mahabharata has powerfully influenced every part of India. 'The Five Pandavas' are still everywhere mentioned as antique heroes of the noblest kind; and any great work in India that appears to surpass ordinary human power is generally ascribed to the wondrous brotherhood. Next to Sita, the wife of Rama, Draupadi—notwithstanding her startling marriage relations—is regarded as a type of true wifehood; and the habitual remembrance of one with such an environment cannot have been without a corrupting influence on the female mind.

Altogether, the potency in the formation of Indian thought of the two epic poems of which we have been speaking has been immense. We hardly know of any parallel case. No book or books had an influence at all corresponding to it in the history of Rome. The poems of Homer may, in popularity and power, have nearly equalled the two great Indian epics, but certainly did not surpass them. It is mainly on the legends contained in these two books that the mind of India feeds

[1] Two of the episodes thrust into the Mahabharata– viz., the Sanatsujatiya and the Anugita—are translated and given along with the Bhagavad Gita in the eighth volume of the *Sacred Books of the East.* Neither of these works has attained much celebrity. Both are probably later than the Bhagavad Gita.

up to the present day. Unhappily the legends have, in very many cases, been conveyed to the popular mind through a polluted channel—that of the Puranas. Of these writings it is now time to speak.

CHAPTER VIII.

THE PURANAS.

THE term 'Purana' properly signifies 'old.' The works so called are generally ascribed to Vyasa, the mythical arranger of the Vedas themselves; so that they would deserve the appellation 'old' if the popular belief as to their authorship had any foundation. But it has no foundation. The Puranas, in their present form at all events, are very modern compilations. It is, however, quite possible that ancient materials may have been drawn upon in the composition of the so-called Puranas; and this may perhaps serve as an excuse for the use of a designation which seems to have been adopted in order to impart the sanction of antiquity to novel compilations.

The Puranas are generally said to be eighteen in number; but the list is differently given by different authorities, and the claims of several usually named are somewhat questionable.[1] There is a division of the Puranas, generally accepted by Brahmans, into three classes: the first includes those relating to Brahma; the second, those that extol Vishnu; the third, those that extol Siva.[2] Each class contains six. But this division is rather unnatural. Seven of the entire number, or even eight, are mainly in praise of Vishnu; six support the honour of Siva; while the rest are certainly in no special way connected with Brahma.

The subjects treated in a Purana are usually stated to be the following five: 1. Primary creation; 2. Secondary creation, *i.e.*, the destruction and renovation of the universe; 3. Genealogies of gods and patriarchs; 4. *Manwantaras*, *i.e.*, the reigns of the Manus; 5. The histories of the kings of the solar and lunar races. But this description does not fully apply to a single Purana, and some of them have hardly any correspondence to it. They seem to have been intended as repositories

[1] The usual list and order are as follows: 1. Brahma P.; 2. Padma; 3. Vishnu; 4. Siva; 5. Bhagavata; 6. Narada; 7. Markandeya; 8. Agni; 9. Bhavishya; 10. Brahma Vaivarta; 11. Linga; 12. Varaha; 13. Skanda; 14. Vamana; 15. Kurma; 16. Matsya; 17. Garuda; 18. Brahmanda. The Kurma P. substitutes the Vayu for the Agni. The Agni substitutes the Vayu for the Siva. The Garuda substitutes the Vayu and Nrisinha for the Garuda and Brahmanda. The Matsya omits the Siva.

The Vaishnava Puranas are Nos. 2, 3, 5, 6, 10, 12, 17, in the above list. The Saiva ones are 4, 8, 11, 13, 15, 16. No. 7 is chiefly in praise of Durga. No. 14 praises both Vishnu and Siva. No. 9 is chiefly in honour of Brahma, Vishnu, and Siva, and also of the god Tvashtri.

[2] It is given by the author of the oldest Sanskrit dictionary, Amara Sinha, probably after the Christian era.

of all existing knowledge on matters connected with religion. Though said to have been written in the first instance only for women and Sudras, yet they became the authorized source of instruction for men also. Religion, philosophy, science, history, geography,—all that came, according to Hindu conception, under these comprehensive designations, belonged to the Puranas. The Agni Purana professes to teach even archery, medicine, rhetoric, prosody, and grammar, and to reveal these sciences with infallible authority.

Generally speaking, the Puranas must have been compiled between the twelfth and seventeenth centuries. One or two may possibly be a century or so earlier than the twelfth.

Along with these compositions we must mention the Upa-Puranas, or minor Puranas. The character of these is almost identical with that of the Puranas themselves. They also are eighteen in number. There is considerable uncertainty about many of these books; and several of them are very seldom met with. They are as sectarian as the Puranas. They are probably, in most cases, later than the Puranas; to which they may be called appendices.

The Puranas and Upa-Puranas draw largely from the heroic poems, the Ramayana and Maha-

[1] Their names are as follows: 1. Sanatkumara Purana; 2. Narasinha; 3. Naradiya; 4. Siva; 5. Durvasasa; 6. Kapila; 7. Manava; 8. Ausanasa; 9. Varuna; 10. Kalika; 11. Samba; 12. Nandi; 13. Saura; 14. Parasara; 15. Aditya; 16. Maheswara; 17. Bhagavata (possibly a mistake for Bhargava); 18. Vasishtha. This is the most usual list.

bharata; but as a rule they are very far inferior, in point of literary merit, to the two great epics. There is a kind of glitter about the Bhagavata Purana; but the style of the books is, for the most part, deplorably bad. All naturalness, and truth, and even common sense have vanished; and little remains but extravagance in thought and extravagance in language.

The religion of the Puranas is exceedingly unlike that of the Vedas.[1] It is an extraordinary blending of pantheism and polytheism. The pantheism is not the spiritualistic pantheism of the Vedanta, which denies the reality of matter; the outward world is believed to exist, and to be a part of God. But again, there is a triad of gods—Brahma, Vishnu, and Siva, in whom the Supreme Spirit, on becoming conscious, manifests himself. It is customary to style these beings Creator, Preserver, and Destroyer, respectively; but this distinction is not at all well retained either in the Puranas or elsewhere. The idea of the unity of the three gods is a philosophical refinement, rather than a popular belief. The partizan of Vishṇu holds his favourite deity to perform the three functions; and the partizan of Siva, in like manner, holds this regarding Siva. Confused and conflicting statements everywhere abound in re-

[1] 'The picture of religion and life unfolded by them is a caricature of that afforded by the Vedic works. It was drawn by priestcraft, interested in submitting to its sway the popular mind, and unscrupulous as to the means it used.'—*Goldstücker.*

ference to this question. The Trimurtti, or union of the three great gods, is not unfrequently represented ; and when this is done the figure contains one body with three heads. The head of Brahma is in the middle ; Vishnu is on his right, and Siva on the left. Perhaps the most famous figure of this kind is the one in the chief cave in the island of Elephanta, near Bombay. In this case Siva seems to have absorbed into himself the two other deities. The famous monosyllable Om, to which, when rightly uttered, most stupendous powers are ascribed, is generally said to denote the triad of gods; being equivalent to *a*, *u*, *m*—*a* denoting Vishnu, *u* Siva, and *m* Brahma. Lastly on this head, it must be remembered that there are said to be three qualities—goodness, passion, and darkness;[1] which are embodied respectively in Vishnu, Brahma, and Siva. The quality of *passion* which belongs to Brahma may be interchanged with *activity ;* but the ascription of *darkness* to a divine being is very startling, inasmuch as, according to the Hindu definition, it is 'the root of folly, delusion, lust, and pride.' It is so far satisfactory that, in the Puranas taken as a whole, Vishnu is more prominent than Siva, who is possessed of such un-divine attributes as these.

We cannot stop to draw nice distinctions between the faith embodied in the two epic poems and that

[1] Sattva, rajas, and tamas. These are the three famous *gunas*, —literally 'fetters.' The unconditioned is where these do not exist —as in the Supreme Being of the Vedanta school.

contained in the Puranas. The great supersession of earlier conceptions which we witness in the former is carried out more fully in the latter ; the difference is in degree rather than in kind. In both classes of writings the divergence from the Vedic faith is very remarkable. Old deities have been obscured ; many entirely new deities have appeared. The 'thrice eleven' divinities of the Vedas are turned into three hundred and thirty millions (or thrice eleven crores) of gods—a fantastic hyperbole, probably grounded on erroneous etymology. Of course, names have not been given to more than a fraction of the mighty host. 'The haughty Indra,' who, as we have seen above, 'takes precedence of all gods,' becomes, in the Puranas, quite a subordinate figure ; and Varuna, who, in point of moral dignity stands unique in the Vedic pantheon, retains simply the regency of the waters. Vishnu in the Veda is often associated with Indra, but is decidedly inferior to him. He became, in the estimation of his worshippers, the greatest of the gods. Krishna, who as time goes on becomes (as in the Gita) not only the greatest incarnation of Vishnu, but the all-comprehending Deity, was not known in early days. Rama, who now stands next to Krishna in popularity, was equally unknown. Siva, Durga, Kali—these also are unknown to the Veda ; but in more modern times they have become mighty divinities. It frequently happens also that there are gods of very great local celebrity, who are not only unknown to the Veda, but unknown to India generally. Thus the glory of Vithoba, who is a form of Krishna, is celebrated by Tukarama and other poets in the most exalted strains; but his name is barely known beyond the limits of the Maratha country. Siva is for the most part worshipped under the emblem of the Linga (or phallus); but regarding such a worship the Vedas are wholly silent.

No dogma of Hinduism, we said above (p. 51), has stamped a deeper impress on the mind of India than that of Transmigration. There is one text in the Veda which some have believed to imply the belief; but there is little probability of this being the true meaning.[1] It is not easy to trace its introduction into Hindu thought; but the wide diffusion of the idea proves that it not unnaturally suggests itself as an explanation of the unequal apportionment of good and evil in the world.[2] The Hindu begins with the assumption that this rests on moral grounds; a man's birth and condition depend on previous character. The Brahmans of later times have carried out this conception, as they do every conception, into immeasurable detail. They dwell on Transmigration with great earnestness, and judicially declare the specific birth that is the award for each specific character. This is done with a

[1] The term *bahuprajah*, which the modern Hindu critic Sayana rendered 'subject to many births' or 'having many children,' very probably means the latter. See Rig Veda i. 164, 72.

[2] Cicero calls it an ancient belief.

minuteness and gravity that provoke a smile. 'Souls endued with the character of truth (sattva) become gods; those possessed of passion (rajas) become men; those that have darkness (tamas) become beasts.' This bold generalization, however, is not very faithfully carried out. Thus, those that possess most of the darkness-character become worms, insects, fish, serpents, etc.; those who have less become elephants, horses, lions, tigers, boars, Sudras, and Mlechchhas (*i.e.*, barbarians, foreigners); while those that have still less of evil become public play-actors, birds, cheats, Rakshasas (a kind of demon) and vampires. (The legislator has apparently forgotten what was said about those who possess the *tamas* quality becoming *beasts.*) 'He who kills a Brahman is born a thousand times as a dog, a boar, an ass, a camel, a bull, a goat, a sheep, a stag, a bird, or as a low-caste man. A Brahman who drinks spirituous liquor will be a worm, an insect, a grasshopper, a fly feeding on ordure, or some mischievous animal.' 'If a man steals grain, he becomes a rat; if milk, a crow; if oil, a cockroach; if salt, a cricket'—and so the list runs on, with a minuteness of specification without a parallel in the annals of legislation. The apportionments of punishment are often rather startling. Every crime committed against a Brahman is especially heinous, and visited with corresponding chastisement. Offences against the rules of caste are equally dreadful. The successive births, we saw already, are all but infinite in number. At last, when (as by a series of purgatorial fires) its sin has been removed and all the merited chastisement endured, the soul is reunited to the Supreme, from whom it originally came—as a drop of water mingles with the ocean and is lost in its immensity. Then cease all individual existence and all consciousness of existence. This is the Indian idea of rest, of peace. But the prospect of attaining this death-like quiet is fearfully dim and distant; and the Hindu mind contemplates with a feeling of unspeakable distress the awful, all but infinite, succession of migrations still awaiting it.[1] And only he who has attained to perfect purity can escape this tremendous doom. So, then, they who are most deeply conscious of imperfection are most overwhelmed by the agonizing prospect before them; while it is the hardened sinner, whose conscience is seared as with a hot iron, that is best able to banish from his mind the thought of coming retribution.

[1] The playful yet pathetic lines are well known in which the Emperor Hadrian addressed his soul, as death was approaching—

> 'Animula vagula blandula,
> Hospes comesque corporis,
> Quæ nunc abibis in loca?' etc.

The feeling of curiosity expressed in Hadrian's lines becomes, in the case of the Hindu, one of terror. He shuts his eyes on the dreadful future.

CHAPTER IX.

THE TANTRAS. THE SAKTI WORSHIP.

WE come now to consider a class of works about which there is a difference of opinion among the Hindus ; some exalting them above all the other Sastras, and others refusing to acknowledge them as in any sense sacred. We refer to the Tantras. The name may mean 'an instrument of faith.' Most of them are probably later in origin than the Puranas. The Tantras have not received the same amount of attention as the works we have already referred to ; and we cannot wonder that so debased a literature should have repelled, rather than attracted, European scholars. We have no accurate list of the Tantras.[1] Five or six are pretty well known ; but the number of Tantrika works is popularly believed to exceed that of the whole of the other Sastras. Properly,

[1] The following are the names of the best known Tantras : Rudrayamala, Kalikatantra, Mahanirvana, Kularnava, Syamarahasya, Saradatilaka, Mantramahodadhi, Kamada, Amnaya, Kalpa.

a Tantra comprises five subjects, viz., creation and destruction of the world, worship of the gods, attainment of the supreme end, means of obtaining union with the highest being. But (as in the case of the Puranas) this theoretical division of subjects is frequently departed from. A Tantra is written in the form of a dialogue between Siva and his wife under one of her many forms. The goddess asks questions, to which Siva replies. The Puranas are intended for popular instruction; but a great air of mystery is thrown around all that is revealed in the Tantras. Their secrets must be communicated only to the initiated.

The Tantras inculcate the worship of the Sakti. This word originally means *power;* and it especially signifies the powers of the gods, particularly of Brahma, Vishnu, and Siva. In the modern form of Hinduism as exhibited in the Puranas, these powers are personalized and regarded as living beings—*wives* of the deities.[1] As Siva is, more than the other two, the deity of destruction, his *power*, as exerted through his wife—especially in the form of Kali—becomes something truly terrific. It is startling to find all that is most horrible and hideous embodied in the character and worship of a female divinity; but the logical Brahman shrinks from no moral consequences flowing from his

[1] Sarasvati, the goddess of speech and the arts, is the wife of Brahma. Lakshmi, or Sri, the goddess of wealth, is the wife of Vishnu. Parvati, or more generally Uma, Durga, or Kali, is the wife of Siva.

assumed premises; he will cut right across the deepest instincts of humanity rather than abandon his theory.

We must not forget that the roots of the dreadful ideas and practices which we are about to describe are found in the Vedas, and still more in the Yoga philosophy; but probably the worship of the aborigines had a great influence on their development. Cruel, obscene, and magical rites, in the worship of female goddesses, appear as early as the third century A.D.

The Tantras, however, are not all equally offensive. The worshippers of the Sakti (or Saktas, as they are usually styled) are divided into two branches—those of the right hand and those of the left. In the tenets and rites of the former there is abundance of mystery, magic, and downright folly; but the extreme of immorality is avoided. In the latter there is a sickening exhibition of the vilest passions of man, all revelling unchecked. The worship of the Paphian goddess, and many of the rites of ancient Paganism, were deplorably immoral; but in the studied, elaborate ritual of the Saktas there is an amount of evil which is certainly unsurpassed, and we believe unequalled, in any other system. In a popular treatise like this it would be unpardonable to give a full account of anything so loathsome; yet, without some distinct reference to it, Hinduism cannot be fully understood.

The right-hand section of the Saktas have departed from the orthodox system in many respects They offer bloody sacrifices, and frequently beat the animal to death with their fists. But the left-hand section plunges into the most revolting excesses. It is indispensable in the rites to employ at least one of five things the names of which begin with the letter M in Sanskrit—which are flesh, fish, wine, women, and certain magical gestures. A woman must be present, as the living representative of the Sakti goddess. She is first stripped of all her clothing; wine and flesh are given to her and the company—which must be composed of both sexes. The women drink first out of goblets of cocoa-nut or human skulls. The men then drink. No regard is paid to caste. Excitement, even intoxication, is produced by the abundant use of liquor. The lights are extinguished; and then follow doings indescribable. Professor H. H. Wilson rightly designates these as 'most scandalous orgies.' The abominable character of the whole celebration is heightened by the declaration of the sect that all is done not for sensual gratification, but as an exalted form of divine worship. Professor Wilson thinks that this declaration may possibly be sincere; but if so, he adds, its promulgators 'must have been filled with a strange frenzy, and have been strangely ignorant of human nature.' It is, in fact, the most appalling exhibition of what is plainly visible in several forms of Hindu worship—an effort to obtain the sanction of Heaven for indulgence in the basest lusts. 'Evil, be thou my good,' exclaimed the lost archangel, knowing that evil was evil still; but when the indulgence of the lowest appetites of human nature is believed to be the sublimest kind of worship, it surely must imply a still deeper fall than his. And yet the left-hand Saktas, in the most varied and repeated terms, declare that evil to them becomes good; and the designation they give to all who do not adopt their creed and rites is that of *pasu* (beasts).

It is distressing to see how little was done by the Sanskrit writers to refute or denounce such abominable practices. The great Sankara Acharya, who was most laborious and vehement in suppressing other heresies, does not seem to notice this worst of all delusions.[1] Of course, any one who is known to indulge in such practices must be expelled from caste, as acting contrary to caste obligations. Still, the number of those who are secretly enrolled as Saktas is believed to be exceedingly great. All castes are admissible, but the members are mostly Brahmans. The sect flourishes chiefly in Bengal.

We have often occasion to state how much Hinduism has drawn from Buddhism. The loan was in some cases repaid. It is sad to see th[at] the Buddhism of Nepal and Tibet had been de[eply] influenced by the obscenity of the Tantras b[y the] ninth century A.D.

[1] Tukarama, the Marathi poet, however, denounces the S[akta] worship as the consummation of all wickedness.

We must still mention that there are practices, less vile indeed, and yet in one sense more horrible; for example, the rites by which power is gained over evil spirits. The worshipper in this case comes alone to a place where dead bodies are burned or buried, or where criminals are executed. He seats himself on a corpse, makes offerings, and uses incantations; and, if he can go through the dreadful ritual without fear, he obtains a mastery over demons, and they become his slaves. But woe to the votary if his courage fail before the awful conjuration is complete!

CHAPTER X.

THE HINDU SECTS.

HINDUISM, as reconstructed after the fall of Buddhism, is split up into a multitude of divisions, or, as we may call them, sects. These are fairly enough classed under two chief heads—the Vaishnava sects, or those that hold Vishnu to be supreme; and the Saiva, or those that ascribe pre-eminence to Siva.[1] It is perfectly possible that divisions pretty nearly corresponding to these may have existed even in Vedic days, and that they assumed far greater prominence while orthodox Brahmanism was engaged in a death-struggle with Buddhism. The history of the sects can be traced with certainty only from the twelfth century after Christ.

The worship of the Trimurtti does not seem at any time to have deeply penetrated the general mind. Even when it was professedly retained, one god—Vishnu or Siva—was represented as supreme;

[1] There are also Sauras, or sun-worshippers; Ganapatyas, or worshippers of Ganesa or Ganapati, and others.

and the dogma of the triad was thus rendered meaningless. Sectarianism has frequently been very bitter, and has proceeded from words to murderous blows—a fact that need not take us by surprise.

I. VAISHNAVA SECTS.

The chief of these are the following:—

1. The *Ramanujas.* These derive their name from Ramanuja, a Brahman, who was born near Madras about the middle of the twelfth century. Their worship is mainly addressed to Vishnu and his wife Lakshmi, or to any one of their many manifestations—especially Rama or his wife Sita, or these two together. The sacred formula by which a member is initiated into the sect is 'Om,' salutation to Rama (*Om Ramaya namah*). They hold the doctrine of duality (*dvaita*); that is, they admit the veritable existence of an external world as well as that of spirit. The latter is not devoid of qualities (as in the Vedanta), and is, in fact, possessed of all good qualities. They admit also the existence of individual souls, though at times they speak of them as being, or to be, identified with God. They are exceedingly particular in the preparation and eating of their food. If a stranger should touch it, or even see it in the process of cooking, or when they are eating it, they throw it away—generally burying it. Marks connected with Vishnu are painted, or occasionally branded, on them, chiefly on the breast and upper arms. They

wear a necklace composed of the berries of the *tulasi* plant (holy basil). Infinite importance is attached to all the symbolic marks they bear; each becomes possessed of a kind of magical virtue. This sect originally spread farthest in the south, and there it retains a powerful influence. In the north of India its sway has been less considerable.

2. The *Ramanandas*. This sect was founded by Ramananda, a follower, if not an immediate scholar, of Ramanuja. His date is uncertain; it may be as late as the beginning of the fifteenth century. He resided at Benares, and it is especially in Northern India that his school prevails. His teaching did not differ very much from that of his master Ramanuja, but it was a system of somewhat greater freedom. He abolished the distinctions of caste among his followers; all men devoted to a religious life were brothers. In this he resembled Buddha, only going somewhat beyond him; and he resembled him also in his employment of the vernacular language. Its likeness in several points to Buddhism explains the prevalence of this system in the north of India. The formula of initiation is Sri Rama (Blessed Rama!). Ramananda had numerous disciples—twelve chief ones, it is said. Several Hindi writers whose writings have been very popular belonged to this sect; and the legends contained in such works as the Bhakta Mala of Nabhaji, are familiar to the Hindu people, at least, in Northern, Central, and Western India. Legends of

saints are almost as popular as those of Rama and Krishna.

3. The sect we have now to speak of is devoted to Krishna, not Rama. It is the sect founded by Vallabha Acharya, who was probably born in 1479. His early life was spent at Gokula, near Mathura, on the banks of the Jumna. He travelled extensively, preaching his peculiar doctrines, and finally settled at Benares, where he had many disciples.[1] His followers have multiplied, especially in Western and Central India. The gurus, or spiritual chiefs, of this sect are known by the name of Maharaj (literally 'great king'); and there may be sixty or seventy who are so designated. The great characteristic of the system is that it inculcates, not fasting and mortification of the flesh, but the indulgence of bodily appetites. It goes, in truth, almost as far in this direction as the Tantras of which we spoke above; and it does so without any sense of shame or attempt at concealment. The gurus themselves soon came to be believed to be representatives, impersonations, of the god, and entitled to the same homage. Everything, therefore, connected with the Maharajas became holy, divine; the water in which their feet were washed became nectar; and even what was ejected from their mouths was greedily devoured. Could human folly go farther? It did. In more systems than one it had been said that *tan*, *man*, *dhan* (body, mind, property), all were to be devoted to the service of the guru; but the

[1] Especially among the trading classes of Bhatias and Banyans.

atrocious doctrine was carried out to its fullest extent by Vallabha and his disciples. We do not need to point out what this implies, especially in the case of female worshippers. Of course, complaints arose. Ever since the writer went to India he was in the habit of hearing vehement denunciations of the wickedness of the Maharajas; and at last, in the year 1871, in a remarkable trial in the Supreme Court at Bombay, the mystery of iniquity was fully brought to light, to the horror of all who were not leagued for its support. Karsandas Mulji, a young man who most boldly exposed the atrocious deeds of the Maharajas, has since then passed away; and in him India has lost a single-minded, energetic reformer whom she could very ill spare. It was hoped that the power of the sect was broken by the merciless exposure made at the trial; but the great majority of the followers of those wretched Maharajas remain as besotted as before. Light, however, is slowly entering even into the Banyan and Bhatia communities; and the system of Vallabha Acharya must pass away ere long. Meanwhile, it gives food for sorrowful musing to see large numbers of shrewd merchants and traders, who have a keen eye to business and are full of enterprise in all their commercial operations, accepting such doctrines, and surrendering their wives and daughters to such horrible degradation. The intellect clear as noonday on ordinary matters, but on moral questions dark as Erebus!

4. The *Madhavacharyas.* This sect was founded

by a Brahman of the same name, who was born in the year 1199 in South India, where his followers are chiefly found. The main characteristic of this school is that they affirm an eternal distinction between the Supreme Spirit and the individual soul. Thus they deny the doctrine of absorption, and the merging of the individual into the universal soul at death. Another peculiarity is a disposition to arrive at an understanding or, if possible, a compromise with the followers of Siva. Images of Siva, his wife, and his son Ganesa, are found in their temples along with those of Vishnu. Asceticism is carried by them to a greater length than by most other Vaishnava sects. They practise celibacy, and generally live in *maths*, or monasteries, under a superior.

5. The followers of *Chaitanya.* These constitute a very large body in Bengal and Orissa; but they have not much influence beyond these provinces. Chaitanya was a Brahman of Nadiya, near Calcutta, born in the year 1485. He is said to have married a daughter of Vallabha Acharya; but at the age of twenty-five he became an ascetic. He was a man of excitable, enthusiastic temperament, who believed he had frequent visions of Krishna and his wives; and it is generally held that, in one of his fits of ecstasy, he went into the sea at Puri, in Orissa, and, dazzled by the glory of the sun shining on the waters, proceeded on till he was drowned. His followers consider him an incarnation of Krishna.

According to Chaitanya, Krishna is the Supreme. The worship consists chiefly in the repetition of the name of the god. One spiritual leader of the sect has been the envy of after times, because, living sequestered from the world in a wood, he was enabled to repeat the sacred name three hundred thousand times every day.

There are two very important characteristics of this sect;—first, the immense importance they attach to *bhakti* or devotion; and secondly, their exaltation of the guru, which often amounts to deification. As, however, other Vaishnavas have the same characteristics, we shall defer our consideration of these two points till we have finished our enumeration of the other sects.

Finally, although the sect has greatly lost both character and influence in Bengal, in which its professed followers were and are most numerous, yet the name of Chaitanya is still held in great reverence. Babu Keshub Chunder Sen never lost an opportunity of lauding him to the skies as a most illustrious and enlightened teacher—one of the greatest of prophets. Mr. Sen's admiration was altogether extravagant; Chaitanya's writings are nothing but wild rhapsodies—emotion without thought. But the people of Bengal are passionately desirous of having 'a prophet of their own;" and the glory of Chaitanya will perhaps only by slow degrees pass away.

6. The followers of *Swami Narayan* have lately risen to considerable importance in Gujarat. The

leader was disgusted with the excesses of the Vallabhacharyas, and inculcated purity of life. He prescribed the worship of Krishna, along with a reverence for the sun as the best symbol of divinity. His followers may be somewhat under 200,000.[1]

Various Vaishnava sects have sprung up of recent years, among which the most remarkable are the Kartabhajas in Bengal. This name means 'worshippers of the Creator.' The Spashtadayakas and the Sahujas are of less importance.[2]

The doctrine of *bhakti*, which is characteristic of all the sects that have been mentioned, is of great importance. The word properly means 'devotion,' or affection fixed on God. In popular Hinduism it is maintained that there are three great means or *ways* to salvation—the way of works, the way of knowledge, and the way of devotion. The 'works' are ceremonial observances—especially as prescribed in the ritual of the Veda. The 'knowledge' is the speculation on the Divine nature exhibited in the Upanishads and philosophical writings. The 'devotion' is attachment to some particular deity. The term is almost confined to the worship of Vishnu in some one of his many manifestations—particularly Krishna. The idea of *bhakti* is not found in early Hinduism. The Vedas, indeed, speak of *sraddha*, or trust in the deities; but of

[1] Bishop Heber had an interesting interview with this man.

[2] The fullest account of the Hindu sects is given by Professor H. H. Wilson. See his works as edited by Dr. R. Rost, vol. i.

the emotional part of religion they are almost or altogether destitute. The introduction of *bhakti*, therefore, and the remarkable extent to which it has influenced later Hindu mind, are matters which have been keenly discussed. Did the idea of love and devotion—so far removed from ancient orthodoxy—develop itself spontaneously in India, or was it imported from without? Professor Weber of Berlin is the great champion of the latter opinion; and his opponents do not appear to us to have answered his formidable arguments. It may be true that the Hindu mind was prepared for its reception by its past experience. It had been wearied by stupendous ceremonialism; it was sick of subtle speculation equally endless and profitless. The mind then was ready to receive the great idea that religion consisted in love to Deity. The doctrine comes into the Hindu system somewhat abruptly. It begins to appear in the Bhagavad Gita, the great eclectic poem of which we have already treated. The idea is developed and systematized in the Bhakti Sutras of Sandilya. If not primarily derived from Christian teachings, we deem it abundantly probable that it was quickened and developed by them. Of the possibility and probability of Hindu thought having been affected by Christianity we have already spoken.[1]

The conception of *bhakti*, or devotion to the god, was soon carried to a wild extreme. It was held to consist of five degrees: 1. Quiet contemplation

[1] See above, p. 79.

of the deity. 2. Slavery, or absolute consecration to his service. 3. Friendship for him. 4. Love to him, resembling that of children to parents. 5. Passionate attachment, like what the Gopis felt for Krishna. When devotion to deity was likened to the last of the five, the Hindu mind had embraced a conception fearfully perilous, or rather, absolutely profane; for the love of the Gopis for Krishna was adulterous. And this melting love was held to be a far higher attainment than knowledge, ceremonial works, subjugation of the passions, or any moral excellence. The worshipper was not to rest until tears of ardent love were streaming down his cheeks. The worship soon became impure. Bold descriptions of the relation between Krishna and his votaries appeared which were utterly licentious. By the twelfth century the poet Jayadeva 'displayed a sensual delirium which defies all translation.' It is a profoundly melancholy task to trace this gradual degradation of the idea of *bhakti*. Originally, the belief that the Divine Being deserved, and demanded, not ceremonial observances or deep thought, so much as the *heart* of his worshipper, seemed a true and important gain to the religious consciousness. But, as time went on, the attempt to resolve all religion into emotion proved an absolute failure. Extravagance succeeded extravagance. The heroic legends of Vaishnavism gave place to the soft, seducing tales of the sports of Krishna. Acts came to be held as indifferent. He who had *bhakti* could not sin; or else, the mere utterance of the name of the god scattered to the winds a thousand crimes.

Along with this development of the idea of *bhakti* came the exaltation of the *guru*, or religious teacher. We saw already how, in earlier days, the man of prayer—the Brahman—came to be raised above his fellows, until the entire Brahmanical race were considered 'gods on earth.' In the sects—which professed to regard all true worshippers as equal—this glorification was reserved for the *guru*. Buddhism, with its teachings about Buddhas and Bodhisatvas, doubtless contributed to this tendency.[1]

All later writings of the Vaishnava school dwell with great emphasis on the necessity of a *sadguru*, or true guru. Thus:

> 'Without a sadguru you can obtain no good;
> First and foremost, let *his* feet be embraced!'

Again:

> 'Your field, your god, you must him call—
> Your father, mother, all in all.'

So say the Marathi poets, expressing the general opinion of their countrymen.

The very gods are said to require gurus. All classes of men, of course, then require them—the men of no caste as well as those of the highest.

It would seem as if, amidst the clashing of opinions, when sect was contending with sect, and the spirits of men were weary of endless doubt, the

[1] Jainism, also, with its *tirthankaras*, and Islam with its prophet, had doubtless an influence. Of the effect of Christianity we have already spoken.

idea of a holy, true teacher as absolutely necessary, almost unavoidably arose in India; but in this case, as in so many others in the unhappy history of the Hindus, a conception radically true was pushed to an absurd and lamentable excess. The homage paid to the guru ere long rose—chiefly, but not solely, among the Vallabhacharyas—to deification. Nay, the guru was even more important than the god; for (so the logic ran) 'if the deity is angry, the guru is our shelter; but if the guru is angry, we have no shelter.' Among many sects the guru is elected because of real or supposed merit; among the Vallabhacharyas and the followers of Chaitanya the position is hereditary, be personal qualifications what they may. Expulsion from the order of gurus does not follow misconduct. The wicked guru changes his place of residence, and seeks for new disciples.

Finally, any man that chooses may become a guru. He first attaches himself to some teacher; and, when he thinks himself qualified, he sets up on his own account. It is true that in various books it is said that only a Brahman has the needful qualifications; but, practically, the rule is disregarded. The lowest castes have their gurus as well as the highest; and many a scoundrel among the lower classes, who *will* not dig but is not ashamed to beg, learns or invents some *mantra*, *i.e.*, word of initiation, which he whispers into the ear of some poor, credulous fellow, and so enrols him as a disciple. The *mantra* is generally the name of a deity or of several deities—as *Rama Sita*, or *Sita Rama*, or *Rama Krishna Hari.*

The people of India, when appealed to, are quite ready to admit that many, or most, of the gurus of whom they have heard are bad men ; but they do not readily see that this interferes with their quasi-magical power. Still, the earnest longing for a True Teacher, and the doubt whether such a one can be found on earth, gives great force to the pleading of the Christian missionary when he points to Jesus Christ as the one Being in whose teachings and character the highest hopes of India regarding the *Sadguru* have been more than completely realized.

II. SAIVA SECTS.

We have now to speak of the Saivas, or followers of Siva. The worship of this deity never penetrated the mass of the people so deeply as that of Vishnu ; there was little in the character or history of Siva that resembled either the heroic exploits of Rama or the seductive sports of Krishna. By the common people Siva was approached with feelings of awe ; admiration or love was out of the question. Remarkably enough, some of the greatest thinkers of India, such as Sankara Acharya, were Saivas. We may perhaps explain this by referring it to the dry, abstract character of Sankara's intellect, which must have been repelled by the highly emotional nature of Vishnu-worship. Sankara was a noted champion of the Vedanta philosophy, and vehemently maintained the dogma of non-duality. His followers have added the teaching of the Yoga; and a very large number follow the revolting doctrines of the Tantras.

It is one proof of the fluctuating character of sectarial divisions in India that we find the list of Saiva sects supplied by one of Sankara's disciples to differ very greatly from any enumeration that could be given in the present day.[1] The most important of the latter are the following:

1. The *Dandis*, or staff-bearers. They are so called from their carrying a small stick, to which is attached a cloth dyed with red-ochre—though this is not an exclusive mark of Saivas. The Dandis, who worship Siva under the terrific form of Bhairava, have an incision made near the knee at their initiation—the blood so drawn being an acceptable offering to the deity. The *Dasnamis* are a sub-section of the Dandis. The term signifies 'the ten names;' it is applied to the ten sections into which the regular followers of Sankara are divided.

2. The *Yogis*. These profess to follow the Yoga philosophy—especially in its most ascetic precepts. Among the most potent of the practices which the Yoga enjoins are continued suppressions

[1] The Rev. Baba Padmanji, who has carefully studied the forms of modern Hinduism, gives the following list of Saiva sects: Dandi, dasnami, yogi, jangam, paramahans, aghori, urdhvabahu, akasmukhi, nakhi, gudad, rukhad, sukhad, ukhad, kadalingi, sannyasi, vairagi, avadhut, nag. Even this long list is not exhaustive.

of the breath, fixing the eyes on the tip of the nose, and various postures, amounting in all to eighty-four. The Kanphata Yogis are so named because, at the time of initiation, their ears are bored and rings are inserted into the wound. These are perhaps the lowest and most ignorant of all. They are of any caste. They smear the body with ashes ; they are fortune-tellers, or quacks who profess to cure disease by incantations ; while many sing and play, exhibiting monkeys and other animals.

3. The *Jangamas*—otherwise called Lingavats, or Lingayits—wear the linga or symbol of Siva on their persons, generally in a box suspended by a string round their necks. They disregard caste and Brahmanical rites.

4. The *Paramahansas* profess to be wholly occupied with meditation on the Supreme Divinity. They go naked, and pretend to be far above attending to any natural want.

5. The *Aghoris* are exceedingly disgusting in their habits. They will eat carrion or the vilest filth. For the bodily tortures to which they subject themselves they demand money. It is probable that formerly human sacrifice formed a part of their dreadful ritual.

6. The *Urdhvabahus* hold an arm, or in some cases both arms, suspended above their heads until the members become quite stiff and will not bend. This is frequently done for a set time ; and then, by friction and lubrication with oil, the stiffened joint

is restored to its former condition. Or, the fist is closed, and by and by the nails perforate the hand.

7. The *Akasmukhis* hold their face up to the sky until the muscles of the neck become rigid, and retain the head in that position.

But we must abandon the attempt to describe, or even enumerate, all the Saiva sects. They are multitudinous; they easily split and split, ramifying endlessly. The Vaishnava sects are more compact and massive. Saiva sects have usually run more than Vaishnava ones into fanatical asceticism. Exorcists, jugglers, charm-sellers, mountebanks of all sorts, are also generally devotees of Siva. The authorities in India have, as a rule, tried to suppress their more indecent and inhuman exhibitions.

There are certain terms which are applied to religious mendicants somewhat loosely—such as Sannyasi, Vairagi (or Byragee, as it is often spelled), Gosain, or, more exactly, Gosavi. Properly, however, the term Sannyasi is a Saiva ascetic: the name denotes one who practises *sannyas*, or renunciation of the world. A Vairagi is, properly, a follower of Vishnu; the name denotes one who has become free from passion. Gosavi is, properly, Go-svami, or 'lord of the cow'—a name of Krishna; so that it ought to denote a devotee of that god; but the name in popular usage is not always so restricted. The term *Fakir* is rightly applied only to Mohammadan mendicants. It properly signifies 'poor.'

III. REFORMING SECTS.

We have seen into what deplorable extravagance the Hindu sects have generally run. It was to be expected that men of purer minds and higher aspirations would from time to time appear, who would strive to purify religion from beliefs and practices manifestly opposed to the dictates of conscience and right reason. We may call Buddha the first great Indian reformer. We must, indeed, speak with caution regarding his teachings, for none of his writings—if such there ever were—have survived. Buddhism originally seems to have contained no theology; but the morality which it inculcated was evidently pure.

When Islam first appeared in India as a victorious, intolerant, and proselytizing system, it compelled attention. It might be hated, but it could not be ignored. Even before the time of the great conqueror Mahmud of Ghazni, about the year 1000, the influence of Arabian thought was felt on the coast of Malabar in South India; and in the great religious movements which occurred in the south from the ninth to the twelfth century, it appears to enter as a factor of some importance. The Arab merchants who visited 'the pepper coast' were often fired with missionary zeal.

But the influence of Islam was still greater in the north. We find unquestionable traces of it in the teachings of the celebrated Kabir. Kabir is usually said to have been one of the twelve disciples of Ramananda, of whom we have spoken above. But if he was really such, he departed widely from the doctrines of his master. Many verses still extant and popular are said to be of his composition; but they probably were the production of his disciples. He flourished about the year 1400—four centuries after Islam had appeared in Northern India, and when multitudes of Hindus must have been familiar with its vehemently iconoclastic character. Kabir has been claimed by the Musalmans as one of themselves; and Hindu writers have sometimes coincided with them in the opinion.[1] He had doubtless come much in contact with Mohammadanism, and had recognized its superiority in many respects to Hinduism. The unity of God, as earnestly proclaimed by Islam, must have strongly impressed him; but he was never able to get rid of Hindu conceptions regarding the illusory character of the world, transmigration, the avataras, and several other points. He inculcates devotion to the guru as earnestly as any teacher; but he holds that all claims to guruship should, in the first instance, be carefully tested. In many respects Kabirism departs widely from Hinduism. It rejects caste, denounces Brahmanical arrogance and hypocrisy, and ridicules the Sastras. Idolatry is sinful. The temple is only a place for men to pray in. Renunciation of the world and

[1] Thus Mahipati, a Marathi poet, or rather chronicler, calls him 'a Yavana devotee.' (Yavana means a Greek, a Greco-Bactrian, or, in later writings, a Musalman.)

contemplation are enjoined. The system runs easily into quietism and mysticism. One noble characteristic of it is the inculcation of moral purity; while of ceremonial purity and outward forms of worship it takes little or no account. It looks on life as almost sacred, and inculcates universal kindness—in this respect reminding us of Buddhism. The worst point in Kabirism is that the disciples are recommended to conform outwardly to the usages of tribe or caste; and they will even profess to worship deities whom in their hearts they scorn. Kabirism is not the stuff of which martyrs are made; it is gentle, yielding, and lacks the stronger virtues. Such as it is, however, it has spread widely over Northern, Western, and Central India; and it has powerfully affected the later developments of Hindu thought. The followers of this teacher are generally called Kabir Panthis.

A second reformer, who in many respects resembled Kabir, was Nanak. He was born near Lahore in 1469, and died in 1539. He had been deeply impressed by Mohammadanism; but, rejecting the Koran as well as the Hindu Sastras, he produced a new Sastra written in the Panjabi language, and called the *Granth* (book). Caste, as a civil institution, was retained. The object of Nanak evidently was to effect a compromise between Islam and Hinduism; but the iron of the former does not readily combine with the clay of the latter. Even in the fundamental question of the nature of Deity there is a gulf between them which it is impossible to bridge over. The sacred book—the Granth—which was to supersede all others, is but a poor production; in so far as it is comprehensible, it is pantheistic much more than monotheistic. The doctrine of *bhakti* is strongly inculcated, as well as absolute devotion to the guru. Morality, however, is not lost sight of.

It is probable that the Sikhs (literally 'disciples'), as the followers of Nanak are called, would have had a history similar to that of the followers of Kabir, had it not been for persecution. Nanak himself was a mystic quietist; and so were the three first of his successors. Arjunmall, the fifth guru, mingled in the political strifes of his age. His successors did the same thing; and the ninth of the series was executed as a rebel by the Emperor Aurangzib. This roused his son, Govind, to vehement opposition. He was a man of no small mental power and immense practical energy. He simplified religion, reducing it pretty much to the adoration of one God and the practice of morality. But both the desire of vengeance and the example of the Mohammadans led him to add that the true faith must be protected and extended by the sword. Every true Sikh must be a soldier. The foolish Hindu he should not condescend to salute; a Musalman he was bound, if possible, to slay. The transformation of simple religionists into ardent warriors has been witnessed in other cases; but in no instance has the change been more complete or equally enduring. It has been maintained by the 'Book of the Tenth King'—a second *Granth*—which Govind added to that of Nanak.

With varying fortunes, yet on the whole gaining ground, the Sikhs fought on during the slow decline of the Moghul empire. In 1764 they formally assumed the position of an independent nation, and issued coin without the name of the Emperor of Delhi. Runjit Singh became virtually head of the community in 1805, and under his strong hand the power of the nation steadily increased. He died in 1839. Confusion followed. Wars with the British came in 1845–6 and in 1848–9; and the territory of the Sikhs was formally annexed to the British dominions in 1849. The Sikh community or nation is still large and important; but its distinctive religious character is slowly passing away. Few or none will become Mohammadans; the vast body will slowly merge in the general mass of the Hindus. Some show a great respect for Christian doctrine; and it is quite possible that this feeling may ere long issue in important movements.

There are various sects which, although not nominally connected with Kabir, have been greatly influenced by his tenets. The most important of these are Dadu Panthis,[1] the Baba Lalis, the Prannathis, the Siva Narayanis, and the followers of Swami Narayan. Each of these systems embodied at the outset an earnest protest against idolatry,

[1] I formed a high opinion of the sincerity of a leader of the Dadu Panthis whom I met at Jeypore in Rajputana. He seemed to have far more sympathy with Christianity than with the gross idolatry around him. His religion appeared to be almost a pure theism.

and the moral corruption that nearly always clings to it; but in the sects, as in orthodox Hinduism, there has always been a deplorable gravitation downwards.

Among reforming sects we may justly reckon the Vaishnavas of the Maratha country. The Marathi literature is of considerable extent; it is nearly all religious, and revolves around the deity Viththal, or Vithoba, who is held to be a manifestation of Krishna. The great place of pilgrimage is Pandharpur—a town about seventy miles north-east of Poona in the Deccan. A commentary on the Bhagavad Gita, composed in Marathi verse by a learned Brahman towards the end of the thirteenth century, has given a marked tinge to all later Marathi poetry; but the influence both of Buddhism and of Kabirism has also been very great. Indeed, there is great reason to hold that Pandharpur was originally a place of Buddhist pilgrimage. There is much vivacity in the writings of Namadeva, one of the more famous Marathi poets; and there is immense emotion in those of Tukarama, the most popular of all. The great subject of the poets now mentioned is to exalt the glory of Vithoba, the glory of his dwelling-place, Pandharpur, and the glory of the river Bhima, on the south bank of which the town is built. Tukarama is perpetually breaking out in exclamations like this:

> 'Much has been heard, much has been seen,
> Much has been said, of the glory of holy places;
> But equal to Pandharpur no holy place exists—
> No, not were even Vaikuntha to be revealed.'

Seeing that Vaikuntha is the heaven of Vishnu, the compliment to Pandharpur is pretty strongly put.

The idolatry of this sect is very decided—none, indeed, more so. The image of Vithoba, standing on a brick with arms akimbo, is extolled in the most hyperbolical strains. A glance at that particular form sends a thrill of rapture through the votary's soul; though it is rather a repulsive image to ordinary eyes. No devotion (*bhakti*) could be more passionate than that of Tukarama; and, when he cannot 'meet' the deity, he is utterly heart-broken. All this is sad enough when we see it in one who really appears to be seeking after God. But the ground on which we have classed the worshippers of Vithoba among reforming sects is that the morality which they inculcate is almost always pure, and generally very decidedly so. There are, indeed, a few unhappy passages in which Tukarama speaks with applause of the lascivious sports of Krishna with the Gopis;[1] but, as a rule, the morality which the Marathi poets uphold is as high as that of Kabir or of Buddha.

The history of Tukarama is partly given in his own writings, but more fully in the works of Mahipati, a Brahman who wrote towards the end of last century. Tukarama lived in the days of the distinguished chieftain Sivaji, rather more than 250 years ago. By the time that Mahipati wrote,

[1] He speaks of their *dhanya dhanya vyabhichar*—*i.e.*, 'the blessed, blessed adultery.'

the compositions of the poet were well known; but his history had become to a great extent mixed with fable. Many miraculous acts are ascribed to him; but the most remarkable thing in the legend is his supposed ascension into heaven, with his body, and without dying. Every year there is a great celebration of the wonderful event. Now, there is nothing else resembling this in Hindu mythology. One thing alone makes the slightest approach to it, viz., the journey which the Pandava warriors, with their wife Draupadi, accomplished up by the Himalaya mountains into the heaven of Indra. But that was a long, laborious ascent, in which the whole party sank under the terrible fatigue, except the eldest brother and the dog. Tukarama, on the contrary, is said to have ascended triumphantly in a blazing chariot. There is documentary evidence that, on a certain day, the poet went on a pilgrimage; and that from this pilgrimage he never returned. The marvellous legend then is explained. We have often pressed the Vaishnavas in Maharashtra with the fact that there is no similar story told of any other saint or poet, and that, for example, Jnanesvara—whom they acknowledge to have been a far greater man than Tukarama—lies in his grave at Alandi, as he has done for nearly six hundred years. We may probably trace the legend to the influence of Christian missionaries. From the beginning of the sixteenth century, Goa—under the Portuguese—was a centre of missionary activity; and there were stations at several places in the Maratha country. Even Tukarama must have heard of the wonderful race of foreigners and of their great achievements under such warriors as De Castro and Albuquerque. Then, religious discussions of an animated kind took place at the court of the Emperor Akbar; and in these, Portuguese missionaries had an important share. Finally, though there was no translation of the Christian Bible into Marathi, there was a Christian Purana—a work actually called a Purana—written in a dialect of Marathi perfectly intelligible to the middle and lower classes of Maharashtra. That work embodies a great number of legends, as well as Biblical narratives, given in a quaint, exaggerated form. That the poet himself may thus have become, to some extent, acquainted with the facts and teachings of the Bible is perfectly possible, and by no means improbable; but we cannot affirm it to be actually proved. But the case of Mahipati, the biographer, is considerably different. He lived, as we have seen, long after the poet, and when a halo had already gathered round him. That Mahipati could have been ignorant of the more striking Biblical narratives is barely possible. The desire which we ascribe to him to exalt Tukarama as a 'world-teacher' (so he calls him) and a great miracle-worker, would imply but a repetition, in very similar circumstances, of the famous attempt made by Philostratus in the third century to magnify Apollonius of Tyana into a form of surpassing grandeur, capable of rivalling, or eclipsing, that of Jesus Christ.

A vast amount of legendary lore exists among all the Vaishnava sects respecting the intercourse which Vishnu, in some of his manifestations, has sought to have with his faithful worshippers. These legends are embodied chiefly in the Bhakta Mala, a work written in a dialect of Hindi by Nabhaji; and this book, being in the vernacular, has profoundly impressed the popular mind where-ever the Hindi language is known. Mahipati, of whom we have already spoken, has imitated these narratives in simple Marathi verse; and this has given them additional currency. The great subject of them is the efficacy—the omnipotence—of devotion to Vishnu. The deity is represented as supremely gracious, supremely condescending; he visits and assists his true worshippers even when they are engaged in the lowest and most despised of occupations, and he enables them to perform the most astonishing exploits. Here, for example, is a noble utterance—

> "'Twixt the low and lofty He no difference knoweth;
> Still to faith He showeth
> All his glory.'

But the poet cannot free himself from the characteristic tendency of the Hindu mind to run to extremes; and, when he has got hold of a fine sentiment, he speedily trails it in the dust. He tells us that the deity stooped even to gather cow-dung with Jani, to bear off dead cattle with Tsokha Mela (a work reserved for outcasts), and even to carry about flesh for a butcher; and so on. Others affirm that, to reward the faith of one of his votaries who was a barber, the deity took his form and shaved the emperor in his stead. Worse than this puerility—Kabir, to entertain a company of devotees, repeatedly stole grain from a shopkeeper's store. On one occasion when he was so employed, along with his son, the shopkeeper discovered the thieves; and the boy, when making his way through the window, was caught by the feet. To prevent discovery, Kabir immediately cut off his son's head and carried it off. Next day the authorities impaled, and publicly exposed, the headless trunk. The devotees, on passing that way, asked for an explanation. The boy's mother told them all, and produced the head; whereupon they fixed it on again, and the boy was none the worse! Every specially holy man is certain to be represented as a simpleton—all but a fool—in the Vaishnava works.

Such are the tales which, in the later days of Vaishnavism, have to a great extent supplanted the legends of the gallantry and gentleness of the conquering Rama and the wifely virtues of the much-suffering Sita.

CHAPTER XI.

MODERN HINDUISM.

WE now proceed to speak of Modern Hinduism as a whole—to take a bird's-eye view of the entire system. But it is by no means easy to convey a correct idea of anything so vast and complicated. The professed adherents of what is broadly called Hinduism are rather in excess of a hundred and ninety millions of human beings; and in so great a number there must—in the nature of things—be immense diversities of belief and practice. We are all the more prepared to expect such diversities when we remember the history of Hinduism. When, more than three thousand years ago, the faith entered Northern India, it found the land tenanted by various races who professed beliefs probably various in character, and certainly very different from Hinduism. The intrusive Aryans conquered the aborigines, but they did not exterminate them; and the victorious race mingled its blood to a large extent with that of the vanquished. In like manner, if not to the same extent, the religions mingled. Original Hinduism would, in any case, have sustained continued change and development from within; but the alteration was greatly accelerated by the operation of causes acting from without, and especially by contact with other creeds. We might almost compare Hinduism to that remarkable effusion of volcanic matter which overspread, at a remote time, many hundreds of miles of the Deccan, entirely covering the sedimentary strata in many places, turning them into metamorphic rocks in others, and not unfrequently allowing them to crop up almost unchanged in character.

What is Hinduism at this day? As to *belief*, it includes a quasi-monotheism, pantheism, polytheism, polydemonism, and atheism, or at least agnosticism.

As to *worship*, it includes meditation on Brahm, the One, the All, without external rites or mental homage; image-worship, fetish-worship, ghost-worship, and demon-worship.

But again, a man may be a good Hindu who avows no belief at all, provided he pays respect to Brahmans, does no injury to cows, and observes—with scrupulous care—the rules and customs of his caste. It has been said that all duty is, to the Hindu, summed up in obedience to the regulations of caste; morality, religion, philanthropy, patriotism, everything. With regard to the other things we have mentioned, it is a very notable historical fact that, when Sivaji, the founder of the Maratha empire, roused his countrymen against their Mohammadan oppressors, he did not summon them to contend for 'altar and hearth'—*pro aris et focis;* he called them to hasten to the rescue of 'Brahmans and cows.' Ay, the shrewd Maratha knew the men he dealt with; and the summons met with an enthusiastic response.

When we first look around us in India, we are deeply impressed with the amazing number of its idols. Images everywhere—in temples and out of them, in the fields, by the wayside; rude figures of stone, each bright and glaring with red paint—trees marked with the same substance. But here is a Maratha village; let us enter, and note the worship. Outside is a circle of stones, all marked as divine by red or white colouring matter—a remnant, doubtless, of the original village faith. Next, near the gate, is a small shrine of Hanuman or Maruti—the figure that of a black-faced monkey, with his tail conspicuously flourishing round his head; he is the special guardian of the village. This deity, too, is probably aboriginal; the strange ways and half-human appearance of the monkey (the forest-man, as they called him) must have surprised and awed the settlers; and, when they took up their abode in or near the woods which he appeared to challenge as his own, they deprecated his displeasure and tried to secure his favour. Gradually he came to be regarded as a mighty warrior and an incarnate divinity; and hence, around the temples of Rama particularly, crowds of monkeys gather, and are held to be sacred.

We now pass into the village. Here is a respectable-looking Brahman sitting, or it may be swinging, on a cot in the verandah of his clean and pleasant house. We address him with the respect we feel; and, with some little delay, he returns the salutation. We find on inquiry that he is conning, not being profoundly versed in Sanskrit, the Viveka Sindhu, a metrical work in Marathi by Mukundraj, which is said by some to be the oldest book in the language. It inculcates the most absolute monism,—there is but one thing in the universe; or as Mukundraj phrases it—'Doer, doing, and deed are all identical.' We politely ask the Brahman if he understands that proposition. He says he does. 'Does he believe it?' He answers, 'Yes.' He declares himself an out-and-out Vedantist: he holds there is but one thing real, and that is Brahm, and he knows enough of Sanskrit to say, *Aham Brahma*—'I am Brahm.' Such men are difficult to argue with; but we would fain inject a feeling into his conscience, and we ask, 'How does your philosophy deal with the great fact of sin?' He quickly retorts, 'What is sin, and what is righteousness? They are illusions, both of them, not real existences.' We explain a very different view of the question, but we seem to make no impression. We part as friends, he telling us at the end that both views are correct—his theory is true to him and our theory to us.

We go farther, and meet a company of people who have just returned from a pilgrimage to Pandharpur, and who are holding a recitation. The party consists of men and women—mostly of the middle ranks, but with one or two Brahmans. They are in the court attached to the shrine of Vithoba. There is a leader in the centre of a company of about sixteen people. He has begun to speak; he holds the sweet, feebly-tinkling *vina* in his hands; he is full of Marathi poetry; he is telling a story about the Princess Mirabai and her supreme devotion to Krishna, and how when, in uttermost distress, she fled for refuge to him, the image of Krishna opened, received the royal votaress within it, and then closed upon her—the god thus taking her into perfect union with himself. Every time that he quotes a line of verse he chants it; the assistants immediately catch it up and repeat it with a loud clashing of the cymbals which every man holds in his hands. The men are dancing with excitement, and the leader may be so carried away that the tears will be seen streaming down his cheeks. This is an exhibition of *bhakti*, or devotion, of which we have had occasion to speak already. It is wonderfully catching; the audience follows every word, and loud shouts are heard from time to time of 'Victory, victory to Viththal!' (or Vithoba). Well, there is food for reflection here. The idolatry is deplorable; the legends are most wild and fantastic; but one seems to see in the devotees a sense of human need, a craving for Divine support, and also an assurance that help is given to true worshippers. This is surely better than the cold, heaven-daring pantheism of the Brahman we first spoke to. These men will admit the great fact of sin; though when we ask how it is to be removed, they unhesitatingly reply, 'By devotion, by gazing on the form of Vithoba, and bathing in the river Bhima.' They, however, listen respectfully to a friendly statement of the True Atonement.

We pass on; and here—is it outside or inside the mouldering village-wall?—is a small shrine with a hideous image, gleaming with the unfailing red lead. What is this? This is Vetal, a devil, a veritable fiend, and worshipped as such. In the far south of India, among the Shanars and other aboriginal races, a small white pyramidal structure that serves both for demon and temple is exceedingly common; but it is rather startling to find demon-worship in a village which is largely Brahmanical.

But it is time to speak of the men who have religious functions to perform in the village. They are two at least, even in the smaller villages. First comes the Bhat, or Brahman priest. He performs the marriage ceremonies, names the children, casts nativities, points out lucky and unlucky days, fixes the proper time to sow and reap, and when the corn is threshed, performs the needful *puja* or worship to it. He also reads the sacred texts over the dead. The bhat is employed in connection with almost every undertaking; for there is always some omen to be explained, or some ceremony to be performed. He is generally well off. He has, at any rate, his regular allowance, which is generally paid in kind. Then, every religious ceremony requires an additional fee; for a poor person it may be as low as a pice or a cocoa-nut, but it is considerable in the case of a rich man. In the month of Bhadrapad, before taking food every devout Kunbi (cultivator) performs the ceremony of *tirth;* that is to say, every one ought to visit a sacred stream and wash his sins away. But no stream of acknowledged sanctity may be within easy reach, and there is a more accessible mode of purification. He has only to drink a little of the water in which the bhat has dipped the great toe of his right foot, and the thing is done. For saith the sacred text—

> 'All the holy streams of the world go to the ocean;
> 'All the holy streams in the ocean are in the Brahman's right foot.'

In the same month also is the ceremony of *pitri paksh*, when offerings must be made to the souls of ancestors. These are represented by Brahmans, and *they* must be fed. If only one can be received, that one must be the bhat; but generally there are several Brahmans—possibly ten or twelve—all of whom must be fittingly entertained.[1]

[1] The sacred men generally get fat at this season. So in the Deccan the proverb runs: 'Plump as a pony in the month of

The next religious functionary is the Gurava—the officiating priest at the village temple. If there are several temples, he attaches himself to the most important; and volunteers are ready to attend the others. The work of the gurava is to wash the idol every morning by pouring water over it, to put red pigment composed of sandal-wood and oil on its forehead, to ornament it with flowers and strew flowers around it. He sweeps the temple, cleans it by smearing the floor over with cow-dung once in seven or eight days, and lights a lamp, or it may be several lamps, before the idol every night. On occasions of feasting, the gurava also prepares the dishes—*i.e.*, leaves cunningly joined together—off which the Hindus eat their food. He is generally also a musician, and plays on the *mridang*, or small drum, both at marriages and when there is a religious recitation at the temple. This functionary is not so generously supported as the bhat; but every family in the village will give him a small quantity of meal, which he offers to the gods after making it into cakes. He then takes it home to his own family. He has also generally some land. His office is hereditary, like that of the bhat. He is a man of respectable caste—higher than a Sudra, and he wears a sacred string. In addition to the homage usually paid by the gurava, the image is often visited by other residents of the village, particularly

Sravan, or a Bhat in Bhadrapada.' (In the month of Sravan there is plenty of green grass for the pony.)

Brahmans. On such occasions some water is poured over the image and prayers are made to it.

There is also in all respectable houses an apartment called the gods' house—a chapel, we may term it—in which the images of the family are kept, ranged for the most part on a shrine in rows. There is almost always a special family idol, a tutelary god or goddess, which has probably been worshipped in the house for generations. In the morning a priest comes, enters the chapel, takes down the deities, bathes them in a pail of water, takes them out, dries them well, sets them again in their places, anoints them with red pigment, offers certain prayers, and, when the worship is over, receives a small fee for his trouble. Or this homage may be paid by the eldest son of the family. The male members of the family then separately pray for a longer or shorter time to the deities. The women and young children will generally throw a few flowers on or near the images, or place some fruits before them. And this is family worship in India!

Idols are made of various materials—such as gold, silver, copper, brass, stone, clay, and occasionally wood. Stone seems the material most frequently used. Pictures are also drawn on the walls, or on paper, which is hung up; and these pictures are worshipped as readily as other images.

Our readers are probably already inquiring what is the Hindu idea of an idol. Is it a deity *per se*, or is it only the resemblance of a deity? In other words, is it a fetish, or an image in the strict sense of the term? Before answering the question we require a careful definition of terms.

We understand by a fetish an object which is regarded as being *per se* a divinity. It is something visible and tangible which is charged with supernatural power—one might say, as a Leyden jar is charged with electricity.

An idol, on the other hand, is properly an *εἴδωλον*, an *imago*—a resemblance, a likeness, or at all events a symbol—of a being distinct from itself.

In theory, fetishism and idolatry are thus quite distinguishable. But, in practice, idolatry very easily runs—certainly in India, and probably everywhere—into fetishism.

An intelligent Hindu, when asked why he worships idols, will generally answer that he does *not* worship idols; he worships the spiritual being who is in the idol. Properly speaking, there is a religious ceremony by which life is communicated to the image; and it is after this that it can be worshipped. The image now is living. It eats or drinks the offerings made to it; smells the odour of the flowers; sleeps, wakes, sometimes speaks; and can move from one place to another.[1]

[1] Avali, one of Tukaram's two wives, had no faith in Vithoba, to whom her husband was passionately devoted. On being told that the image drank milk when offered, she said, 'I will put that to the test.' So she made some milk 'hissing hot,' put it on a vessel and held it to Vithoba's lips. The poor god was burnt; he turned his face

All this is clearly fetishism. The idol is no longer a mere symbol; it is itself a god. The 'life,' which by one ceremony has been brought into it, can by another ceremony be taken out; but unless that is done, the image is an independent deity. And thus images of the same deity may possess very different powers. We have seen the image of a god carried in procession to pay a visit of high ceremony to another image of the same god, like a friend visiting a friend. But the fetishism of India goes much farther than this. Any object whatsoever, if of very remarkable appearance, is sure to be worshipped. It will probably be marked with a red pigment to indicate its supernatural character. Any shape, if not easily explained, any object strikingly beautiful or strikingly the reverse, is marked and worshipped. There was fetishism in ancient Vedic days, but evidently it has increased in the lapse of ages; and it often appears in as gross a form in India as among the lowest savages of Africa or Polynesia. Soon, around the object that has attracted homage by its singularity, there collects a mass of legendary lore. The strange position, or fantastic shape, is due to some god or other who visited the spot; and the low fetish thus gradually obtains a place in the orthodox Hindu system. There is nothing

to one side, and lo! a blister appeared on his lip. And if any person doubts the truth of the story, why, let him go to Dehu, Tukaram's village, and there to this day he will see the image with the wry-neck. 'Seeing is believing,' says the Hindu devotee.

it comes in contact with, which Hinduism cannot absorb and partially assimilate; and thus the stupendous pantheon becomes every day more stupendous still.

It is wholly impossible to enumerate all the objects worshipped in India. It is not easy even to classify them.

We may first mention the sun, moon, and stars of heaven. Next may come certain human beings; especially Brahmans. But any very extraordinary man, even if not a Hindu, may be recognized as 'a descent,' or incarnation, of a divinity;—as happened in the well-known case of General Nicholson. Among animals the cow is pre-eminently a goddess. Monkeys, peacocks, serpents, tortoises, are also worshipped. So is the wild boar, as a representive of the Boar Avatara,—but we have also seen the animal hunted, killed, and eaten; whereas the domestic swine is held by Hindus in almost as much horror as by Mohammadans. Again, certain animals are vehicles of certain gods, and so become *quasi* divine; as, for instance, the bull of Siva and the rat of Ganesa.

In the vegetable kingdom the *tulasi* (holy basil) may be said to stand pre-eminent. But the *pipal* (*Ficus religiosa*) is also worshipped; its leaves quiver like those of the aspen, and thus indicate the presence of a divinity or divinities.[1] The Banyan (*Ficus Indica*), too, is sacred; probably on account of its very remarkable mode of growth—

[1] Bishop Heber speaks of 'the peepul's haunted shade.'

> 'a pillared shade,
> High overarched, and echoing walks between.'

But there are at least six or seven other trees which are hardly less divine; as, for example, the beautiful asoka,[1] the kusa grass, the custard apple, and so on.

Of the productions of the natural world, the one most frequently worshipped is the salagram—a small black stone, with markings like those of the ammonite—which is found in various rivers. This is more than a mere symbol; Tukarama calls it 'Vishnu's self.' Nearly every deity has some object especially dear to him, and therefore sacred—some tree, or herb, or stone. The objects that are, or may be, worshipped, are thus, as we have said, altogether countless.

We may indeed affirm that the Hindus will worship anything and everything *except* the Supreme Being.[2] A maxim which one hears every day in India is this: *Where faith is, there is God.* Believe a thing to be divine, and it is divine. Thus, a swine is regarded as utterly unclean; yet we have asked this question, 'If a man believed a swine to be a god, would it be so?' and the answer, perhaps somewhat slowly given, has been, 'Yes, if a man really believes it, the swine is a god.' 'And,' we have gone on to ask, 'would his faith in that case

[1] 'Best of trees the asoka, blooming, in the forest she espied,
Gemmed all o'er with glittering blossoms, vocal with the song of birds.'—Kalidasa, *Raghuvansa*, bk. i.

[2] Bossuet has somewhere said of classical antiquity: 'Tout était Dieu, excepté Dieu lui-même.'

save him?' and the answer has been, 'Most certainly.'

So much for the immensity of Indian idol-worship. But with regard to the non-existence of the worship of the Supreme. We have frequently asked, 'Where is the temple of the Supreme?' and the answer, given with evident surprise at a question so unexpected, has always been, 'Temple of the Supreme? What do you mean? there is no such temple.' 'Why?' 'Because He can have none. He is formless, nameless, inconceivable; and we cannot worship Him.' 'And therefore you worship idols?' 'Certainly. An idol is indispensable. We need some visible object on which our minds can rest.'

At a first glance India thus appears to be utterly, infinitely, exclusively polytheistic. But, on entering into conversation even with the simple villagers, you are startled by the discovery that another system of thought, which at first seems wholly irreconcilable with polytheism, has been wrought into the very texture of the Hindu mind. We mean pantheism. Polytheism and pantheism are the warp and woof of Hinduism. We have asked a hundred times, 'Who is it that speaks in you and me?' and the answer has always been, 'The Supreme.' The commonest man will say that his soul is a part of God. He will even reason with you, and ask whether the Supreme is not omnipresent; and when you answer 'yes,' he will say that the case is therefore clear, for the Divine

Spirit which is in man necessarily excludes every other spirit.

The pantheism which has extended so widely, and sunk so deeply into the popular mind, is not indeed the sublimated system of the Vedanta. We saw above that the Vedanta denies the reality of an external world, and affirms the existence of one Self, one sole Spirit, in the universe; or rather, there is no universe—nothing but the one Self and its illusions. But the popular pantheism allows the existence of matter. The Puranas speak of matter as the body of God—the mountains being His bones, the rocks His nails, the trees His hair, and so on. The common people seldom do this; and they believe in their own bodies, though not in their own souls. But, in truth, all is inconsistency. Even Tukaram, who at one time contends earnestly for the doctrine of *dvaita*, or dualism, at another declares that his soul has blended with Deity, as salt dissolved in water is blended with the water.

No characteristic of any religion can be more important than the manner in which it deals with the great fact of Sin. Many a Brahman will assert that he holds sin to be a mere appearance, an illusion; and this is in accordance with Vedanta doctrine. Yet the same man will go through a round of ceremonies every morning and evening, and confess that he is a sinner from his birth. The common Hindu will not go to the extreme of asserting the non-reality of sin; though he is wholly unable to explain how the Divine Spirit, which dwells in him instead of a soul, is led into the commission of evil. He is therefore quite consistent in using means for the removal of sin.

But when we speak of sin, we need to explain with some care what the Hindu conception of sin actually is. We referred already to the declaration of Professor Weber, that in the Vedas the religious notion of sin is altogether wanting; and various writers of note have used equally strong language in regard to the Greek and Roman writings. But there was what we may call a vacillating sense of sin in Greece and Rome; and there is as much among the Hindus now. St. Paul declares that 'God has never left Himself without witness': and that 'the Gentiles show the work of the law written on their hearts.' There are differences. In some cases conscience appears, to quote St. Paul again, 'to be seared with a hot iron;' familiarity with evil has in many destroyed the moral perceptions and emotions. Yet all the Hindus are not such. Conscience, alas! is frequently asleep, often drugged with opiates; but it is not dead, and it is generally capable of being roused. Undoubtedly the ordinary Hindu sees that there is a distinction between right and wrong; he fully admits also that he is bound to do the right and shun the wrong; although he is often sorely astray as to what is right and what is wrong. We therefore do not say that 'the religious notion of sin is altogether wanting.' The man will at once concede that he ought to worship God, and that he sins unless he does so. He will at once admit that he ought not to injure his neighbour; and that stealing, lying, adultery, and such-like deeds, are sins which Heaven will punish. Yet when all this is said, how much is left unsaid! One deplorable and fundamental error into which Hindu teachers have fallen is that they have inculcated an endless number of ceremonial observances and rules of caste as of equal importance with the clearest moral duties—nay, in many cases, as of greater importance. Conscience has thus been bewildered; although from time to time there has come a reaction from extreme ceremonialism, and the fundamental truths of morality have been recognized and raised again, for the time, almost to their proper place.

The ancient ascetics, whose questionings and aspirations are contained in the Upanishads, paid comparatively little attention to external rites. Meditation on the Divine constituted to them nearly the whole of religion. Salvation was attainable only through knowledge. Farther, the important school of thought which exalts devotion (*bhakti*), makes, in theory at least, equally little account of ceremonies; devotion is all in all, and through devotion salvation is obtained. Still, viewed as a whole, Hinduism strikes every observer as a most colossal system of outward rites and ceremonies; one stands in blank amazement to think that human beings could willingly bend their necks and bear a yoke so crushing. Salvation by works—that is, by ceremonies—is the doctrine held by an overwhelming majority of the people.

The means of purification from sin and of acquiring righteousness are very numerous. The following are the most efficacious and customary:—

1. Pilgrimages to holy places, washing in a sacred stream, and beholding a deity.
2. Giving food, or money, to Brahmans.
3. Frequent repetition of the name of a deity.
4. Bodily austerities.
5. Eating the five products of the cow.

Pilgrimages were not known in Vedic days; no one spot was deemed more sacred than another. Rivers, indeed, soon began to be held in reverence, and this doubtless on account of their manifest and manifold utility; and it was the holiness of the river that made the town on its banks holy. First the Indus, 'the most copious of streams,' as the Rishis called it, attracted admiration; then, as the race moved on, came the Sarasvati: but both of these were afterwards eclipsed by the Ganges. We trace the idea of sacred places from the time of the Mahabharata, about 200 B.C. It has gradually attained immense development, and is still developing. India is covered with holy places, or *tirthas*; they are found from the lake Manasa in Tibet to Ramesvar, over against Ceylon; from Dwaraka in the west to Puri in the east. Benares, on the Ganges, still holds the pre-eminence it attained in pretty early, though not the earliest, days. All the territory around, within a radius of ten miles, is equally holy. Next come in importance Prayag (Allahabad), at the confluence of the Ganges and Yamuna (Jumna); Haridwar (also written Hardwar), at the point where the Ganges breaks out into the plains from among the mountains; and Ganga Sagar, where the Ganges joins the ocean. These are very celebrated *tirthas*. Nearly equal in importance to Benares is Puri, in Orissa, with its notorious temple of Jagannath (Juggernaut); the region around for twenty miles is all holy. Dwaraka, in Gujarat, said to have been the capital of Krishna, is also famous. Nasik, on the Godavari, is sacred, as being associated with the history of Rama. Pandharpur, on the Bhima, which is a tributary of the river Krishna, has been for above four hundred years a centre of immense attraction to the Marathas. Ramesvar, situated on an island between India and Ceylon, is visited by great multitudes from all parts of India; and devotees carry vessels of water from the Ganges for the purpose of pouring it on the image. The last-mentioned place contains one of twelve celebrated *lingas*, or symbols of Siva—among which Somnath in Gujarat; Omkar, on an island in the river Narmada (Nerbudda); Badari Kedar, near the source of the Ganges; and Tryambak, at the source of the Godavari, are among the most popular.

The numbers that frequent the *tirthas* differ in different places. Those on the Ganges are visited at certain recurring times by more than a million, or occasionally two millions. The holy season extends over a considerable time—crowds coming and going daily. At Pandharpur there gather twice every year, in July and December, from a hundred thousand to a hundred and twenty-five thousand. The attendance at Puri is also very great, amounting to about three hundred thousand.

The ceremonies of purification differ somewhat in different places. Very generally at a *tirtha* there are men who call themselves *Gangaputra*—sons of the Ganges—whose duty it is to help the pilgrims in the performance of the customary rites. Every family of these has a book in which are marked down the names and residences of pilgrims who have in former days visited the spot; and, on the arrival of any visitant, these men eagerly ask his name, turn over their records, and try to discover that he or his family having formerly availed themselves of their ministrations, he must do so now. They help the pilgrim to find a suitable place in which to pitch a tent or bit of cloth as a kind of shelter; take him to the temple, or temples; perform the ceremony of shaving his head [1]—a matter of much importance in many places; and, above all, help him in the washing away of his sins by bathing. They stand beside him in the stream, repeating the appropriate prayers in Sanskrit. A price is paid, which varies according to the circumstances of the pilgrim or the importunity of the priest.

[1] This is not performed everywhere. It obtains at Benares, Gaya, Nasik, Pandharpur, etc. Women who are not widows cut off a portion of their hair.

The great prevalence of the system of pilgrimage is truly remarkable. One cannot look upon it with any satisfaction. No doubt it relieves in some degree the dull monotony of every-day existence; it enables a man whose horizon has been limited to his village to see a little of the outside world. But the evils accompanying it are exceedingly great. It is expensive; it makes a man neglect his daily work, which, in the case of the Indian cultivator, is a very serious matter; it makes the pilgrim run a serious risk as to health and even life. At all the great festivals wretched accommodation is certain, and an outbreak of disease is frequent.[1] In the rainy season the dangers are aggravated. In Bengal, husbands and fathers have often occasion to resist the attempts made by female members of their families to go on pilgrimage to Puri or elsewhere; for, when the caged bird escapes, there is the danger of its never returning. Men sent out from Puri traverse India, proclaiming the glories of Jagannath and the blessedness of going on pilgrimage; and it is against the representations of such men that the heads of families require to be on their guard. Regarding the deplorably erroneous view of true religion which is fostered by the whole

[1] Until of late the Government of India did very little with a view to secure the simplest sanitary arrangements. The consequence was that in a few days the neighbourhood became utterly disgusting, and the whole atmosphere poisoned. Latterly, Government has interfered to a much greater extent; and, when cholera has broken out, has issued proclamations warning the people against attending the infected place.

system of pilgrimage, it is unnecessary to speak. It is a great corruption of the earlier and simpler faith of India. Finally, it ought to be noticed that the mind of the pilgrims is much more set on acquiring merit than on being purified from sin. The idea of acquiring merit, righteousness, is very deeply implanted in the mind of every Hindu; and pilgrimages are among the most meritorious of works.

With regard to ascetic practices as a means of purification. They are far more general among the Saiva than among the Vaishnava sects. We have already spoken of asceticism, when treating of the Yoga system and the Saiva sects.

One of the most powerful means of purification is eating the five products of the cow. The cow being holy, everything that issues from her body is holy; even the dust raised by her feet will purify from sin.[1] The five-fold mixture is called *pànchagavya*. Marvellous is its potency:

> 'Piercing through my bones and marrow, dwelleth sin within my flesh;
> But the *panchagavya* burns it, as the fire consumes the wood.'

Being not only potent, but easily accessible, this means of purification is more frequently had recourse to than any other. Sacred streams may be at some distance, but the cow is always at

[1] So Kandasa—

'Rising from her holy footsteps, lightly curled the dust around;
But it purified the monarch, like the *tirtha's* sacred wave.'
Raghuvansa, bk. i.

hand. A feast given to Brahmans generally accompanies the purifying rite, and is its suitable completion.

Regarding this practice, which will appear to our readers one of the most irrational of the innumerable observances of Hinduism, it may be well to note in conclusion that we see something very similar in the Parsi ritual. One of the products of the animal—we do not mean milk or butter—is greatly used as a means of purification among the professed followers of Zoroaster. It is applied to the body every day, and a small quantity is drunk. There is, indeed, this difference between the Hindus and Parsis: it is the cow that is specially sacred to the former, but it is a bull that the Parsis keep in their temples, in order that the purifying liquid may never fail. It is regretfully we write of such things; but to omit a point so characteristic would be to give an imperfect account of these religions.

We may here mention the purifying rites[1] which must be performed by all Hindus who belong to the three highest castes. 1. A ceremony to cause conception; 2. On the first indication of vitality, and to secure the birth of a male child; 3. At the time of birth; 4. At the time of naming the child; 5. On taking the child out to see the moon, and to see the sun; 7. On feeding it with

[1] They are called *sanskara—i.e.*, perfecting, completing. The word 'sacrament' is generally rendered in Indian languages by *sanskara*.

rice, especially in the fifth or eighth month; 8. The tonsure of the hair except one lock, in the second or third year; 9. Investiture with the sacred string on the tenth or twelfth day after birth; and 10. Marriage. These ceremonies amount to ten. Some authorities give two more;—arranging the mother's hair in the fourth, sixth, or eighth month of pregnancy; and the return of the young man to his home after completing his studies under a *guru*. Investiture with the sacred string takes place in the case of a Brahman in the eighth year; in that of Kshatriya in the eleventh, and in that of a Vaisya in the twelfth. The youth thus enters the honoured rank of the twice-born. In the case of a female the rites are much fewer.

The legislator Gautama enumerates forty sacraments or purificatory rites.

Ceremonies connected with the dead are regarded as of great importance. First come the funeral rites. The spirit of the deceased is understood to hover for some time after death over the place where the corpse is burned or buried. The spirit is unhappy, and in its nakedness impure; and all the relatives of the deceased are also impure. The funeral rites, which are celebrated after death for ten days, pacify the troubled spirit. Balls, generally made of rice and milk, along with water, are offered; and the spirit feeds on their essence. It acquires in this way a covering, or body, more substantial than the 'subtile body' which it possessed when it quitted the one of flesh and blood. The spirit is no longer a *preta*, or ghost; it is now exalted into a *pitri* (ancestor), and can be worshipped. Offerings are made to it, consisting as before of balls chiefly of rice and milk; and these are accompanied with the recitation of sacred texts. This ceremony is called *sraddha*.[1]

The prescriptions connected with the observances of the *sraddhas* run into infinite complexity. A book which has lately appeared in Bombay contains on this single subject more than a hundred closely-printed pages. We will not weary our readers by going into details that are as meaningless as they are endless. Suffice it to say that there are daily offerings to the *pitris*; offerings on particular days of the moon; occasional offerings, such as for a relative recently deceased, or on domestic occurrences, such as the birth of a son. These may all be called obligatory. There are also voluntary *sraddhas*, which are performed for the acquisition of merit. The proper times for *sraddhas* are during the 'dark half' or waning moon, the day of new moon, at the solstices, eclipses, etc.

It is interesting to note that, in more ancient days, as appears from the legislation of Manu, offerings were made which have been discontinued in modern Hinduism. Thus Manu informs us that the *pitris* have their hunger satiated for two months by the offering of fish; deer's flesh satisfies them for three; sheep's flesh for four; bird's flesh

[1] Derived from the Sanskrit *sraddha*—faith.

for five; wild boar's for eleven; cow's milk for twelve; red goat's flesh for ever. Other specifications on this subject are no less precise.

It is the office of the nearest male relative to present the ball of food to the deceased and to his forefathers, both in the male and female lines. He who does so establishes a claim to the inheritance.

It is the greatest of misfortunes that there should be no male descendant. In that case no one is qualified to present the *sraddha;* and the *pitris* are reduced to the uttermost distress,—so greatly are the dead dependent on the living.[1] Adoption, however, remedies the evil; an adopted son (if the statutory prescriptions have been exactly complied with) is fully qualified to present the necessary offerings to the *dii manes.*

We must still refer to caste. It has been termed the very stronghold of the religion Dr. Wilson of Bombay says it is 'the soul as well as the body of Hinduism.' In truth, a man may believe anything or nothing, and he may neglect other precepts of the faith as much as he chooses; and yet, if he attend to the rules of caste, he remains a good Hindu. A tuft of hair on the crown of the head is, in most places, the great outward badge of his being so. But still more important

[1] Kalidasa puts this conviction in a somewhat grotesque form. King Dilipa had no son; wherefore he sorrowfully says—

'Soon must cease the holy *sraddha;* and my fathers, seeing this,
Drink the water of the offering, warming it with sighs of woe.'

Raghuvansa, bk. i.

is compliance with the prescribed rules as to what he eats and drinks. A man is defiled by what goes into his mouth—especially by eating food prepared by a man of lower caste. Contact with such a man is also polluting.

The orthodox legislation, as we saw above, was one that highly exalted the Brahman, and sternly depressed the Sudras, and the still lower divisions of the people. Of course, under a Mohammadan or Christian government, the measureless pretensions of the Brahmans could not be conceded. For example, such precepts as these—'Never shall a king slay a Brahman, though convicted of all possible crimes;'[1] 'Whatever exists in the universe is all the property of the Brahman,'[2] could only be treated with contempt. But, under purely Hindu rulers, it is amazing to what extremes the Brahmans have insisted on the maintenance of the ancient rules. Thus, before Poona was taken from the Marathas by the British, no Mhar was allowed to enter the city before nine o'clock or remain in it after three; and this for the remarkable reason that before nine, and after three, he cast too long a shadow,—and if his shadow fell on a Brahman, it polluted him.

The kingdom of Travancore in Southern India is the part of the country in which Brahmanical ideas now rule most strongly. The Namburi Brahmans number only a little more than ten thousand; but their will is law. The late

[1] Manu viii. 379, etc. [2] Ibid. i. 93-10.

Maharaja had received a good English education; but, either from choice or necessity, he acted precisely like a bigoted Hindu. Various public improvements, such as roads and bridges, were urgently required, but such things must wait; for the Brahmans must be fed and receive largesses which the country can ill afford. Meanwhile, certain classes which, until the British Government interfered, were in a condition of abject slavery, are not allowed to enter courts of justice nor public markets, nor to remain on the public road if a man of higher rank is using it. A Pulaya must remain sixty-nine steps away from a Brahman; otherwise the latter is polluted, and the former visited with condign punishment.

Thus the idea that some classes are inherently holy, and others inherently polluted and abominable, has taken complete possession of the mind of the higher castes in Travancore, and also in the neighbouring region of Cochin. The fact may seem extraordinary, seeing that in the Veda there is no trace, or the least possible trace, of caste. Yet we can see in the language used regarding the aborigines—which breathes only passionate hatred or contempt—how ready the Aryans were, even in early days, to trample their enemies in the dust. History is sorrowfully full of proofs of 'man's inhumanity to man;' but it strikes us (not forgetting the case of the Helots of Sparta) that perhaps the most flagrant instance of high treason against the rights of man as man is seen in the legislation of Manu, and the practice of the 'orthodox' kingdom of Travancore.[1]

Feasts and Fasts.—One of the most characteristic features of Hinduism is the immense number of feasts and fasts which it prescribes. It is quite impossible to give even a brief description of the whole of them; and, were it possible, it would greatly try the patience of the reader. But a fairly correct idea of these observances may be obtained from a short statement regarding ten or twelve of the most important. We shall describe them especially as they are observed in Western India. We shall take them in their chronological sequence.

1. *Makar Sankranti*—corresponding to 12th of January. The celestial sign *makar* answers to Capricorn. On that day the sun is said to begin his journey northward. To the early Hindus, living in a cold region, the approach of spring was an occasion of the greatest joy; and the commencement of the sun's northward progress could not pass unmarked, for then opened the auspicious half of the year.[2]

The sun especially is worshipped in this festival. Bathing in the sea is prescribed wherever it is possible. Rejoicings abound in public and private. Great gatherings take place—as at Prayag, where the Ganges and Jumna mingle; and at Ganga Sagar, where the Ganges meets the ocean.

[1] The number of distinct castes in Travancore is said to be 420. The most degraded of the outcasts are the Pulayas.

[2] According to correct astronomy the sun enters Capricorn and commences his northward journey on the 21st of December.

In the Tamil country the festival is called 'Pongal.' Great attention is paid to the cattle. Their horns are painted and adorned with chaplets, and the poor beasts have, for once, a grand holiday.

2. *Mahasivaratri—i.e.*, the great night of Siva (12th of February). The linga (*phallus*) which is the emblem of Siva, is especially worshipped on this occasion. A legend of great celebrity is connected with it. A wicked hunter, to escape the wild beasts, mounted at night into a *bel* (*bilva*) tree, which is sacred to Siva. Leaves were broken off, and fell on a linga that stood below. Moreover the hunter had fasted all day, for the sufficient reason that he had nothing to eat. Siva was delighted at the honour paid him by the falling leaves and the fast, and sent a heavenly chariot to convey the hunter to heaven. This event is commemorated in the festival. First there is a fast during the day; at night the worshippers repair to the temples of Siva, and remain there from about eight o'clock till five next morning. Worship is performed for them by a priest on four different occasions; and thus the vigil lasts the whole night. Generally the priest reads a list of Siva's many names; and as each is mentioned, the worshipper throws a leaf of *bel* on the linga.

3. *Holi.* This festival properly lasts ten days in the end of February and beginning of March. It is exceedingly popular in all parts of India. It corresponds in many respects to the ancient Satur-

nalia, of which the modern carnival is a mild survival.

The most marked feature of the Holi is the extreme licence with which it is attended. Red powders or red-coloured liquids are thrown about; people are sent on absurd errands (as on All-Fools' day in Europe); dances are kept up in commemoration of the sports of Krishna with the Gopis (the female cow-herds of Vrindavana). Bonfires are kindled for the last three days. Matters get worse towards the end of the festival, and on the last day it is hardly possible for a respectable woman to leave her own house: she is at once assailed with volleys of the vilest language conceivable. Legends had to be invented to justify, or at least explain, so disgusting a practice. We are told that a female demon who was injuring children had to be driven away by the use of such abominable words [1]—and certainly they are enough to disgust even a demon. But there can be no doubt that originally this was a spring festival—a season of universal rejoicing at the revived life of nature. It is sad to see it celebrated, not with innocent gladness, but with obscene and riotous excess.[2] When the bonfires at the conclusion are extinguished, the ashes are distributed, and people rub their bodies over with them.

[1] In the Bhavishyottara Purana, ch. xvii.

[2] It deserves to be noted that, in the Roman festival of Anna Perenna, which was also celebrated in spring, the same evil practice prevailed. As Ovid expresses it, '*joci veteres obscænaque dicta canuntur.*'

4. *Rama navami.* This is commemorative of the warrior-god Rama. It ends on the ninth day of the light half of the month Chaitra ; hence the term *navami*, which means 'ninth.' For eight days previous the temples of Rama are illuminated and largely attended ; the history of Rama is read or recited ; and the images of the god are arrayed with costly ornaments. The last day is the anniversary of the birth of the deity. At noon, when the birth is believed to have taken place, the preacher, as we may call him, who has been descanting on the greatness of Rama, exhibits a small image of the god, and puts it into a cradle. The assembly prostrates itself before it. Acclamations rise all around ; handfuls of red powder are flung in token of joy; and all go home exulting.

5. *Naga panchami.* This festival is held on the fifth day of the light half of the month Sravan. It is in honour of serpents. The figure of a serpent is made of clay, or drawn on the wall, and worshipped. Living serpents are brought, and supplied with milk and eggs. All this is done to deprecate the wrath of the venomous reptile.

6. *Narali paurnima.* This festival is observed chiefly by those who dwell on the sea-coast. It is held on the 23rd of August, when the more stormy period of the rainy season is believed to be over. Flowers, and especially cocoa-nuts, are thrown as offerings into the sea, in order to secure its favour, or else as a thank-offering because its rage has abated.

7. *Krishna* (or *Gokul*) *Janmashtami*, is celebrated on the eighth day of the dark half of Sravan (=August 31st), in commemoration of the birth of Krishna. It is one of the greatest of the sacred seasons. The worshippers fast the whole day—that is, they can eat only certain kinds of food uncooked. Boiled rice, for example, is prohibited. At night they bathe, worship a clay image of the infant Krishna, and adorn it with leaves of the *tulasi* and flowers. Next day is a great occasion among all keepers of cattle, as Krishna in his boyhood lived among such.

In Western India a deity, probably aboriginal, called Kanhoba, has been identified with Krishna. The chief devotee, on the night when Krishna is supposed to have been born, becomes excited, uses wild gestures, mutters strange sounds, his whole body quivering. This is a sign that 'the god has come'—*i.e.*, he has entered the body of his worshipper. This man is now himself worshipped. Others become equally frantic, and are worshipped in their turn. Sick persons are brought; Kanhoba's devotees rub ashes on their heads, pass their hands over them, receive money, and dismiss them as healed.

8. *Ganesa chaturthi*, celebrated on the fourth of the light half of Bhadrapad (September 10th), is in commemoration of Ganesa or Ganapati—'the remover of difficulties'—a god with an elephant's head. His vehicle is a rat; and therefore the clay image of a rat, saddled and bridled, is often placed

beside him. The image of the god is gilded and glittering. The deity has to be brought into the image, which is done by elaborate consecration. It is then worshipped. The exploits of Ganesa are enlarged on, friends and relatives attending. A sumptuous feast is then given to Brahmans. The deity remains as an inmate of the house for several days, amounting in some cases to ten. Thereafter he must depart. First, the divinity which had been brought into the image is extracted by the repetition of appropriate formulæ. The image is then seated in a palankeen, and carried to the sea or a tank in a gaily attired procession. It is flung into the water with the expression of much regret at parting and of hopes to meet next year.

Once Ganesa, when riding on his rat, had a fall; and the moon, who saw it, laughed at his equestrianship. Whereupon the offended god cursed the moon and all who should look at her; but he condescended afterwards to restrict the curse to those who should behold her on his birthday. Accordingly, if any Hindu accidentally or forgetfully sees the luminary at that time, he becomes terribly afraid of the consequences; which he probably seeks to avert by provoking some neighbour to pour on him a flood of maledictions. These are held to be a substitute for the curse he has incurred.

9. The *Dussera*, properly *Dasahara*, ending on the tenth of the light half of Asvin (October 16th), seems to be connected with the autumnal equinox.

It commemorates the victory of Durga, the wife of Siva, over a buffalo-headed demon. In Bengal it is called the Durga puja, and is a very splendid festival. The clay image of the goddess, highly bedizened, is treated with much the same ceremonies as have been described in the case of Ganesa, and, after nine days' worship, is conveyed with immense pomp and flung into the river.

As it is believed that the warrior god Rama marched out on this day against Ravana, the demon-king of Ceylon, the Marathas selected it as the proper time to begin the great plundering expeditions to which that warlike race was so much addicted. To this day the implements of war are worshipped. The bright flowers of the *palasa* (*Butea frondosa*) and other trees—which are held to represent gold—are offered to the gods, and by friends to each other.

10. *Diwali* (from *dipavali*), 'the feast of lamps,' is celebrated on days corresponding to the 2nd, 4th, and 5th of November. The houses are cleaned, whitewashed, and illuminated. In front of the house a quadrangular space is marked with pretty figures, drawn with variously coloured kinds of chalk. This is done on most festivals, but especially at the Diwali. To draw the figures well is deemed a high accomplishment of the women. Gambling is permitted—almost enjoined—during the feast. Fireworks abound. The merchant closes his accounts, gets new ledgers and account-books, which are consecrated and

worshipped. It is the commencement of the Hindu year.

11. *Bali pratipada* is celebrated on the first day of the light half of Karttik (November 6th). The people clean their houses, bathe, fill baskets with the rags and rubbish lying about, and throw it out of the house. In the Maratha country they repeat the words given above in the note to p. 113.

12. *Champa shashti*, on the sixth of the light half of Margasirsh (December 11th), is sacred in Western India to the god Khandoba of Jijuri, near Poona. This used to be a great occasion for men or women, in the performance of vows, being suspended by a hook run through the back and swung round in front of the temple. But this cruel practice has been forbidden by the British Government.

CHAPTER XII.

RECAPITULATION.

We have thus endeavoured to trace the history of the Hindu religion from the commencement up to the present time—through a period amounting to more than three thousand years. It may be well to give a brief summary of the conclusions to which we have been led.

The foundation of the Hindu faith is laid in the Veda, otherwise called the four Vedas. But from the facts which the Veda supplies we are able to draw some inferences regarding an earlier form of religion which we may designate pre-Vedic. It thus cannot be doubted that the Indo-European race, before it parted into five or six separate branches, recognized the existence of a Supreme Divinity—a Being powerful, wise, and good. He was held to be the arranger (we cannot say, the creator) and the ruler of all things. Offerings were a very important part in the worship of this Being; and, among these, animal sacrifice held a high place. We can hardly suppose that the Supreme Divinity was the only Being to whom worship was paid ; yet we may well hesitate before we call the religion polytheistic.[1] Idolatrous it almost certainly was not; if images were used at all, it could only have been very sparingly. The Supreme Divinity was in all probability a spiritual Being, but localized in heaven ; and we may believe that, with many, Heaven and the God of heaven were conceptions separable, but in fact not always separated. Worship was, to a very large extent, domestic. We have little or no evidence of the existence of a priestly order.

It is evident that the Hindus and Iranians (old Persians) remained together for a considerable time after the other divisions of the race had migrated towards the West. Reverence for the fermented juice of the *Soma* plant (in Zend *Homa*) is very marked in the Veda and the Avesta ; but it does not appear in Greek or Roman writings. It may have been of very early origin ; in the tribes migrating to the West, it would cease when the holy plant was no longer visible ;—or it may have begun after the eastern tribes had parted from the western. It seems to have been offered to the divinity as being the most wonderful and precious beverage they knew.[2]

[1] Thus, we do not tax the Roman Catholics with polytheism, notwithstanding the invocation of saints and angels.

[2] In the parable of Jotham (Judges ix. 13) wine is said to 'cheer God and man.'

We come now to the Vedic religion. The earliest hymns are 'racy of the soil;' there is little, if any, remembrance of the time when the Aryans lived beyond the great mountains that form the northern battlement of India. The religious thought of the Vedic poets is deeply affected by their environment. Varuna, the god of heaven, is still a mighty being and possessed of high moral attributes; but a very different deity has begun to overshadow him. Indra, the god of the lower sky —the region of cloud and storm—is now spoken of as supreme, and the lofty, supersensuous attributes of Varuna begin to pass out of view. Deities multiply, yet slowly; the Veda generally speaks of them as 'thrice eleven.' None has any ethical character except Varuna. The worship is mainly nature-worship. Every part of nature is regarded as divine; while there is some conception of nature as a whole: so that we have polytheism, and the commencement of both pantheism and fetishism. Everything connected with religious rites becomes also sacred, divine; thus, the Soma juice is now a god—and one of the mightiest gods. Worship is highly ritualistic. Sacrifice is both eucharistic and propitiatory; it has developed in extent and deepened in meaning, and mystical ideas gather thickly round it. Sacerdotalism has commenced; the selection and arrangement of the hymns has been made by priestly hands. Domestic worship still retains a high place; but there are great public celebrations made in the open air, which require a vast array of sacrificers, singers, and assistants. As the ceremonies become more complex, and the knowledge of the old language gradually fades, these men grow into a priestly caste. The 'men of prayer' thus begin to be exalted above their fellows; and a foundation is laid on which posterity will build the great structure of Brahmanism. It is almost exclusively for temporal benefits that the deities are approached. Thus the ethical character of the Vedic faith is decidedly low.

The preceding remarks apply to the Rig Veda; but we have to take into account the Atharva also. Deterioration must have gone on rapidly; for the latter book cannot well be more than a few hundred years later than the former, and yet the far greater number of its hymns stand morally on a much lower level than those of the more ancient work. We may indeed explain the inferiority of the one collection to the other, by supposing that there existed from the beginning two forms of the religion—the higher being embodied in the Rig V., and the lower in the Atharva. But that corruption did go on is unquestionable; and when the Atharva, in process of time, was put in the same place of honour, with the more ancient hymns, it became impossible to separate the better from the worse, since all was alike divine.[1] The Atharva abounds in incantations,

[1] Professor Max Müller is never a harsh critic of Indian thought or institutions; yet one of his latest utterances is the following: 'That the Veda is full of childish, silly, even to our minds monstrous conceptions, who will deny?' He evidently includes the Rig Veda in this censure.

imprecations, and prayers for the destruction of enemies. The Rig V. acknowledges no evil divinities; but the Atharva deprecates, by prayer and offerings, the wrath of demons. This is a great descent from earlier conceptions.

The early ritual is unfolded to us in that part of a Veda which is called the Brahmana. The earliest can hardly be much older than the sixth century B.C.; but the ceremonies which they explain and inculcate may, in many cases, be considerably more ancient. The Brahmanas are intellectually very poor productions. The writers were occupied with a round of ceremonies which extinguished, or excluded, thought. The rites came to be regarded as all in all; the deities addressed were of little importance in comparison. If the sacred texts had been rightly uttered, and the sacred ceremony duly performed, the incantation was complete, and the end was sure to be gained. Worship was thus degraded into magic. The moral character of the worshipper was of little or no consequence.

Towards the end of this period—perhaps about 500 B.C.—the doctrine of Transmigration began to appear, and to exercise a continually deepening influence. This implied an immense departure from earlier ideas. Asceticism also became prominent, chiefly in connection with the worship of the god Siva. This had probably existed before; but it became more and more influential as Vedic conceptions faded away.

A tendency to speculation—to musing rather than to action—seems inherent in the Aryan mind ; or else it has been infused into it from very early days. The growth of this tendency was kept in check during the earliest period of the Aryan invasion of India ; but as the Hindus steadily pressed eastward and southward, following the course of the Jumna (Yamuna) and Ganges, it began to assert itself. Moreover, excessive ritualism necessitated a reaction. Speculation was thus contemporaneous with ceremonialism. The development of the latter was the work almost exclusively of the Brahmans ; but the former engaged the minds of kings and other members of the Kshatriya caste—probably even of the Vaisya, or third caste. Still, it is probable that the leaders of thought were generally Brahmans.

These hermit philosophers were no systematic thinkers. Aspirations, guesses, rhapsodies—these are all we get from them, perhaps all we could reasonably expect. They did not mean to be heretical, and they assumed the truth of the Vedic faith ; but their whole strain of thought lessened the authority of the established ritual. The ceremonies were well enough for the vulgar ; but there was another 'way,' far nobler, for the truly wise to follow. That was the way of knowledge.

The teaching of the Upanishads is not self-consistent ; but on the whole the current of thought is strongly pantheistic. It maintains a spiritual unity, and generally regards all things else as mere appearance, unreality; the soul being not really distinct from Brahm, the One, the All. But Illusion, or Ignorance, is said to be co-eternal with Brahm; so that the doctrine is self-contradictory—asserting in the same breath one, and two, eternal existences.[1]

After the doctrine of the Upanishads seems to have come that of an original void, out of which all things arose. This doctrine was formally enunciated in the metaphysics of Buddhism. The fully developed Sankhya doctrine of the existence of two eternal agencies, Soul and Nature—a system essentially dualistic—was probably later in origin.

All along, there were schools of thought opposed to the orthodox—sceptical and scoffing systems, which ridiculed earnest thought and inculcated the pursuit of worldly enjoyment. Among these the materialistic school of the Charvakas was preeminent.

The formulated philosophy is usually said to consist of six *Darsanas* or exhibitions,—which are arranged in pairs. These are the Nyaya and Vaiseshika; the Sankhya and the Yoga; and the former and later Mimansa. Of these six the first two are closely related, the latter being a kind of supplement to the former. The Sankhya and Yoga agree in much; but the former is agnostic, while the latter acknowledges a deity. Of the

[1] In the fully systematized philosophy Ignorance (or Illusion) is said to be properly neither existent nor non-existent. In the Bhagavad Gita—as we saw above—the same thing is asserted of Brahm.

two Mimansas the former treats only of Vedic interpretation, under heads logically arranged. The latter, which is usually called the Vedanta (end, or scope, of the Vedas), is a development of the doctrine of the Upanishads; which, though containing doctrines very different from the Hymns, had come to be called a part of the Veda. Hence the name Vedanta. The bracketing together of schools so widely different as those of the two Mimansas is thus intelligible.

The former Mimansa has thus no philosophical doctrine. The later Mimansa inculcates a spiritualistic pantheism, and requires separate consideration.

All the other systems seek to unfold the means of attaining salvation—that is, the emancipation of the soul. Salvation, they assert, can be attained only through knowledge. All works, whether good or bad, hinder salvation; virtue is to be discarded as earnestly as vice.

Vedantism is now by far the most prevalent system of Indian philosophy; and it has affected the thinking even of the common people, so far as to make them say that their souls are portions of God. It affirms the existence of the sole Spirit or Self. There is no material world save in appearance: it *seems*, but *is* not. An eternal illusion or ignorance 'projects' its appearance. The one Self is 'thought and bliss' (not a thinking or blissful being). So the Vedantists say, and try to think. The practical effect of such thoughts (or words) is evil. A thorough-going Vedantist looks on right and wrong as mere semblances, and easily breaks through all moral restraints. Farther, even a moral Vedantist must be all for himself. Endeavour for the good of others is to him impossible; he is entirely occupied with the effort to know and feel his identity with the Self. Without any wish to play on words, we are compelled to say he cannot but be supremely selfish.

The lover of his kind cannot but be deeply saddened by the spectacle of successive generations of men dreaming life away in such unprofitable and foolish dreams. To the sum of true thought Indian philosophy has contributed nothing that is of permanent value. The great lesson which we have to learn from it is the lesson of humility. In the review of all those systems of philosophy—so contradictory, presumptuous, and futile—what an emphasis of meaning do the words of St. Paul receive: 'After that, in the wisdom of God, the world by wisdom knew not God, it pleased God by the foolishness of the preaching to save them that believe.' In the strength of its own fancied wisdom the mind of India sought to scale the heaven of heavens, and there blend itself with God. Vain attempt! But now a hand is outstretched from the heaven of heavens to raise it to that height, and there impart to it a fellowship, yea a union, with Deity more vital and more blissful than, in their wildest dreams, the ancient sages ever ventured to expect.

So much for the philosophy, or esoteric faith, of

India. With regard to the popular system that still reigns over nearly two hundred millions, we need not, in this recapitulation, say much. The Puranas, in which the orthodox system is embodied, have exceedingly little merit; they are tasteless and extravagant productions. The faith which they inculcate is an incongruous mixture of pantheism and polytheism. The polytheism often runs into the grossest fetishism. Each divinity has a history; but, for the most part, it is a history of sin and shame. The fundamental distinction between god and devil is not recognized; that is to say, the characters and doings ascribed to the divinities are often diabolical. The worship runs into endless ceremonialism, which in most cases is as childish as it is complex. Religion is thus transformed into magic. Prayer is an incantation.

True, sects, and what we have called reforming sects, dissatisfied with the orthodox system, have so far modified it. The followers of Siva tend to extreme asceticism and self-torture. The followers of Vishnu have brought forward the doctrine of *devotion*; but in most cases the devotion is paid to Krishna, whose worship leads necessarily to corruption. Viler practices, as a part of religion, have flourished among the followers of Vishnu than among almost any other class of religionists. The Vallabhacharya sect affords a conspicuous example of this.

Of the worship of the Sakti, as enjoined in the

Tantras, we need say nothing more; it is painful even to think of the moral degradation it involves.

These remarks may seem severe; and it may be contended that Christians can hardly do justice to a faith so unlike their own as Hinduism is. Let me quote then the testimony of a writer who cannot be suspected of any bias in favour of orthodox Christianity. Mr. Moncure Conway has lately visited India, and has seen Hinduism with his own eyes. Of Hinduism as it *was* he has a very high opinion—far higher than we have; but we are now concerned with his estimate of Hinduism as it *is*. He thus writes:

'When I went to the great cities of India . . . . the contrast between the real and the ideal was heart-breaking. In all those teeming myriads of worshippers, not one man, not even one woman, seemed to entertain the shadow of a conception of anything ideal, or spiritual, or religious, or even mythological, in their ancient creed. . . . To all of them the great false god which they worshipped—a hulk of roughly carved wood or stone—appeared to be the authentic presentment of some terrible demon or invisible power, who would treat them cruelly if they did not give him some melted butter. Of religion in a spiritual sense there is none. If you wish for religion you will not find it in Brahmanism.'

Coming from such a quarter, this is a terrible indictment; and we do not know that, in speaking of Hinduism, any Christian missionary has used sterner words. Yet assuredly such is the estimate which every truth-loving man must form of the religion, provided his eyes are open. The contemplation is profoundly saddening.

> 'O miseras hominum mentes, O pectora cæca!'

CHAPTER XIII.

RECENT HINDU RÈFORMERS.

WE have had occasion to refer to men who, in past ages, strove to purify Hinduism from some of its more erroneous doctrines and debasing rites. The most noted of these was Buddha; but, quite possibly, he was preceded by others whose names are now forgotten.

We have above adverted to the interesting question whether Christian ideas are incorporated in that striking work the Bhagavad Gita, which has so powerfully influenced the later Sanskrit literature. Again, religious movements occurred in Southern India from the ninth to the twelfth century, in which we can trace with considerable probability not only Christian, but Mohammadan, influences.

We have also seen that, from about the year 1000, in Northern India, Islam, vehemently iconoclastic and generally victorious in battle, exerted a powerful influence on Hindu faith.

We must now come down to more recent days.

It was to be expected that the large influx of Christian ideas, and Western ideas generally, which has lately taken place, would powerfully affect Hinduism. Christianity is advancing in some places even rapidly; and, in every place where it is proclaimed, the progress is steady. The time when the higher Hindus regarded with supreme contempt the efforts of Christian teachers to proclaim the Gospel has for ever passed away; although indifference may still occasionally be professed. But the influence of Christianity extends far beyond the circle of the baptized. The Gospel is now performing among the people of India that work which, before and after the Christian era, was performed by ancient Judaism among the inhabitants of the Roman Empire. Speaking of the Jews, Seneca uses the strong language: 'The vanquished have given laws to the victors'—*Victoribus victi leges dederunt.* The great conceptions which were entertained by the Jews regarding God, and the soul, and holiness, and sin, and heaven and hell, could not but tell powerfully on all thinking men. Even so in India at the present day, wherever Christianity is preached, the great truths in which it stands opposed to Hinduism are steadily making way. The unity of God—the evil of idolatry—the evil of caste—the goodness of God—the surpassing elevation of the character of Christ; a conviction, or half conviction, of these and other fundamental verities is gradually extending among the people. Ideas change before institutions, and old customs moulder away but slowly, even when the belief on which they were based has broken down; but the mighty change goes on—silently, yet irresistibly. The change commenced more than a century ago in Bengal, in which the most noted reformers of recent times have appeared.

The first of these innovators who attracted public attention was Rammohun Roy, a Brahman, born in 1774. He was, from the outset, a man of inquiring mind; and as early as the age of sixteen he wrote a tract against idolatry. Apparently the monotheism of Islam had impressed him even before he knew much of Christianity. He had a good knowledge of Arabic and Persian. The cruel practice of widow-burning called forth his earnest opposition; and he began to denounce other cruel and superstitious observances as corruptions of the ancient Hindu faith. To be a reformer in those days entailed both obloquy and persecution. His own nearest relatives were strongly opposed to his revolutionary movements. Nevertheless he persevered. In 1814 he settled in Calcutta; and meetings were soon held in his house for the discussion of religious subjects. In 1818 he published a pamphlet against widow-burning. In Calcutta he had frequent intercourse with missionaries and other Europeans. He seems to have first attended to Christianity in 1817. He studied Greek and Hebrew, that he might read the Bible in the original languages. In 1820 he published a book with the remarkable title—*The Precepts of Jesus a Guide to Truth and Happiness.* He often gave expression to the sentiment that the teachings of Christ were the best and deepest he knew; but he maintained that precious truth was also contained in the ancient Hindu book the Veda. It is important to remember that by the Veda he meant the Upanishads—the philosophical treatises appended to the Veda proper.

Meetings continued to be held at his house; they were now weekly, and largely attended. In January, 1830, a hall for public worship was opened. Every Wednesday extracts from the Vedas (*i.e.*, Upanishads) were read in Sanskrit, hymns sung in Bengali, and a discourse was delivered, generally in the same language. Caste, however, was to some extent maintained; the holy texts were chanted by the holy men (the Brahmans) in an adjoining room, into which none but Brahmans could enter. The society called the Brahmo Somaj—more correctly Brâhma Samâj—was thus formed. We may translate the name *Assembly of believers in Brahm.*

The hymns sung at the meetings were usually of Rammohun Roy's own composition. He was not devoid of poetic sentiment, and he had much devotional earnestness.

In November, 1830, being commissioned by the Emperor of Delhi to proceed to England as his envoy, he sailed for Liverpool, which he reached in April, 1831. He was now a great man in public estimation, having received from Delhi the title of Raja. Much notice was taken of him both in London and Paris. But health gave way, and he died at Bristol in 1833.[1]

We have dwelt at considerable length on the events in Rammohun Roy's history, because he occupied a very conspicuous place as the pioneer of reform in modern days, and because also of the high moral courage which he exhibited in declaring his convictions even when he stood single against a host. Intellectually, though by no means a small man, he was still not so great as he was morally. On some important questions he held opinions that were mutually irreconcilable; or else, from time to time, his views fluctuated.[2] He never was an orthodox Christian; he did not believe in miracles

[1] It is interesting to note that Rammohun Roy had continued to be on very friendly terms with Christian missionaries, notwithstanding a passage-at-arms which he had with Dr. Marshman of Serampore. When Dr. Duff opened his educational institution in 1830, he received hearty sympathy and very valuable help from Rammohun Roy. Dr. Duff and his missionary associates took the deepest interest in his movements, and showed him all possible sympathy in his trials. His earnest pleadings against idolatry had aroused the most violent opposition; and even Europeans thought he was going too far. Speaking of this period, he says: 'This roused such a feeling against me that I was at last deserted by every person except two or three Scotch friends, to whom, and the nation to which they belong, I always feel grateful' (*Lecture on Rajah Rammohun Roy*, by Rev. K. S. Macdonald, p. 9).

[2] Such was the opinion of the late Rev. Krishna Mohun Banerjea—himself a very distinguished reformer.

nor in the full divinity of Christ. But he believed in Christ as divinely commissioned, and as a Being whom God had 'anointed and exalted above all creatures and prophets.' He even spoke of Christ as 'the Redeemer, Mediator, and Intercessor with God on behalf of His followers,' and held that He will judge the world at the last day.

The cause for which Rammohun Roy had earnestly laboured suffered a great loss on his removal. But in the year 1839, Debendernath Tagore, a young man of great wealth and earnest character, had come forward in the cause of religious reform. He joined the Brahmo Somaj in 1841 (some say earlier), and gave it a kind of constitution, introducing important new rules. By 1844 the society was fully organized. Every member now bound himself to abandon idolatry and pray daily to the One God. No distinct declaration had yet been made regarding the authority of the Vedas; but it was felt that so important a question must now be decided. Four Brahmans were sent to Benares for the study of the sacred books. In four or five years they returned to Calcutta; and, after earnest discussions, the doctrine of the infallibility of the Veda was rejected by Debendernath and a majority of members in 1850. This was a bold step—indeed, a radical revolution. He published a short confession of faith, consisting of four articles. The Brahmos discarded belief in any written revelation, and declared the works of God in nature a sufficient exhibition of truth and duty. 'The rock of intuition' ere long began to be spoken of; and every attack made in Europe on what was called 'book-revelation' was eagerly repeated in India. In fact, it would be a serious mistake to hold that the changes we have been chronicling were spontaneous movements of the Hindu mind; they seldom, or never, were so.

But a new champion now appeared in the person of Keshub Chunder Sen. He was born in November, 1838, not of a Brahmanical, but a Vaidya family—the members of which were so far imbued with English views, yet remained, in practice, orthodox Hindus. He received a fair English education. By the year 1855 he had begun to interest himself in reform; and his whole character seems to have deepened. He now gathered knowledge from all sides, courting the society of Christian teachers. We heard from his own lips that his religious views were drawn in the first instance from the Bible and the writings of Dr. Chalmers. But he read extensively; and, among other books, he evidently studied the writings of Theodore Parker, who for a time was very popular in India. He joined the Brahmo Somaj in 1857. Soon after this, Debendernath Tagore returned to Calcutta after three years' absence, and a mutual affection sprung up between him and Keshub. The latter was pressed by his family to conform to orthodox Hindu rites, but he firmly refused. He taught a school in Bengali, and lectured in English to the Brahmo Somaj, under Debendernath's patronage.

In 1861 he abandoned all secular work, resolving to devote himself to religious reform. Up to a certain point his friend and patron could go along with him. Thus, Debendernath allowed his daughter to be married in 1861 without any idolatrous rites. Idolatry was now rejected, and religious ritual was remodelled. Debendernath farther agreed to discard his own sacred thread. But here he drew the line. Ancient customs not openly idolatrous he would at all events allow. The friction between the old man and the young became more and more painful. Ardent, ambitious, self-reliant, Keshub was uncontrollable; and when a marriage was celebrated by him in August, 1864, between two persons of different castes, Debendernath informed him that their co-operation must cease. Keshub and his friends were separated from the Somaj in February, 1866; and they formed a new society in November of the same year. By August, 1869, they had built and opened a new *mandir*—a place of worship—of their own.

Since the separation, the original Somaj (Adi Samaj) has been very little heard of. Rajanarayana Bose, one of its leading members, has committed the serious mistake of including the Tantras among the recognized Hindu Scriptures. If the Adi Samaj has moved at all, it has moved back towards orthodox Hinduism; and its influence in advancing practical reform has not been appreciable.

Keshub now called his section 'The Brahmo Somaj of India.' He gave public lectures—especially one great lecture every year. That delivered in May, 1866, on *Jesus Christ: Europe and Asia*, attracted much attention, and was believed to indicate on Keshub's part a strong leaning to Christianity. Another lecture, on *Great Men*, which was delivered a few months later, was held to imply a renunciation of some of his advanced positions regarding Christ. His followers largely shared his own ardour. Religious festivals, attended with a large measure of excitement, began to be held—the first of them in November, 1867. The services contrasted strongly with the languid worship of the old society. At the same time, practical efforts in the direction of social reform were energetically made. A Missionary Institute was set up. Much was accomplished on behalf of women. A Female Normal School was established; and in March, 1872, a Brahmo Marriage Act was passed by Government which legalized the union of two persons of different castes, and fixed on fourteen as the lowest age for the marriage of females. This was a most important measure; for the custom of child-marriages is one of the worst and most inveterate of Indian ills. Efforts were also made for the promotion of temperance; many of the younger generation of Hindus, when educated, having yielded to the temptation of drink. Before this, however, Keshub had paid a visit to Britain. He did so pretty early in 1870, and, in April of that year, a remarkable meeting was called in London to welcome him; in which Dean Stanley, Lord Lawrence, James Martineau and other distinguished men took part. He was also granted a private interview with the Queen. He was allowed to preach in a good many places of worship connected with the Unitarians.

By the year 1873 it was becoming plain that an explosion among the members of the Somaj was at hand. The autocracy exercised by Mr. Sen was felt by many to be a heavy yoke. He believed in 'Great Men' as fully as Carlyle did in 'Heroes;' and from him, indeed, Keshub had drawn much of his teaching on the subject. He held that, from time to time, Divine Providence raises up men endowed with special powers, and intended to introduce new forms of religion; and he evidently expected—if he did not exact—the homage due to a teacher so commissioned. Yet, all the while, his words disclaimed the personal authority which he exercised. The murmurers were in a minority, but the disaffection was steadily increasing.

Regarding the Somaj and its doings, the language employed by Keshub, and still more by his followers, was always that of the loftiest self-assurance. Every effort was called a victory, and celebrated in strains of triumphant exultation. This tone of exaggeration alarmed many of his friends outside, as much as his new ideas—though some of these were certainly strange enough.

He had instituted important practical reforms; but to several innovations demanded by not a few he was strongly opposed. He held that many were rushing on too fast in the emancipation of women; whose visible attendance at public meetings he disliked as, at all events, premature. Perhaps he was right; but many Brahmos, and Brahmo ladies, thought otherwise. The crisis which was certain to come arrived early in 1878, when Mr. Sen's daughter was married to the Raja of Kuch Bihar. The bride and bridegroom were both somewhat under the age which had been fixed as the earliest allowable by the Brahmo Marriage Act,' which he himself had been mainly instrumental in getting passed. Vehement remonstrances were addressed to him; and a party proposed his deposition as minister of the Brahmo Mandir. Keshub called in the police, and only by their aid was he able to keep possession of the building.

A great revolt from his authority immediately succeeded; and the Sadharana Brahma Samaj was regularly constituted on May 15th. An appeal had been made to the provincial societies; and no fewer than twenty-one of these, consisting of fully four hundred members, male and female, joined the new body. This number amounted to fully two-thirds of the whole. It must have been a terrible blow to Mr. Sen. He and his friends denounced the rebels in very bitter language; and the strife became scandalously hot. 'The irony of fate' was in it; the Brahmos had often reprobated the divisions among Christian churches; and now 'the church of the future,' as Keshub had begun to denominate the Somaj, was carrying on civil war, and with poisoned weapons.

Calmly looking back on the whole struggle, it is plain that both sides were to blame. The seceders took the unkindest view of everything Keshub did, and attributed it to sordid motives. On the other hand, although, in general, by no means wanting in power of accommodation, he scornfully tossed aside all remonstrances, and declared himself guided in the whole proceeding by an express intimation of the will of Heaven.

In one point of view, the great secession was a relief to Mr. Sen. Men of abilities equal, and education superior, to his own, had hitherto acted as a drag on his movements. He was now freed from their interference, and could deal with his remaining followers very much as he pleased. Though undoubtedly there were among these some able men, yet their admiration of the leader was unbounded; and perhaps they hardly sought to check his inventiveness. Ideas that had been working in his mind now attained rapid development.

Within two years (in 1880), the old name of the Society was changed into that of the 'New Dispensation.' In a public lecture regarding this new creation, Mr. Sen used very daring language. He claimed equality for it with the Jewish and Christian dispensations—nay, virtually, if not formally, superiority; and for himself a Divine commission and 'singular' authority. 'When men,' said he, 'are hopelessly gone in the way of misery and ruin . . . it is then that Providence sends to the world one of those men whose life has been sold to

His almighty will.' Such a man he fully believed himself to be. He described the New Dispensation as 'the harmony of all scriptures and prophets and dispensations; . . . the science which finds, and explains, and harmonizes all religions.' Its function, as Mr. Sen understood it, was certainly a marvellous one. 'It gives to history a meaning, to the action of Providence a consistency, and to successive dispensations a continuity. . . . It is the wonderful solvent which fuses all dispensations into a new chemical compound.'

As Mr. Sen put it, all religions are true. He did not say merely that there is truth in all. The two propositions are, of course, widely different; but Mr. Sen dealt with them as interchangeable. Much of a rhetorician and a poet, he never was an accurate thinker. But how could he confound things so greatly diverse?

In May, 1879, Mr. Sen had expressed himself in remarkable words regarding the claims of Christ. 'None but Jesus, none but Jesus, none but Jesus ever deserved this precious diadem, India; and none but Jesus shall have it.' Such language, of course, arrèsted attention in Europe, and awakened high expectations. But the Jesus of whom Mr. Sen spoke so earnestly was an imaginary being, and not the historic Christ. And notwithstanding his continual cry for catholicity, this conception became more and more one-sided—more and more national. The real Christ is neither Asiatic nor European; He realizes the highest ideal of humanity. The

Christ to whom Mr. Sen seemed more and more to turn was not only an Asiatic, but a Hindu—a Hindu ascetic—in fact, a *yogi*. Every Christian belief and rite Mr. Sen, in like manner, contrived somehow to Hinduize. Was all this from policy, or was his mind beginning to give way?

It seems strange that the name of Christ does not occur in the formally enunciated Creed of the New Dispensation (1880). The creed inculcated belief in the following articles:—

1. One God, one Scripture, one Church. 2. Eternal progress of the soul. 3. Communion of prophets and saints. 4. Fatherhood and Motherhood of God. 5. Brotherhood of man and sisterhood of woman. 6. Harmony of knowledge and holiness, love and work, *yoga* and asceticism, in their highest development. 7. Loyalty to Sovereign.

This strange summary suggests many questions; but we content ourselves with remarking that it contains no reference to Sin or Redemption, any more than to the name of the Redeemer. All along Mr. Sen had spoken earnestly of the Fatherhood of God and Brotherhood of Man; although assuredly it was to Christianity, not Hinduism, he owed these great conceptions. He now added the 'sisterhood of woman' (needlessly, since the brotherhood of man implied it), and the 'Motherhood of God.' I presume he drew this last item from his old favourite, Theodore Parker; but he probably would have called it a repetition, or exaltation, of the old Hindu belief that there is a female counterpart of every divinity. Some have said that it was probably introduced with a view to conciliate the worshippers of Durga and Kali—those great goddesses of Bengal. If it was for the latter reason, Mr. Sen doubtless would have said that there is an element of truth even in the worship of these sanguinary deities.

As early as 1868 a great leaning to Ritualism had been noticed in the services of the Somaj; and this had gone on ever increasing. Under the New Dispensation it became altogether extravagant.

A public proclamation was now issued, purporting to be from God as 'India's Mother.' The whole thing was very startling; and many, even of Keshub's friends, had declared it really, if unintentionally, profane.

Next, in the 'Flag Ceremony' on January 30, 1881, the flag or banner of the New Dispensation received a homage which was barely distinguishable from adoration.

One of the great deities in the Veda is Agni (*ignis*), the god of fire; and the ceremonies connected with this ancient worship retain a high place in Hinduism to this day. It was painful to see the New Dispensation give its sanction to it in the following way. A pile of wood was lighted; clarified butter, such as the old Rishis used, was poured upon it, and prayers were addressed to it, ending in these words, 'O brilliant Fire, in thee we behold our resplendent Lord.' In a land wedded to idolatry, as India is, such things were fearfully perilous.

In March, 1881, Mr. Sen and his friends introduced celebrations in imitation of the two Christian sacraments. To all Christian minds this was unspeakably distressing; yet we are far from saying that Mr. Sen intended anything like mimicry. He had noted the beauty and solemnity of the rites of Baptism and the Eucharist; and he imagined he could secure what was essential in them in a way more in accordance with Indian usages.[1] Instead of bread and wine he employed rice and water. Round both were flowers and leaves. He read part of the twenty-second chapter of the Gospel of St. Luke; but, in the prayer which he offered, there was no reference whatsoever to the death of Christ, or to the commemorative character of the Eucharist. But we cannot dwell on this part of the subject; even the few things we have said will deeply pain our readers, as assuredly they do ourselves. It is strange that Mr. Sen never seems to have thought that Christians could be offended by this parody of an awfully solemn rite. Other institutions followed, mostly copies of Christian ones. One of the most notable of these was the Apostolic Durbar, or Court of Apostles, who were to be the commissioned heralds of the New Dispensation.

An attached friend and adherent of Keshub—Mr. P. C. Mozumdar—wrote in August, 1881: 'Keshub is continually becoming more metaphysical and

[1] As the organ of the New Dispensation expressed it, 'The ceremony of adapting the Sacraments to Hindu life was performed with due solemnity.'

more mystical. . . . Recently he has very much given himself up to symbolism. There has been a good deal of flags, flowers, fires, and sacraments of all kinds.'[1]

In January, 1883, Mr. Sen delivered a public lecture on Asia's message to Europe. This was the last time he spoke publicly in English. We had seen him shortly before in a private interview; and hopes of his future usefulness, which had begun to fade, had been somewhat revived by the way in which he had expressed himself. But the lecture was in no way satisfactory. For one thing, it was too evident that Keshub's powers were failing. There was no fire, no rush of feeling, in his utterance; there was a sort of fluency, but no real eloquence. And the great ruling sentiment of the lecture was that Asia is the mother-land of religions; that Europe must accept what has been already given to Asia; and that the thing requisite to constitute the faith of the future—the religion of humanity—is the blending of all Asiatic systems into one. One could not help thinking at the time what the prophet Elijah would have said, if he had been told that Baal and Jehovah were but two forms of one divinity. Could the speaker himself really hold that the stupendous confusion he recommended was desirable or possible? He had said, when in England in 1870, 'Hinduism has degenerated into a most horrid and abominable system of

[1] Max Müller's *Biographical Essays*, p. 154.

idolatry and polytheism'; and was not that his opinion still? If he meant that the religions to be fused together, 'into a new chemical compound,' should first be purified from their corruptions, why did he not honestly say so? Many came away from the exhibition very sad at heart.[1]

I do not profess myself fully able to understand Mr. Sen's character. I would by no means tax him with insincerity; but I found it difficult to reconcile his private and public utterances. I have spoken of an interview I had with him shortly before the lecture just referred to. Two missionary friends were with me. Our conversation extended over two hours; and all the characteristic truths of Christianity were considered, such as the Trinity; the Divinity of Christ; the atonement wrought by Him; salvation by faith in Christ; regeneration and sanctification as effected by the Holy Spirit; communion with God and Christ; —and on these great doctrines none of us could discover any palpable difference between Keshub's views and our own. Two points, indeed, remained on which the diversity was great. He did not believe in miracles; therefore not in the bodily

[1] On August 5, 1882, Keshub wrote to Prof. Max Müller: 'There was a time when an aggressive warfare had to be kept up, and we had to put down idolatry with iconoclastic fury. But the New Dispensation is a work of construction. It fulfils, does not destroy; it builds, does not demolish.' Translating this into plain English, does it not mean that henceforth he would tolerate idolatry? We must ask again: Was this said from policy, or was Keshub's mind giving way?

resurrection of Christ. But the whole interview was deeply solemn ; and, at the end, we all united in prayer for Divine teaching. None of the survivors can forget that remarkable evening, and the brotherly fellowship which we all had together.

One of the latest expressions which we have seen of the views of the 'New Dispensation' is contained in the following passage :—

'Sakya [Buddha], Chaitanya, Mahomed, and Jesus, spoke the harmonious truth while they lived ; but they never lived together in the world. In heaven, however, they do—in solid, compact, and loving fellowship. May their united spirit shed its genial influence upon those troubled and sinning brethren of the New Dispensation Church who are trying to imitate what they are doing in heaven, but do not succeed.'[1]

Such language, to say the least, does not indicate any inclination on the part of the Somaj leaders to turn to the teaching of the New Testament.

It is only right to say that Mr. Sen's references to Missionaries were ever most kind and friendly. He had controversies with some of them ; and, on several occasions, his Brahmo shield was pierced by the Christian spear. But the sense of defeat never ruffled his temper. He said when in England, 'Honour, all honour, to that sacred band of energetic and self-sacrificing missionaries who have gone out to India on a sacred mission. Honour, all honour to them.' And all honour, say we, to the Brahmo leader who, both in England and India—and sometimes in opposition to the feeling

[1] Quoted in *Bombay Guardian*, July 11, 1885.

of his audience—could boldly utter such sentiments as these.

Since the death of Mr. Sen there has been a great misunderstanding between his family and the so-called 'Apostolic Durbar' on the one side, and some of his old followers on the other—particularly Mr. Protap C. Mozumdar, who has been already referred to. Mr. Mozumdar is closely connected with Mr. Sen's family, but has been unable to fall in with the extravagant veneration with which they and the 'Durbar' cherish Keshub's memory. They hold his pulpit too sacred to be entered by any other person—it must remain unoccupied; the carpet on which he stood in the Mandir is treated as a sacred object; indeed, what threatens to become relic-worship begins to appear in distressing forms in connection with the memorials of Keshub Chunder Sen. Mr. Mozumdar is an enlightened man, and far more logical than Keshub. He will probably run into few extravagances, and will speak the language of consistent Theism. But we have reason to fear the glowing words in which Keshub spoke of Christ will not be heard from his lips. And without true and deep devotion to Christ as a Person, no series of propositions on religious subjects is likely to stir the heart of India or prevent the Somaj from sinking into insignificance.

The Sadharana Somaj, which broke off from Keshub's party in 1878, is a body of considerable influence. It has gone on for seven years with no small vigour. What we have just said regarding

Mr. Mozumdar's section of the Brahmos will largely apply to the Sadharana Somaj also. It will probably perpetrate no follies, and will keep clear of mysticism. As a reforming, philanthropic society, it may accomplish much good. It has gone farther in what it would call the emancipation of woman than Keshub's party has done, or is likely to do. But that it will meet the spiritual wants of the human soul, or produce any great results in India, we certainly do not expect. It may amount to a kind of Unitarian Christianity, and exist rather than live. We desire, however, to speak with high respect of the two leaders of this Somaj. One of them is a graduate of Cambridge, now a Calcutta barrister; he is an able, thoughtful man. The other is a Brahman, well acquainted with English, and also possessed of no small measure of Sanskrit lore.

Movements not unlike that of the Brahmo Somaj have occurred in other parts of India. One of the earliest attempts at reform was made in Bombay from about the year 1846, by Mr. Dadoba Pandurang. He and his friend Mr. Nana Narayan, as well as his brother—now Dr. Atmaram Pandurang—and Mr. Ramachandra Balkrishna, had much intercourse with missionaries; two of the four, indeed, asked to be received into the Christian Church by baptism, though they afterwards drew back. It was in or about the year mentioned that Dadoba Pandurang, who was superintendent of the Government Normal School, formed the *Parama hansa Sabha*, which was a kind of eclectic society. The members met once a week, and commenced their proceedings with prayer. They pledged themselves to disregard the distinctions of caste. Branch societies were formed at four or five out-stations, and the society was somewhat lively for a time. It became extinct in 1860. But about 1850, an association more distinctively religious had been formed in Bombay under the name of the Prarthana Sabha, or Prayer Union. The main articles enumerated in its constitution were the following:—

1. I believe in one God. 2. I renounce idolatry. 3. I will do my best to lead a moral life. 4. If I commit any sin through the weakness of my moral nature, I will repent of it and ask the pardon of God.

The society, after some time, began to languish; but in 1867 it was succeeded by the Prarthana Somaj, which still exists in Bombay, with branches in Poona, Ahmedabad, Surat, and a few other places. Able men have joined the Somaj; but it has by no means exerted in Western India the influence wielded by the Brahmo Somaj in Bengal. It has kept considerably far away from distinctive Christianity; and the allusions to the Gospel in any lectures or meetings have been made in a somewhat grudging way. Doubtless there are differences among the members in their feelings; but the glowing tributes which Mr. Sen delighted to pay to Christ and Christianity seem entirely unknown in the Prarthana Somaj. Brahmanical intellect mainly rules it.

A similar movement, not powerful yet interesting, has taken place in Madras. Mr. Sen paid a visit to the city of Madras in February, 1864, and produced a deep impression by his lectures. Shortly afterwards a society was formed under the name of Veda Samaj, in connection with which weekly lectures were held, and considerable activity exhibited. Branches were formed in various cities of Southern India. By 1868 the leading men in tne society had passed away, and a reconstruction took place under a young man whose name deserves special notice—Sridharalu Naidu. He had been impressed by what he had heard of the Brahmo Somaj in Bengal, and resolved to study the system at headquarters. His means were scanty, and it was with difficulty he could make his way to Calcutta. After about eight months' earnest inquiry into the principles of the Somaj, he returned to Madras, and in June, 1871, formed 'The Brahmo Somaj of Southern India.' The Somaj sent a memorial to the Viceroy in favour of the Brahmo Marriage Bill; and when it had passed the Legislative Council, Sridharalu performed the first Brahmo marriage in September, 1871. He was diligent in the use of the press, and in making missionary tours. The record of his doings leaves on the mind the impression of a single-eyed, very earnest man, who nobly devoted his life to the prosecution of high, unselfish ends. Our so-called Indian reformers have often been mere talkers; but he was a true reformer, and his deeds were in accordance with his words. The funerals of former secretaries of the Madras Society had been conducted with idolatrous rites; but, before his death, Sridharalu wrote with his own hand the words: 'My funeral should be simple, with only Brahmic prayers.' He died in January, 1874.

We are not aware that the Madras Somaj, since the removal of this interesting man, has made much impression on the community.

Another remarkable movement of the Indian mind has been exhibited in the formation of what is called the Arya Samaj. Its founder was a Gujurati Brahman, born in Kathiawar. His father was a devoted worshipper of Siva, and taught his son to be the same. The son was of an inquiring turn of mind, and soon began to doubt whether the idols were real deities. He paid much attention to the Vedas. The sudden death of a sister led him to very serious thoughts about the world to come. His father was preparing to get him married, and, to avoid this, he fled from home—was recovered, but again escaped. Ere long he joined the order of religious mendicants called Sannyasi, receiving the name of Dayananda Sarasvati. He continued to travel about for years, still intent on acquiring religious knowledge. By the year 1880 the man and his opinions began to attract public attention. By this time he had come to see that only the Hymns of the Veda could be received as fully authoritative—as the Brahmanas and Upanishads (the ritual and philosophical treatises) contained much that was wrong, or at least doubtful. He declared that the Hymns taught strict monotheism—the many names, Agni, Indra, and all the rest, being merely various designations of one being. Idolatry he renounced. He said he found in the Vedic Hymns express references to many principles which only modern science has discovered.

The Hymns, as we saw when treating of the Veda, certainly do not recommend idol-worship; but the hope of Dayananda to prove them monotheistic was founded on an entire delusion—as much so as the attempt to see the latest discoveries of science in them. All real Sanskritists scouted these ideas as preposterous; it was a desperate effort to save the reputation of the Veda at all hazards. Dayananda carried on disputations, like the schoolmen of mediæval times, in many places; and his eloquence secured a following of young men who were not well acquainted with ancient Hindu literature. But at a great convocation of learned Brahmans at Calcutta, his views—in so far as they differed from the ordinary belief—were declared to be unsound. This was a heavy blow; nevertheless the indefatigable Pandit continued travelling, lecturing, publishing, till he died in Rajputana, in October, 1883. That his school can long continue is exceedingly improbable; it rests on a foundation of sand. Vedism can never be built up again.

CHAPTER XIV.

SUMMARY AND CONCLUSION.

THE systems of reformed Hinduism to which we have been adverting are all of them interesting and instructive. We may also call them hopeful—hopeful in the sense that they seem to be transitional and preparatory. They form a middle ground between Hinduism and Christianity, from which more earnest souls will gradually find their way to the Gospel.

But other systems of thought are at work in India, on which we cannot look with any measure of complacency. Their presence was, doubtless, to be expected; but their influence is mainly, or wholly, evil.

Thus, for a considerable time the works of Comte were extensively read in India; and some, if not many, professed to accept the tenets of Positivism. One, however, hears little on the subject now.

But for several years past the people who call

themselves Theosophists have been bustling and loquacious—most eager to be accepted as interpreters of ancient Indian lore. As they are atheistic, their natural ally is Buddhism, but (unless our memory fails us) they assert that esoteric Buddhism, esoteric Hinduism, and esoteric Zoroastrianism all coincide [1]—a proposition that manifests gross ignorance on the part of those who advance it. A lady—Madame Blavatsky—is the moving spirit in this school; but she professes to be in communication with certain Mahatmas—personages residing on the Himalaya mountains, possessed of much occult science and various astonishing endowments. These gentlemen, in addition to ordinary bodies, rejoice in astral ones (the nature of which is not explained); and in these they reveal themselves in very amazing ways to those who believe in them or Madame Blavatsky. We have read a good many numbers of the organ of this sect, *The Theosophist;* but there is much in it which we do not profess to understand. One thing only is plain—that the lady and her coadjutor, Colonel Olcott, are determined to oppose in every possible way the victorious march of Christianity in India. It would seem, however, as if the whole thing had collapsed. A lady who was associated with Madame Blavatsky has come forward and publicly declared that the letters and appearances (astral bodies and all) of the so-called Mahatmas were an imposture from first to last.

[1] So it was certainly affirmed in *The Theosophist.*

As one reads the evidence, the feeling of indignation is quenched only in a sense of the infinitely ludicrous character of the whole exhibition. Can such things be in this scientific, nineteenth century of ours? For not a few actually believed in the lady and her Himalayan sages. But, as Pascal said, *Les incredules les plus credules.*[1]

To add to the terrible confusion of Indian thought, books inculcating decidedly atheistic principles are largely circulated. There has been for years an atheistic propaganda, chiefly in Britain, which supplies such publications as Mr. Bradlaugh's to Indian students.[2] Of course Christians and Brahmos make common cause against such offensive productions.

Such, then, is the strange conflict of opinion which we now witness in India. It has often been noticed that there is a remarkable similarity between the state of religious belief in the Roman Empire in the first and second centuries of the Christian era, and what exists in India at the present day. There is doubtless a striking similarity; yet there is also a dissimilarity. The obstacles to the spread of Christianity in India

[1] In exposing this amazing folly, and worse than folly, the *Christian College Magazine* of Madras has done important service.

[2] So also in Japan. It was a remarkable and touching thing to be asked, as we were, by a Japanese theologian, whether it was not possible for Christians and Buddhists to unite in an effort to repel the evil principles inculcated by books sent from Britain and America. He belonged to the Shin-shiu sect, which has exalted Amida Buddha to the rank of Deity.

seem decidedly greater than they were in ancient Greece and Rome.

The population of India is more than double that of the Roman Empire. In Greece and Rome there were no books holding the position which is assigned to the Sastras. In India religion is made to consist of an infinite number of minute observances. Authority and ceremonialism have combined to crush the religious consciousness. Caste is all but omnipotent. The soul is in fetters. There is no individuality in India. Farther, foolish and evil as much of ancient Paganism was, it was not so wicked or so childish as modern Hinduism.

In the Empire a period of scepticism had been followed by a reaction to superstition, which is traceable at least from the time of Augustus Cæsar. Eastern and Western beliefs then became strangely mingled together; the blending which Keshub Chunder Sen, in his later days, so earnestly contended for, was begun. But the great fusion of creeds soon threatened to turn out a great confusion, only enhancing the distress of truth-loving souls.

Christianity had arisen, and was slowly advancing, not in rural districts so much as in cities. In India the advance of Christianity is witnessed both in cities and in rural districts—rather more in the latter. Judaism, also, as we have seen, was spread throughout the Empire, and was to some extent the forerunner of the Gospel. In India the Gospel is its own forerunner. The great truths of natural religion which it republishes are widely accepted, even while its distinctive doctrines are still repelled. This is like the dawn preceding, and heralding, the sunrise.

One important point of difference between the ancient Empire and India is the extent to which education is carried—or likely to be carried—in the latter. Education in its higher branches is entirely subversive of Hinduism. As conducted in schools directly connected with Government, it exercises on belief an influence simply destructive. Therefore one must watch with anxiety the extension of purely secular instruction over India. Still, an infidel *nation* is hardly conceivable ; and Christianity must, ere long, come in to fill the intolerable void. A national system of education will involve, sooner or later, a national renunciation of Hinduism.

Should infidelity spread widely in Europe, it is certain that the conversion of India will be indefinitely delayed. But the signs of the times do not seem to us to betoken the triumph of unbelief in the West. On the contrary, the missionary spirit—which is essentially a spirit of faith and love—is continually deepening in Europe and America ; and if so, it will tell more powerfully every year on the worn-out religions of the East.

At the present rate of progress, the whole of India would be Christian in less than a century. We are far, however, from affirming that such systems as Brahmanism and Mohammadanism will by that time have wholly perished. In

Europe, the final triumph of the Gospel came after a struggle of centuries; and it may be so in India. Yet, on the other hand, the Hindus are a gregarious people; and they may probably ere long, begin to move in masses into the Christian Church.

The case of Japan is in some respects analogous to that of India—only the former is accepting Western thought with more rapidity than the latter. It seems probable that Japan may profess itself a Christian nation by the year 1900. Such a revolution would deeply impress the minds of all educated men, and accelerate the advent of a similar change in India.[1]

The last great attempt—apart from persecution—to arrest the onward march of the Gospel in early days, was made by the Neo-platonists, Plotinus, Porphyry, and others. In several respects this school resembled the Brahmo Somaj. Its philosophy tended more and more to a vast eclecticism—or rather syncretism—in which the tenets of all religions and all believing schools were run into one crude mass. The reaction from a chilling scepticism (which was itself a reaction from its opposite) carried them very far into superstition.

[1] It is also quite possible that the expectation of the Japanese Christians regarding India may yet be fulfilled—they may send missionaries to help in its evangelization. 'Tell the people of India,' they said, when we were lately among them, 'to become Christians without delay. If they do not, we must go and persuade them. They sent us Buddhism. We shall more than repay the obligation: we shall give them gold for brass—the pure doctrine of Christ for the mixed teachings of Sakhya Muni.'

Philosophers began to talk of ecstasy and raptures, and the felt, yea visible, presence of Deity. In opposition to the Christian Church, they excogitated a catholic church of philosophy, speaking much of a 'golden chain' of sages who had all taught the same pure theology. How like is all this to Mr. Sen's attempt to reconcile all systems of belief! We must not, indeed, overlook one point of difference. The Neo-platonists ignored Christ as far as possible; the New Dispensation has not done so, though it too much projects a Christ of its own devising. But in other respects the parallel is very striking and instructive. Neo-platonism failed, as the successive forms of Gnosticism that preceded it had failed; and the march of the Gospel was ever steadily onward. Even so, we believe that the Brahmo Somaj, in all its forms, must fail. God forbid that we should say this boastfully, or as if it were only one school of human thought vanquishing another! We know full well the exceeding reluctance of India to adopt foreign systems of belief, and the pride she takes in her own ancient sages. Well, we do not ask her to submit to the reasonings of men; but we do beseech her to listen to the message of love and reconciliation which Christ has brought from heaven. And when she has done so, oh then let the heavens rejoice and let the earth be glad; for a new day will have dawned both on India and the world. And that thrice blessed consummation may not be so far off as many say it is.

CHAPTER XV.

HINDUISM COMPARED WITH CHRISTIANITY.

IN the preceding pages we have had occasion from time to time to draw a contrast between the Hindu Sastras and the Bible; and the difference between these two books must have not unfrequently suggested itself to the reader even when no express comparison was made. But it is right to consider this important topic at greater length.

The first thing that strikes us is the difference in the size of the books. The Bible is composed of about forty different compositions, but is not a large work. The Sastras, though much smaller than the authoritative Scriptures of the Buddhists, are yet exceedingly voluminous. Many of them are written in a style which even educated men find very difficult to understand; and, if they have to be studied in the original, only a small part of them can possibly be mastered by one man.

The component parts of the Sastras are, in some

respects, not unlike the component parts of the Bible. Prose and verse are found alike in the Hindu and Christian books. Hymns, as the expression of devotional sentiment, abound in both scriptures. Ritual to regulate worship, and political and social laws, form an important part of the Sastras and also of the Hebrew Scriptures.

So far, in the form of composition, there is resemblance between the books. But the diversities are not small. Science is largely introduced, and authoritatively taught, in many of the Sastras; while it is most sparingly introduced, and never authoritatively taught, in the Bible. Then, history, except in the form of wild poetic legends, is absent from the Sastras. So is prophecy—wholly so in its predictive form. There is, farther, nothing in the Sastras corresponding to the epistolary portions of the New Testament.

It is interesting to observe that both Hinduism and Christianity can historically be divided each into two great periods. The rise of Buddhism was a great cataclysm in the history of Hinduism; and the system that was constructed on the fall of Buddhism was widely different from the more ancient faith. So the religion presented in the Old Testament is, in several respects, different from the Christianity of the New Testament. We believe, then, that we ought to compare ancient Hinduism with the faith unfolded in the Old Testament, and then contrast modern Hinduism with Christianity. We do this, in order that we may be thoroughly just to Hinduism; since, for example, it would not be fair to compare Vedic conceptions with those of the New Testament, which were expressed a thousand years or so later. Yet let it be remembered that, on the part of a Christian controversialist, this concession would be too large; inasmuch as, to an orthodox Hindu, the Veda contains the supreme Revelation authoritative to all ages, whereas the Christian believes in a progressive Revelation, in which the earlier part is related to the later as the flower-bud to the expanded flower.

We have seen that modern Hinduism differs widely from the ancient faith. But in the ancient faith itself there was no unity. It grew less by development from within than by the accretion of foreign elements from without. We have spoken above of the startling contrast between the first and fourth Vedas. But even in the Rig Veda—the oldest and best—there is no consistency. We have in one place something like monotheism; in another, the germ of pantheism; in a third, polytheism. The Upanishads, which are associated with the Hymns, contradict each other; but with a strong tendency to pantheism, which differentiates them from the earlier writings. Gods go on multiplying with time; some wholly unknown in the Veda assume a high position, others are degraded or even wholly disappear. Institutions change; thus, idol-worship and caste, which were unknown at first, become universal.

On the contrary, one form of religious thought pervades the whole Old Testament from Genesis to Malachi. Men of the most varied ranks—from kings to herdsmen, and during the long period of a thousand years—give utterance to the same high thoughts regarding things spiritual and divine. The Bible is not a collection of units; it is one—an organic whole. The first verse of Genesis expresses a grand conception which was also the belief of the latest of the prophets: 'In the beginning God created the heavens and the earth.' Progress, development, there was; but never by the absorption of foreign and incongruous elements. Event succeeded event, each full of instruction; prophet succeeded prophet; clearer light was shed on the Divine character and government; the mind of the people was educated;—but the old belief was never cast aside—it was only more fully appreciated and more firmly held. Clearly this wonderful unity is a most convincing evidence that the Old Testament is of Divine inspiration.

The one form of religious thought to which we have been alluding is the strongest, strictest monotheism. Polytheism is now, to any educated mind, an impossible belief; but the monotheism of the nineteenth century is not more absolute than that maintained by Moses or Abraham, fifteen hundred or two thousand years before the Christian era.

Again with regard to the character of God. The deities in the Sastras are *un*moral—often *im*moral. Even in the Vedas they are so—the only deity to whom moral excellence is ascribed being Varuna; and, as time went on, the gods became worse and worse. They demand homage; when that is given, they support their votaries through right and wrong. On the contrary, the God of the Hebrew Scriptures is pure—thrice holy; He is as much opposed to evil as light is to darkness. Power, wisdom, and goodness belong to Him in an infinite degree. Being holy, He demands holiness in His worshippers. He demands 'truth in the inward parts;' and outward homage, when the heart is impure, is a gross offence.

In the Vedic religion there was at first no image-worship; but in the course of generations it became more firmly rooted among the Hindus than perhaps in any other nation. Scattered over India there are probably a full thousand millions of idols. In form the divinities are often monstrous—in this, very different from the gods of ancient Greece. Max Müller somewhere speaks of 'the hidden wisdom of the second commandment.' History testifies that there is, at least in all earlier stages of religious thought, a strong tendency to *externalize* religion, and to surround it with symbols which, in common minds, soon usurp the place of the thing signified. The idolatry of India easily runs into the grossest fetishism—than which there can be nothing more debasing to the human mind. Now, few things in the Hebrew Scriptures are more remarkable than their perpetual, stern denunciations of idolatry. Most wisely, and not too vehemently, did the

Hebrew prophets thunder against the worship of images. The Jewish people, like other nations, were long prone to yield to the sweet seduction of idolatry; but the scathing denunciations of the prophets, and also the strict discipline through which Divine Providence made them pass, at length converted them into a nation of earnest monotheists.

What we have said of discipline reminds us of another important difference between Hinduism and Judaism. The expression *God in history* is full of significance. God reveals Himself in providence as well as in the works of creation; and few subjects are more deserving of study than what is called 'the philosophy of history.' Now, the Vedas and Upanishads contain no history; and the same thing holds of the philosophical books. They express *thoughts*, not *facts*. In the Epic poems and Puranas what is put forward as history stands self-convicted as the lawless product of imagination. But how different is the Bible! Dean Stanley has justly said that 'Christianity alone of all religions claims to be founded not on fancy or feeling, but on fact and truth.' In the Bible there stands recorded a long and lofty succession of *events*, *facts;* and these fitted to convey the most important lessons regarding the Divine character and will. If the historical details were struck out of the Bible, the loss would be infinite. Deeds are often more important than words. Accordingly, we find that the events recorded in the earlier part of the Bible made a most profound impression on the mind of the Israelites, not only at the time, but during after ages. And they are full of instruction still.

We have seen how Sacerdotalism, from exceedingly small beginnings, gradually shot up in India into rank luxuriance, and became a veritable Upas tree, distilling poison. Nothing of this kind ever occurred in Judaism. The priest held a place of honour, but could not act the tyrant over the bodies or consciences of men. Had the priests remained the only religious instructors of the people, this would have been an almost necessary result; and farther, religion would have consisted mainly in external things—rites and ceremonies. But in Israel the order of prophets perpetually recalled the people to the inner soul of religion—asking, 'What doth the Lord require of thee, but to do justice, to love mercy, and to walk humbly with thy God?' The functions of the prophetical order were thus of immense importance, both for individuals and for the community. Milton affirms of the prophetic writings—

> 'In them is plainest taught and easiest learnt
> What makes a nation happy, and keeps it so,
> What ruins kingdoms and lays cities flat.'

But in speaking of the prophets we can by no means overlook the importance of their *predictions*. The Bible speaks of past, present, and *future*. The character of the references to futurity is truly remarkable. While the prophets perpetually threaten sinful men and sinful nations with chastisement from the hand of God, they delight to dwell on the future with exulting hope. They disclose a Divine purpose—a purpose of mercy formed before the foundations of the world were laid, running through the ages, and steadily advancing towards a glorious consummation. Even when, to all human appearance, the cause of God and the cause of man seemed lost, the prophets of Israel never despaired of the future of the world. All would come right at last. Heaven's high degree should stand in spite of the rage of God's enemies; and the heart of the long-sinful earth should beat at last in full unison with the heart of heaven. Emphatically, the Bible is the book of hope. In this it is entirely unlike the Hindu books. They are marked by a despondency ever ready to darken into despair. At present the Kali Yuga is advancing; and the world is plunging deeper and deeper into ignorance, vice, and misery. The patriot may die for his country—the martyr for his God; but their doings and sufferings are of no avail to stem the tide of evil. True, after æons of misery, the Age of Truth comes back; but it does so only to pass away again, and torment us with the memory of lost purity and peace. The experience of the world is thus an eternal renovation of hope and of disappointment. Progress towards abiding good there is none. The whole conception which Hinduism forms of human life is overwhelmingly sad. Hope for ourselves, and effort for the good of others, are rendered impossible.

The summary of duty contained in the Decalogue, as has often been observed, is singularly brief, clear, and comprehensive. There is no summary in the Sastras at all corresponding with it.

The rest of the Sabbath can be proved, on physiological grounds, to be needful both for man and beast. Politically, too—as Adam Smith has expressed it—it is 'of inestimable value.' Its spiritual value is equally inestimable, as producing a break amidst the engrossing avocations of life, and affording time for calm reflection and the undisturbed worship of God. But in Hinduism there is no such institution. Rest to man and beast comes irregularly; at one time there is too much of it, and at another time too little.

It would be very instructive to compare throughout the legislation of Manu with that of Moses. We can notice only some outstanding points. One of the most prominent things in Manu is the place assigned to caste. Some men are held to be essentially, and in virtue of their blood, pure; others are neither pure nor impure; others are essentially, and in virtue of their blood, impure. The idea of the dignity of man as man would have been scouted by Manu as utterly ridiculous.[1]

[1] The frightful extent to which the idea of birth-pollution is carried by Brahmanism lately came under our notice in Southern India. Some high-caste men said to the lowest classes: 'We who are men cannot endure the presence of such impure wretches as you. Do you think the gods will allow you to approach them? They will kill you, if you do. You had better make the best terms you can with the devils, and worship them.'

One becomes sick at heart when he thinks of what caste has done and is doing. Even politically it is a curse. It goes on multiplying divisions; men of the same caste, if from different localities, will not eat with each other. Society splits and splits. All feeling of brotherhood is destroyed; that of nationality is also destroyed; and if the Hindus are ever to become one nation, they must first cast off Hinduism.

On the contrary, the Hebrew legislation recognized nothing resembling caste. All Israelites were brethren—all equally children of Abraham; ay, Jehovah had said of Israel as a whole, without exception, 'Israel is My son, even My first-born.' Such a thought ennobled a man, even the poorest man—

> 'cœlumque tueri
> Jussit, et erectos ad sidera tollere vultus.'

We do not assert that the Mosaic institutions were intended for all stages of advancement; but for a society like that which existed in ancient Palestine they seem the wisest possible. The Jews were occupied partly with agricultural, partly with pastoral, pursuits. The land was divided among the families according to their size, and it could not be permanently alienated from its possessors. Ownership and occupation of land generally went together; the evils of absentee landlordism were unknown. Extreme wealth on the one hand and pauperism on the other were as far as possible guarded against. The poor were few, and were sufficiently cared for. Millionaires and 'lapsed masses' seem to have been equally unknown. Various perplexing questions regarding land-tenure which are hotly discussed in the present day, were solved, or superseded, in ancient Israel. Michaelis and other writers have shown that, viewed even as sanitary and police regulations, the Mosaic institutions were full of wisdom; and the question has been repeatedly asked whether the remarkable longevity of the Jews is not dependent on the extent to which they are still able to carry out these requirements.

In the various matters now mentioned Hindu legislation was immensely inferior to the Hebrew.

It has been noticed that the position of women in India, which was originally somewhat honourable, became more and more degraded as time went on. Gradually there came in such dreadful institutions as the burning of widows—the prohibition of the marriage of widows, and their cruel treatment—child-marriages—the practice of Kulin Brahmans in Bengal marrying fifty or a hundred wives. There is nothing in Hindu law rendering polygamy illegal.[1] Nowhere have the rights of women been more disregarded than in India. The true idea of the family is destroyed.

It was not so in Israel. Woman occupied from the first a place of respect, which she never lost. The pictures which are given of family life are

[1] H. Cowell's *Lectures on Hindu Law*, p. 164.

exceedingly attractive. The wife was honoured. 'The heart of her husband doth safely trust her': 'in her tongue is the law of kindness'—such a description rises to the highest ideal of domestic love and happiness.

It is true that polygamy was in certain circumstances allowed, though not approved; and so was divorce. Evidently customs already existing had, in certain circumstances—and to prevent worse evils—to be retained. The Mosaic institutions were disciplinary—intended to elevate and fit a people whose souls had been debased by slavery, to become the true worshippers of the true God.

The ceremonial systems both of ancient Hinduism and Judaism were complex, though that of the former was especially so. We do not find fault with this in Hinduism, any more than in Judaism. Positive precepts (which rest simply on authority) seem indispensable for the rousing of conscience at a certain stage of society; and that they should be at first intermingled with moral precepts need cause us no surprise. The distinction of animals and meats into clean and unclean appears to be very ancient. In Parsiism, for example, certain animals are pure, as being made by Ahuramazda; certain others are impure, as being the work of Ahriman (Angro-mainyus) the Evil Power. No such idea as this ever appears in the Bible. According to Hinduism, certain animals, particularly the cow and the monkey, are sacred; certain other creatures are by nature unholy. The distinction of clean and unclean in Judaism was not based on any such ground as this; when feelings of natural repugnance or sanitary ideas did not rule, the distinction rested on the Divine command. It served to keep conscience on the alert and test obedience, until the time should come when it could safely be laid aside.

There are some remarkable similarities in the view of Sacrifice taken by both the Hindu and Jewish systems. In both it occupies a very important place; and in both its origin is referred to primeval times.

But the dissimilarities are very great. Human sacrifice probably existed in Vedic days—though rarely practised; and, while not enjoined, was winked at. Among the Hebrews it was sternly prohibited; and they were solemnly warned against being seduced into the commission of the dreadful rite by its frequent occurrence among the surrounding nations.

Animal sacrifice gradually attained a prominence among the Hindus far greater than among the Hebrews; everything in heaven and earth was held to be affected by it. It was believed to be mighty *per se;* it had no typical meaning. Then, after it had risen to colossal dimensions, it was gradually undermined by philosophic speculation, and finally overturned by Buddhism. It perished; being now held to be not only unmeaning, but wicked and absurd. Nor has it revived in orthodox Hinduism; the sacrifices that are still offered in connection with Kali and other goddesses are not survivals of Vedic worship, but corruptions borrowed from sanguinary aboriginal systems of demonolatry.

In Judaism, sacrifice was intended to 'sanctify to the cleanness of the flesh'[1]—that is, it removed ceremonial defilement, and restored a man to the privileges of citizenship in Israel. But farther, it was typical,—prophetic of the great sacrifice of Jesus Christ; a picture, so far as any picture could be given, of the sublimest event in all history—the self-sacrifice of the Son of God. This is not an interpretation forced on Jewish sacrifices by Christian writers; 'the typical import of sacrifice did actually develop itself in the heart of Judaism without any New Testament influence.'[2] The cessation of sacrifice in Christianity thus implied nothing wrong in its past existence;—on the contrary, it implied its utility and even necessity for the time; but, when the prophesied event took place, the prophecy necessarily ceased. The type was useless when the great Antitype had come.

But it is time to speak of Hinduism as contrasted with the fully developed faith presented in the New Testament.

Were we to compare the New Testament only with the Puranas, we should be selecting for criticism the weakest part of Hinduism. Let us, therefore, now take into account the Hindu Sastras generally—only excluding the abominable Tantras.

[1] So the Revised Version.

[2] Kurtz on *The Sacrificial Worship of the Old Testament*, p. 121. (Clark's Theological Library.)

Much that has been already said regarding the Old Testament applies with equal force to the New; for example, there is the perfect harmony that reigns through all its parts. Nor is it only consistent with itself; it is equally so with the Old Testament;—the two Testaments form a whole—a perfect unity. On the contrary, the Puranas are for the most part intensely sectarian; one denounces beliefs and rites which another enjoins. The Puranas thus make the great confusion we have already spoken of still worse confounded.

Again, as into the Old Testament so into the New, history largely enters. And what a history! The life, and death, and resurrection of Jesus Christ: these chiefly. If the facts recorded in connection with these things are true—and that they are so we must now assume—then they are infinitely the most stupendous, the most glorious, events which this earth has witnessed. If it were possible to prove them false, how would the universe be impoverished!

One of the most important points in later Hinduism is the doctrine of the Avataras—the 'descents' to earth of the divinity Vishnu. When we turn to contrast with these the Christian doctrine of the Incarnation, we almost feel rebuked, as if guilty of profanation. We need not repeat the Hindu teaching regarding the Avataras;- -oh, how has it sullied and defiled the great conception from which it probably arose—that of man requiring the presence and help of Heaven! Even when the doctrine rises to its greatest height—which it does in the Gita—it affirms that Vishnu is periodically born to 'rescue the good and destroy the evil.' It is enough, as a contrast, to remind our readers that Christ came from heaven to earth 'to seek and save that which was lost.' The idea of man seeking God is not foreign to Hinduism; but it knows nothing of God seeking man—seeking fallen man, pitying him and restoring him.

We might say much of the teachings of Christ; but we forbear. Men who are far from orthodox Christianity have spoken with eloquence and high admiration of the Sermon on the Mount, His parables, and all His doctrine; and they have affirmed that there is no probability of any future age hearing purer and loftier thoughts expressed. We therefore pass on.

Christ not only spoke the truth; He lived it. He exemplified in act what He taught in words.

> 'He wrought
> In human form the creed of creeds;
> In loveliness of perfect deeds
> More strong than all poetic thought.'

There is a most beautiful commingling in His character of the stronger and the softer virtues; fortitude above heroic, reconciled with a tenderness more than motherly. And far more than this. Self-denial and self-sacrifice—for God, for man, for truth—this we all regard as the highest reach of the human spirit, as the blossom and fragrancy of created excellence; and there are names in history

—that of the martyr dying for his God, or the mother, it may be, dying for her children—on which 'attend the tears and praises of all time.' But, after all, what is the highest and holiest exhibition of such heroic goodness but a dim and distant reflection of the self-emptying and self-sacrifice of the Son of God?

It would be easy to quote from many writers of the most 'liberal' schools of thought the strongest possible declarations regarding the matchless excellence of Christ's character, and the immense influence which it has exerted, and must exert, on the human race. Let one testimony suffice. 'It was reserved for Christianity to present to the world an ideal character which, through all the changes of eighteen centuries, has inspired the hearts of men with an impassioned love, and has shown itself capable of acting on all ages, nations, temperaments, and conditions; has not only been the highest pattern of virtue, but the highest incentive to its practice, and has exercised so deep an influence that it may be truly said that the simple record of three short years of active life has done more to regenerate and soften mankind than all the disquisitions of philosophers and all the exhortations of moralists.'[1]

We therefore cannot force ourselves to contrast the Incarnation of Christ with the so-called Hindu incarnations—in which the divinity successively takes the form of a fish, a tortoise, a boar, a man-

[1] Lecky, *History of European Morals*, vol. ii. p. 8.

lion, a dwarf, a destroyer, a warrior, a licentious cow-herd, and an arch-deceiver. 'When we turn from such representations to the "Word made flesh," we seem to have escaped from the pestitential air of a charnel-house to the sweet, pure breath of heaven.'[1]

It is important to remark that, among the Hindu sages also, whose doings are recorded, there is not one who could be taken as a pattern of conduct. Nearly all of them were guilty of flagitious deeds; most of them were excessively irritable—ready to pour out curses on any one, god or man, who crossed their imperious will. If then 'example is better than precept,' it will easily be seen how sorrowfully poor is the Hindu.

No question is more important than that of the mode in which a religion deals with the great fact of Sin. So far as our experience goes, every sin is ascribed by the Hindus to the Divine Being as its ultimate cause. This dreadful blasphemy destroys all sense of personal demerit, or at best renders it exceedingly slight. Where it exists, the idea of sin seldom rises above that of ceremonial impurity; which ceremonial cleansing can fully remove. What a contrast between this shadowy conception and the Christian doctrine of sin! Of evil as wholly opposed to the Divine character, as a violation of Eternal Right, as hateful to God, and as poisonous to the human soul, the Hindu Sastras speak not. Of the majesty of conscience as the vicegerent of

[1] *Hinduism; a Sketch and a Contrast*, p. 53.

God—which the philosopher Kant likens to the awful magnificence of the starry heavens—they also speak not; nor have they any conception of the magnitude of the catastrophe when conscience, like a dethroned monarch, is chained and blinded by evil, rebellious passions.

And having no right sense of the character of sin, the Sastras fail to recognize either the difficulty or the preciousness of pardon. They indeed speak of atonement—yes, of many atonements. But what is a Hindu atonement? Some paltry device such as we have mentioned above—such as pilgrimage, washing in a sacred stream, feeding Brahmans, or seeing an idol and passionately praising it. Such things leave no impression on the heart either as to the character or desert of sin.

And when these miserable 'atonements' fail, then there really is no pardon. Indeed, the doctrine of transmigration implies that there is no forgiveness with God, and that the transgressor must himself drink to the lowest dregs the cup of bitterness which he has filled. Oh, when conscience is really awake, and evil is seen in its true character, with what a rapture of relief does the sinner turn to the Christian Scriptures and their revelation of the great atoning sacrifice of Christ! The Cross, steadily gazed upon, fills the human spirit at once with contrition, and hatred of sin, and overflowing joy. The love of God in Christ—in Christ the crucified—when once apprehended, cleaves the hard heart in twain, and summons forth the far-down streams of penitence and love. Love is love's recompense. We love Him because He first loved us. We live to Him who died for us. The atonement made by Jesus Christ is the divinest revelation of Divinity; a manifestation of the highest perfections of the Eternal Mind in their highest exercise.

And the redemption wrought for man implies not only pardon but spiritual renovation.

Salvation denotes deliverance from the power, as well as from the punishment, of sin. The perfection of the individual and, through that, the perfection of society—these are the ends in view. Christ taught His disciples thus to pray: 'Our Father which art in heaven, Hallowed be Thy name. Thy kingdom come. Thy will be done on earth, as it is done in heaven.' The Christian waits in fulness of expectation, and continually strives for the realization of this magnificent ideal. It may not come soon; but it will come. As for himself, he looks forward to death without fear. To him it is a quiet sleep, and the resurrection draws nigh. Then, glorified in soul and body, the companion of angels and saints, strong in immortal youth, he will serve, without let or hindrance, the God and Saviour whom he loves.

How different from this sublime hope is the belief of the Hindu! His great effort—if he has embraced the Vedanta philosophy—is to persuade himself that he is, even at present, identified with

Brahm, and to get rid of all conscious existence. And the expectation of the ordinary Hindu is that, after passing through almost innumerable births, the soul—like a drop of water mingling with the ocean—will be absorbed or swallowed up, and lost in the One, the immeasurable All.

Again, one of the greatest facts in man's experience is suffering. Hinduism acknowledges this, and gives, as we have seen, a strongly pessimist view of human life. It affirms all suffering to be penal. Many an innocent sufferer has the trials of life fearfully enhanced by this belief.[1] And when death comes to tear from their embrace those whom they love, they sorrow as those 'who have no hope.' Tell the mother who is clinging desperately to the body of her dead child, refusing to part with it, that there is another world in which she may hope to meet that child again, and she will only think you are adding mockery to her woe. No, her belief is this—parted once, parted for ever. No reunion is possible. But when the Christian commits his loved ones to the dust he does so in the full assurance that 'those who sleep in Jesus will God bring with Him.' He calmly waits for a blessed resurrection.

Even so, amid the varied trials of life, Hinduism can supply no comfort; whereas Christ's invitation

[1] For example, young widows (so called, though many of them were never wives), who are subjected to dreadful oppression by Hindu law, often torture themselves with the fear of having committed some horrible offence in a previous birth. Otherwise, they ask, how could they be made so miserable?

—His entreaty rather, and command—is this: 'Come unto Me, all ye that labour and are heavy laden, and I will give you rest.' What a marvellous promise! Yet innumerable breaking hearts have put it to the test, and found it true.

Of the 'enthusiasm of humanity,'—the holy passion of philanthropy,—Hinduism can, of course, know nothing. Its theology declares that good works as well as bad works hinder final salvation. Apathy, cessation from all action, is the natural result. Christianity, on the contrary, exhorts man to action: 'Show me,' it says, 'thy faith by thy works.' The Christian is to be a worker for God—ay, a fellow-worker with God. Hence Christianity, when true to her original, continually strives to teach the ignorant, to comfort the sorrowful, and to recall the erring to God and goodness. She scorns not the meanest, she despairs not regarding the vilest, of the human race. Every individual soul is precious, and must be lovingly and perseveringly dealt with, if haply it will turn and live.

These remarks are lengthening out too much, and we must touch with a rapid pen what yet remains.

There are very striking declarations in the Bible regarding the connection between Christ and His true followers. This is represented as far more than communion; it is actual union. He is in them; they are in Him. He is the Vine; they are the branches. He is the Head of the body; they are the members. The union is generally expressed in figurative language; but it is nevertheless a fact. 'I live,' said the Apostle Paul, 'yet not I, Christ liveth in me.' We cannot possibly attempt an explanation here of this wondrous union. We content ourselves with noting that there is no conception in the Sastras which at all resembles it. Both philosophical and religious teaching in India often refer to connection between the deity and the worshipper; but it is not a union of spirit with spirit which they assert, but a personal identification of the divine and human,—pantheism in the strictest sense.

We have not in Hinduism any doctrine which resembles the grand conception of the Church—whether the Church visible, or the Church invisible. Nor have we anything like the sublime doctrine of the indwelling of the Holy Spirit in the individual members, and in the united body of believers.

We have had occasion to speak of caste—which is a main characteristic of Hinduism—in terms of strong reprobation. It is utterly foreign to Christianity. We saw above how the Old Testament inculcated a feeling of brotherhood which should link Israelite to Israelite, and, so far as the selfish passions of the human heart allowed, make the nation one great family. In the New Testament the view is widened, and the family is to consist of all believing men of all nations. 'In Christ there is neither Greek nor Jew, Barbarian, Scythian, bond nor free; neither male nor female.' All believers are equal in the Father's sight,—all are brethren. Nay, the feeling must overpass the limits of the professing Church; we are commanded to 'add to brotherly kindness, charity'—that is, a love co-extensive with the human race. What is, if possible, more remarkable still, Christians are commanded to 'honour all men.' Respect must be paid to man as man; and, while we mourn over the fall of those who have surrendered themselves to evil, we must hopefully labour for their recovery.

We have been speaking of the great moral blemishes of Hinduism. Of less importance, but still notable enough, is its opposition to scientific truth. The Sastras do not refer to science incidentally; they formally teach it—that is, they communicate, as authoritatively revealed from heaven, such science as existed at the times in which they were written. And, so doing, they go continually astray.[1]

The Christian Scriptures, as we have mentioned, come—if they ever do come—on scientific questions only incidentally; they never authoritatively state them. This reticence is truly remarkable. All other writers of the first century blunder perpetually in questions of science. Thus Josephus

[1] Thus, in astronomy, the planets are said to be nine in number. The sun is one of them, and Rahu and Ketu (the ascending and descending nodes) are also planets, and cause eclipses by swallowing the sun and moon. The sun is nearer us than the moon. In the works called Siddhantas a different system of astronomy is taught; but it is the Ptolemaic, not the Copernican. We must not waste time by detailing the geography. It represents the world as composed of seven concentric islands or continents, which are surrounded by as many oceans, consisting respectively of wine, clarified butter, milk, fresh water, etc.

the Jewish historian, Greek and Roman authors, and the Christian Fathers, all introduce scientific matter, and necessarily go wrong. This makes the silence of the New Testament the more wonderful and significant.

Nor is it only on matters of science that this majestic silence is maintained. Even in connection with religion there are many questions that the Hindu Sastras largely discuss, on which Christianity preserves an exceeding reticence. Whatever bears on man's necessities and duties is inscribed in characters of light on the pages of the Bible; but whatever is purely speculative and fitted only to gratify curiosity is carefully withheld. Hinduism revels in physical descriptions of heaven and hell. The Bible plainly states their existence, but does not describe either the physical enjoyments of the one or the physical sufferings of the other; and, when it refers to these things, it does so almost exclusively in figurative language.

Finally, one striking feature of the Hindu books is the way in which good and evil are strangely mingled in them. It would be quite possible to make a selection of sentiments from the Sastras which would command respect and even admiration. But, in the original, it happens in cases innumerable that a true thought is linked with falsehood, and a pure sentiment stands side by side with one that is dishonourable or disgusting. Max Müller says that he has long tried in vain to explain this strange inconsistency. The learned professor has a much higher idea than we have of 'what India can teach us;' but even he confesses that the Sastras contain 'much that is not only unmeaning, artificial, and silly, but even hideous and repellent.'

Of the Christian Scriptures we need only say, in the words of the Psalmist, 'The words of the Lord are pure words, as silver tried in a furnace of earth, purified seven times.'

NOTES.

HYMNS OF THE VEDA.

We have given various quotations from the Veda; but lest it should be said that detached paragraphs give no proper idea of the work, it may be well to subjoin an entire hymn. We select the first in the Rig Veda, as translated by Prof. H. H. Wilson.

The hymn is addressed to Agni, or Fire—

1. I glorify Agni, the high priest of the Sacrifice, the divine, the ministrant, who presents the oblation [to the gods], and is the possessor of great wealth.
2. May that Agni who is to be celebrated by both ancient and modern Sages conduct the gods hither.
3. Through Agni the worshipper obtains that affluence which increases day by day, which is the source of fame and the multiplier of mankind.
4. Agni, the unobstructed Sacrifice of which thou art on every side the protector, assuredly reaches the gods.
5. May Agni, the presenter of oblations, the attainer of knowledge, he who is true, renowned, and divine, come hither with the gods.
6. Whatever good thou mayest, Agni, bestow upon the giver [of the oblation], that verily, Angiras, shall revert to thee.
7. We approach thee, Agni, with reverential homage in our thoughts daily, both morning and evening;

8. Thee, the radiant, the protector of sacrifices, the constant illuminator of truth, increasing in thine own dwelling.
9. Agni, be unto us easy of access, as a father is to his son; be ever present with us for our good.

But as a prose version necessarily gives an imperfect idea of any hymn, we subjoin part of a metrical translation of a hymn addressed to the winds (Maruts). The version is Prof. Whitney's, who follows Roth's metrical version in Cerman, with a few slight changes—[1]

THE POET SPEAKS:

1. Upon what course are entered now together,
Of common age, of common home, the Maruts?
With what desire, and whence, have they come hither?
The heroes make their whistling heard for longing.
2. Whose prayers and praises are the youths enjoying?
Say, who hath turned the Maruts to his offering?
As they go roving through the air like falcons,
How shall we stay them with our strong devotion?

THE MARUTS SPEAK:

How comes it, Indra, that thou goest lonely,
Though else so blithe? Tell us what ails thee, master.
Thou'rt wont to talk with us as we go onward;
Lord of the coursers, what hast thou against us?

INDRA SPEAKS:

I love the prayers, the wishes, the libations;
The odours rise; the Soma-press is ready;
They draw and win me with their invocation;
My coursers here carry me forward to them.

Whereupon the winds offer to go with him; but Indra rather testily complains that, though eager to join him in feasting, they had let him formerly go forth alone to slay the demon. But they flatter him; and he expresses pleasure. Finally

THE POET SPEAKS AGAIN:

Wh(hath exalted you like us, ye Maruts?
As ıriends go forth to friends, so come ye hither.
Ye bright ones, fan to ardour our devotions;
Of these my pious labours be ye heedful.

[1] *Oriental and Linguistic Studies*, p. 144.

This is your praise, and this your song, O Maruts!
Made by Mandāra's son, the singer Mānya.
Come hither with refreshment for our strength'ning!
May we win food and meadows rich in water!

Of the poetical merit of such hymns we shall leave the reader to form his own opinion. As to their religious character, it is evident that they are devoid of all true spiritual feeling.

THE GAYATRI.

The most holy prayer—if prayer it be—occurring in the Veda is called the Gayatri. The name is derived from the metre in which it is composed. It is thus rendered by Prof. H. H. Wilson—

We meditate on that desirable light of the divine Savitri, who influences our pious rites.[1]

Prof. Monier Williams translates it—

Let us meditate (or, we meditate) on that excellent glory of the divine Vivifier. May he enlighten (or stimulate) our understandings.

This prayer is repeated by Brahmans many times every morning and evening, and also at noon. It can hardly be omitted in any important rite. The Gayatri is clearly a prayer to the sun, or rather a meditation on him.

THE ATHARVA VEDA.

There has recently been discovered in Kashmir a text of the Atharva Veda, which is considerably different from the one hitherto known. It contains a greater mass of matter, liturgical and legendary, and abounds more in charms and incantations. Dr. Roth holds that this is very probably the genuine text of the Atharvana; and that the shorter text is only an expurgated edition of the original. If the opinion of this distinguished scholar be correct—and that it is so can hardly be matter of doubt—then still stronger expressions of censure are required than those which we have used in our references to the poor, low, magical character of the fourth Veda.[2]

[1] Rig V. iii. 62, 10.

[2] See the *Report of the Congresso Internazionale dei Orientalisti, Firenze*, 1878, p. 89.

THE UPANISHADS.

We submit one or two specimens of these compositions. We select from the Chhandogya Upanishad a very celebrated passage, beginning with the text which Keshub Chunder Sen continually quoted as teaching monotheism. This was assuredly a mistake ; it asserts absolute pantheism.

'In the beginning, my dear, there was that only which is, one only, without a second. Others say, in the beginning there was that only which is not, one only, without a second ; and from that which is not that which is was born.

'But how could it be thus, my dear?' the father continued. 'How could that which is be born of that which is not? No, my dear ; only that which is was in the beginning, one only, without a second.

'It thought, may I be many—may I grow forth. It sent forth fire. That fire thought, may I be many, may I grow forth. It sent forth water. And therefore whenever anybody anywhere is hot and perspires, water is produced on him from fire alone.

'Water thought, may I be many, may I grow forth. It sent forth earth (food). Therefore, whenever it rains anywhere, most food is then produced. From water alone is eatable fruit produced.' [1]

But let us select a portion of an Upanishad which has been rendered into verse. We take Prof. Monier Williams's rendering of part of the important Isa Upanishad—

Whatever exists within this universe
Is all to be regarded as enveloped
By the great Lord, as if wrapped in a vesture.
There is one only being who exists,
Unmoved, yet moving swifter than the mind ;
Who far outstrips the senses, though as gods
They strive to reach him ; who, himself at rest,
Transcends the fleetest flight of other beings,
Who, like the air, supports all vital action.
He moves, yet moves not ; he is far, yet near.

(It would be more literal to substitute in these lines *it* for *he* and *him*, and *which* for *who*.)

[1] Chhandogya Upanishad ; Prapathaka 6 ; Khanda 2 (see *Sacred Books of the East*. Upanishads, Part I.).

THE CODES OF LAW.

The *Manava Dharma Sastra* (Law Book of Manu) has attracted attention ever since it was rendered into English by Sir W. Jones. His Hindu friends assured him that it was the basis of all sacred law in India, having been dictated by a divine being, Manu, at the creation of the world. It is now held to be a late redaction of the usages of a particular *gens*, or clan, the Manavas. Its date has been, and still is matter of high dispute. Sir William Jones believed it might be as ancient as 1280 years B.C. The late Dr. Burnell contended that, even in its original form, it was not composed before 400 A.D. The date we have assigned (p. 85) may provisionally be accepted as more probable than either of these extremes.

As to the mode in which law was developed in India, Sir H. Sumner Maine compares it to what would have happened in Western Europe if the Canonists had gained a complete ascendency over common lawyers and civilians. In that case, Western law would have been 'deeply tinged in all its parts with ecclesiastical ideas,' as all Hindu legislation is.[1]

We have referred to the two great codes of Manu and of Yajnavalkya. There is another code, but later and of less importance—that ascribed to Parasara.

VIRODHA BHAKTI.

One of the most singular modes of dealing with the gods is what is called *Virodha bhakti*—literally, antagonistic worship. The deity is reviled, defied, or, it may be, beaten. He is thus either compelled to grant the worshipper (!) his request, or else he is provoked and destroys the daring wretch. In the latter case the votary is absorbed into deity, or, at all events, is translated to heaven.

I am not sure whether we can bring under this head the not unfrequent habit of ridiculing the gods. In Western India the following satire on the awkward figure of Ganesa is very well known—

[1] *Early Law and Custom*, p. 44.

Poor Ganpati bewails his rat,
Borne off by vile felonious cat;
'My legs are short; how can I trudge?
And how shall this big belly budge?'

Ganapati, or Ganesa, it must be noted, usually rides on a rat.

MODERN BRAHMANICAL WORSHIP.

This ritual has become, in the lapse of ages, immensely complicated. A full description would be intolerably tedious. The following statements will suffice.

We speak first of worship in the temple. In the case of the god Siva the rites are as follows—

The Brahman first bathes, then enters the temple, and bows to the god. He anoints the image with clarified butter or boiled oil; pours pure water over it, and then wipes it dry. He grinds some white powder, mixing it with water; dips the ends of his three fore-fingers in it, and draws them across the image. He sits down, meditates, places rice and *durwa* grass on the image—places a flower on his own head, and then on the top of the image; then another flower on the image, and another, and another—accompanying each act with the recitation of sacred spells; places white powder, flowers, *bilwa* leaves, incense, meat-offerings, rice, plantains, and a lamp before the image; repeats the name of Siva with praises, then prostrates himself before the image. In the evening he returns, washes his feet, prostrates himself before the door, opens the door, places a lamp within, offers milk, sweetmeats, and fruits to the image, prostrates himself before it, locks the door, and departs.

Very similar is the worship paid to Vishnu—

The priest bathes, and then awakes the sleeping god by blowing a shell and ringing a bell. More abundant offerings are made than to Siva. About noon, fruits, roots, soaked peas, sweetmeats, etc., are presented. Then later, boiled rice, fried herbs, and spices; but no flesh, fish, nor fowl. After dinner, betel nut. The god is then left to sleep, and the temple is shut up for some hours. Towards evening curds, butter, sweetmeats, fruits, are presented. At sunset a lamp is brought, and fresh offerings made. Lights are waved before the image; a small bell is rung; water is presented for washing the mouth, face, and feet—with a towel to dry them. In a few minutes the offerings and the lamp are removed : and the god is left to sleep in the dark.[1]

The prescribed worship is not always fully performed. Still, sixteen things are essential, of which the following are the most important—

1st. Preparing a seat for the god, invoking his presence, bathing the image, clothing it, putting the string round it, offering perfumes, flowers, incense, lamps, offerings of fruits and prepared eatables, betel nut, prayers, circumambulation. An ordinary worshipper presents some of the offerings, mutters a short prayer or two, when circumambulating the image ; the rest being done by the priest.[2]

We give one additional specimen of the ritual—

As an atonement for unwarily eating or drinking what is forbidden, eight hundred repetitions of the Gayatri prayer should be preceded by three suppressions of the breath, water being touched during the recital of the following text : 'The bull roars ; he has four horns, three feet, two heads, seven hands ; and is bound by a three-fold cord ; he is the mighty, resplendent being, and pervades mortal men.'[3]

The 'bull' is understood to be justice personified.

All Brahmanical ceremonies exhibit, we may say, ritualism and symbolism run mad.

The prescribed forms of worship out of the temple are equally minute. We extract a few things from the very lengthened statement by Colebrooke—

On rising, the Brahman rubs his teeth with a twig of a particular fig-tree, praying. If no proper twig be procurable, he rinses his mouth twelve times with water. He then bathes, in a river if possible. He sips water, sprinkles some water before him, utters three prescribed prayers, throws water eight times on his head, or towards the sky, and concludes by throwing water on the ground to destroy demons. He plunges thrice in the stream, repeating sacred texts, washes his mantle, puts it on, and sits down to worship the rising sun. He ties the lock of hair on the crown of his head, recites the Gayatri prayer, holding much

[1] We have condensed this statement from Ward. The description applies chiefly to Bengal.

[2] So writes Van Kennedy, a good authority. The rites, however, vary somewhat with varying places.

[3] *Asiatic Researches*, V. p. 356.

kusa grass in his left and three blades of it in his right hand, or wearing a ring of it on the third finger of the right. He thrice sips water, repeating the Gayatri, each time rubbing his hands as if washing them, finally touching with his wet hand his feet, head, breast, eyes, ears, nose, and navel. If he happen to sneeze or spit, he must touch his right ear; 'for,' saith the legislator Parasara, 'fire, water, the Vedas, the sun, moon, and air, all reside in the right ears of Brahmans.' Impurity is removed by the touch. He closes his eyes and meditates on Brahma, Vishnu and Siva. He then meditates the Gayatri, during three suppressions of breath. Closing the left nostril with the two longest fingers of his right hand, he breathes through the right nostril. Then closing likewise that nostril with his thumb, he holds his breath, while he meditates the Gayatri; then he removes both fingers from the left nostril and emits the breath he had suppressed. He sips water and prays; throws, as before, water eight times on his head, or towards the sky, and once on the ground, and prays. He fills the palm of his hand with water, holds it to his nose, draws in the fluid by one nostril, retains it for ome time, then expels it by the other nostril towards the north-east. Sips again and prays. Worships the sun, standing on one foot, resting the other against his ankle or heel, and looking towards the east. Prays. The Gayatri is invoked, and then it is inaudibly muttered a hundred or a thousand times, the repetitions being counted on a rosary; etc., etc., etc.[1]

We really must pause for the reader's sake and our own; but the description of morning worship is only half finished.

It will afford room for earnest reflection to note that an intellectual race like the Brahmans should have prescribed, and largely practised, observances so utterly childish and fantastic, deeming them worship acceptable to heaven.

THE BRAHMO SOMAJ.

The most recent accounts of the Brahmo Somaj do not indicate any approximation towards each other of the three parties into which it has divided. Mr. P. C. Mozumdar writes: 'Most unfortunately there is so much personal rancour, such exclusiveness and embittered party feeling still in them all, that I see as little hope of future harmony and progress in one as in the others.' He adds: 'I will, for that reason, have no Somaj of my own.'

[1] *Asiatic Researches*, vol. v. p. 345, etc., or *Colebrooke's Essays* (edited by Cowell), vol. ii. p. 141.

INDEX.

In the following list of words, the vowels *a*, *e*, *i*, *o*, *u*, and the diphthongs *ai* and *au*, are to be pronounced as in Italian—very nearly as in the following words:—f*a*ther, th*e*re, pol*i*ce, t*o*ne, r*u*le, a*i*sle, *ou*t (English), or *au*s (German). The mark (–) denotes that the vowel is long. The chief difficulty in the case of the vowels is with the letter *a*, when short. It then sounds nearly as in *A*meric*a*.

The consonants *d*, *dh*, *t*, *th*, *l*, *n*, make the tongue strike the teeth. In *ḍ*, *ḍh*, *ṭ*, *ṭh*, *ḷ*, *ṇ*, it strikes the roof of the mouth.

Ś is pronounced as in the English word *sure*. Thus the often-recurring word *Śāstra* sounds as if written *shāstra*. *Ph* always is as in u*p*-*h*ill, *th* is as in no*t*-*h*ere.

ADITI, worship of, 29.
Age of Truth, 121.
Aghorīs, sect of, 161.
Agni, the Fire, worship of, 26.
Ahura, or Ahura mazdā = Varuṇa Asura, 30, 265.
Ahura mazdā, 30, 265.
Ahrimān (Āngro-mainyus), 265.
Ākāśmukhīs, sect of, 162.
Akbar (emperor), 171.
Akshapada, 53.
Alandī (village), 170.
Amara Sinha, 133.
Anna Perenna, 204.
Anugītā, 130.
Apollonius of Tyana, 171.
Apostolic Durbar (so-called), the, reverence of, for Mr. Sen, 241.
Araṇyakas, the, or 'forest treatises,' third part of a Veda, 16.
Arjuna, story of, 74, 128.
Arjunmall, the Sikh guru, 166.
Ārya Samāj, the, 245.
Aryans, probable date of entrance of, into India, 19; original faith of, 22.
Asceticism in Upanishads, 54.
Aśoka tree, worship of, 186.
Aśoka, Emperor of India, 103.
Astronomy (Hindu), 275.
Aśvamedha, the, sacrifice of the horse, 38.
Aśvinas, the two, worship of, 27.
Atharva V., the contents of, 18; recently discovered recension of, 282.

Atheistic propaganda in India, 249.
Augustine, 65.
Avalī, wife of Tukārāma, story of, 183.
Avatāras, or Descents, the, 107.
Avestā, the, worship taught in, 28.

Bābā Lālīs, sect of, 167.
Baba Padmanji, Rev., 160.
Bādārāyaṇa, 53.
Bali, legend of King, 112.
Bali pratipadā, feast of, 208.
Banyan tree, worship of, 185.
Barth on the Veda, 40; on the Yoga, 64.
Bentinck, Lord William, 93.
Bergaigne on Varuṇa and Indra, 24.
Berkeley, Bishop, 61.
Bhagavad Gītā, the, date of, 72; author of, 73; the story of, 74; dialogue between Arjuna and Kṛishṇa, 74; teachings of, 75; contradictions of, 77; glories in caste, 77; exaltation of Kṛishṇa, 77; language of, resembles the Bible, 78; theory of Dr. Lorinser, 79; judgment of M. Cousin on, 80; probable influence of Christianity on, 118.
Bhakti, or devotion, doctrine of, 154.
Bhakti Sūtras, 155.
Bhakta-Mālā, the, contents of, 172.
Bhaṭ, or Brahman priest, 179.
Bhīma, strength of, 127.
Bhīmā river, 168.
Birth-pollution, extent of, 262.
Blavatsky, Madame, opinions of, 248.
Boar, Vishnu becomes a, 111.
Brahmā, duration of life of, 122.
Brahma, or Brahman, and Brahmā, distinction between, 66.
Brāhmaṇ, the necessity of the, 41; pride and usurpations of, 42; education of, 42; position of, 86; supremacy of, 87; life of, 89.
Brāhmaṇa, the second part of a Veda, 16; description of, 35; date of, 35; no temple worship, 36; worship, personal or social, 36; consisted of offerings, prayer, and praise, 37; sacrifice of the horse, 38; of human beings, 38; ideas connected with sacrifice, 38.
Brāhmaṇaspati, the lord of prayer, 32.
Brahmanism, development of, 84; supremacy of, 87; struggle of, with Buddhism, 95.
Brahmo Somaj (properly Brāhma Samāj), formation of, 225; full organization of, 227; Mr. Sen separates from, 229; decline of, 229.
Brahmo Somaj of India, formation of, 229; services of, 230; revolt from, 232; *see* New Dispensation, 233.
Brahmo Somaj of S. India, the, formation of, 244.
Bṛihaspati, the guru of the gods, 82.
Buddha, date of death of, 99; teachings of; 99; tenderness of, 100; character of, 102;

counsels of, 103; brotherhood taught by, 104; an incarnation of Vishṇu, 108.
Buddhism, philosophy of, 101; atheism of, 102; faults of, 102; superiority of, 103; missionary spirit of, 103; contest of, with Brahmanism, 103; defeat of, 104; persecution of, 105; disappearance of, from India, 105; influence of, 107.
Bühler on codes of law, 85.
Burnouf, on the Hindu mind, 81.
Butler, Archer, on Hindu philosophy, 81.
Byron (quoted), 27.

CARO (quoted), 53.
Caste, incubus of, 77.
—— tyranny of, 88.
—— in Travancore, 200.
Castrén, 23.
Castes, the four regular, 86.
Chalmers (Rev. Dr.), 226.
Champā shashtī, feast of, 209.
Chaitanya and his followers, 152.
Chārvākas, the, teachings of, 81.
Cicero on transmigration, 138.
Coleridge on ritualism, 36.
Comte, influence of, on India, 247.
Conway, Mr. Moncure, estimate of Hinduism by, 220.
Cousin, M., judgment of, on the Gītā, 80.
Colebrooke, 286.
Cowell (Prof.), 59.
Cow, five products of the, a means of purification, 195.
Custard apple, worship of, 186.

DĀDŪ Panthīs, sect of, 167.
Daemon, 33.
Daṇḍaka forest, the, 115.
Daṇḍīs, sect of, 160.
Darśanas, the six, list of, 55; the Sūtras, 55; pairs of, 56; contradictions of, 57; the Nyāya system, 58; the Vaiśeshika system, 59; refinement of Hindu schools, 60; the Sānkhya system, 60; doings of Prakṛiti, 61; the system of Kapila, 62; the Yoga philosophy, 62; the Mīmānsā, 64; the Vedānta philosophy, 65; influence of Śankara Achārya, 65; four conditions of the soul, 67; necessity of knowledge, 67; importance of meditation, 67; contradictions of, 68; ethical character of the Vedānta, 69: summary of, 70; points of agreement in, 70.
Darśanas, the six, description of, 13.
Daśaratha, King of Ayodhyā, or Oude, legend of, 114.
Dasnāmīs, sect of, 160.
Daśyus, 86.
Dayānanda Sarasvati, history of, 245.
Dead, ceremonies connected with the, 33, 197, 198.
Debendernath Tagore, history of, 227.
De Quincey (quoted), 4[illegible].
Dalton, 59.
Democritus, 59.
Deva (god), etymology of, 33.
Devakī, mother of Krishṇa, 116.

Devotion, or bhakti, doctrine of, 154.
Dhṛitarāshtra, father of the Kauravas, 125.
Draupadī, story, 125.
Dravidian race, the, civilization of, 20.
Diwālī, feast of, 208.
Drupada, King, 125.
Droṇa, the tutor, 125.
Duff, Dr., friendship of, for Rammohun Roy, 226.
Durgā (goddess), 142.
Duryodhana, plots of, 126.
Dussera, or Daśaharā, feast of, 207.
Dvāpara Yuga, the, 122.

EARTH, the (Pṛithivī), worship of, 28, 29.
Education, spread of, 251.
Ekamevādvitīyam, 66, 68.

FAKIR, meaning of the term, 162.
Feasts and Fasts—
 Makar Sankrānti, 202.
 Mahāśivàratri, 203.
 Holī, 203.
 Rāma navamī, 205.
 Nāga panchami, 205.
 Nārali paurnimā, 205.
 Kṛishṇa, or Gokul, Janmashṭamī, 206.
 Ganeśa chaturthī, 206.
 Dussera, or Daśaharā, 207.
 Diwālī, 208.
 Bali pratipadā, 209.
 Champā shashṭī, 209.
Female deities, 29.
Fish, worship of, 110.
Fliedner, Pastor (quoted), 100.
Forest life in India, 45.
Four ages of the world, the doctrine of, 121.
Funeral rites, 197.

GAMBLING, legislation respecting, 95.
Ganges, 41.
Gaṇapati or Ganeśa, 206.
Gaṇapatyas, 147.
Ganeśa chaturthī, feast of, 206.
Gangāputra, duties of, 193.
Gāyatrī, the, 282.
Gautama—(philosopher), 55.
Gautama (legislator), 197.
Geography, Hindu, 275.
Gopīs and Kṛishṇa, legend of, 117.
Goldstücker on Purāṇas, 40, 135.
Go-swāmī or Gosāvī, a, description of, 162.
Gospel of the Infancy, the Arabic, description of, 79.
Gough, 51, 54, 67.
Govarddhana, the mountain, legend of, 117.
Govind, the Sikh guru, 166.
Granth, sacred book of the Sikhs, 165, 167.
Gurava, the, work of, 181.
Guru, the exaltation of, 157; training of, 158.

HADRIAN'S address to his soul, 140.
Haug, Dr., 31.
Hanumān the monkey, legend of, 115.
Heaven, ancient worship of, 23.
Heber, Bishop, 101, 154.

Hegel (quoted), 76.
Hinduism, antiquity of, 10; approaching end of, 10; spirit in which it should be studied, 11; to be fairly treated, 12; to be studied chronologically, 12; the Śāstras, 13; the four Vedas, 13; the six Darśanas, 13; the eighteen Purāṇas, 13; direct and indirect revelation, 13; Śruti, 14; Smṛiti, 14; Sanskrit dramatic literature, 14; the Tantras, 14; uncertainty of Hindu canon, 15; reconstruction of, 106.
Hinduism, modern, number of followers, 174; belief, 175; worship, 175; number of idols, 176; a village Brahman, 177; a company of pilgrims, 178; duties of the Bhaṭ or Brahman priest, 179; ceremony of *tīrtha*, 180; of *pitṛi paksh*, 180; duties of the gurava, 181; the gods' house, 182; idol worship, 182; fetishism, 183; other objects of worship, 185; pantheism, 187; conception of sin, 188; means of purification, 191; pilgrimages, 191; holy places, 191; numbers of pilgrims, 192; ceremonies of purification, 193; evils of pilgrimages, 194; eating the five products of the cow, 195; ten purifying rites, 196; funeral rites, 197; offerings to ancestors, 198; importance of male descendants, 199; rules of caste, 199; means of defilement, 200; Brahman pretensions, 200; feasts and fasts, 202; Makar Sankrānti, 202; Mahāśivarātri, 203; Holī, 203; Rāma navamī, 205; Nāga panchamī, 205; Nāraḷi paurnimā, 205; Kṛishṇa, or Gokul, Janmāshtamī, 206; Ganeśa chaturthī, 206; Dussera, or Daśaharā, 207; Diwālī, 208; Bali pratipadā, 209; Champā shashṭi, 209.
Hinduism compared with Christianity: size of the Śāstras and the Bible, 254; contents of, 254; diversities of, 255; rise of Buddhism, 255; inconsistency of Hinduism, 256; unity of the Bible, 257; monotheism of the Bible, 257; character of God, 257; idolatry, 258; God in history, 259; thoughts, not facts, 259; facts of the Bible, 259; sacerdotalism, 260; prophecy, 260; the Bible a book of hope, 261; Hindu books despairing, 261; summary of duty, 262; the Sabbath, 262; legislation of Moses and Manu compared, 262; curse of caste, 263; Mosaic land laws, 263; position of woman, 264; polygamy, 264; ceremonial systems, 265; sacrifices, 266; New Testament history, 268; the Incarnations (avatāras), 268; teachings of Christ, 269; character of Christ, 269; testimony of Lecky to Christianity, 270; differences as to views of sin, 271;

atonement, 272; pardon, 272; hopes of the Christian, 273; belief of the Hindu, 273; suffering, 274; comfort, 274; philanthropy, 275; union of Christ with His followers, 275; brotherhood of Christians, 276; science, 277; inconsistency of the Śāstras, 278; God's Word pure, 279.
Hindus in Northern India, life of, 95.
Hiraṇyaksha, legend of, 111.
Holī, feast of, 203.
Homa of the Iranians, connected with Soma of the Hindus, 30.
Horse, sacrifice of the, 38.
Hymns of Rig V., 18.
Hymns, the, contents of, 39; language of, 41; confessions of ignorance in, 47; speculations on the origin of the world, 47.

IDOLS, amazing number of, 176.
India and the West, intercourse between, 72.
Indra, conception of, 24; character of, 25; his love of Soma, 37; anger of, against Kṛishṇa, 117.
Islām, influence of, in India, 163.
Iśwara, the supreme ruler, 62.

JACOLLIOT, M., 120.
Jaimini, 53.
Jainism, 157.
Jumna river, 31.
Jamshid (king), 33.
Jayadeva (poet), 156.
Janaka, King of Mithilā, legend of, 115.
Jangamas, sect of, 161.

KABĪR, story of, 163; theft of, 173.
Kabirism, doctrines of, 163.
Kālī (goddess), worship of, 142, 265.
Kali Yuga, the, 122.
Kālidāsa (quoted), 186, 195, 199.
Kalkī avatāra, the, 121.
Kalpa, a, length of, 122.
Kānhobā, 206.
Kansa, king of Mathurā, legend of, 116.
Kapila, the philosophy of, 62.
Karma, 102.
Karsandas Mulji, 151.
Kartābhaja sect, the, 154.
Kauravas, the, wars of, 125.
Keshub Chunder Sen, history of, 228; separates from Somaj, 229; forms new Brahmo Somaj, 229; services of, 230; visit of, to Britain, 230; autocracy of, 231; marriage of daughter of, 232; revolt from, 232; forms the New Dispensation, 233; on the claims of Christ, 234; creed of the New Dispensation, 235; ritualism of, 236; proclamation of, 236; the 'Flag Ceremony,' 236; the fire ceremony, 237; introduces two sacraments, 237; last lecture by, 238; conversation with, 239; references of, to missionaries, 240; reverence for m mory of, 241.

Khaṇḍobā, 209.
Kolarian race, the, civilization of, 20.
Kṛishṇa, story of, 74, 128; exaltation of, 77; Vishṇu, incarnated as, 116; legend of, 116; popularity of, 118; evil influence of, 119; death of, 120.
Kṛishṇa, or Gokul, Janmashṭamī, feast of, 206.
Krishna Mohun Banerjea, Rev., 224.
Kṛita or Satya Yuga, the, 121.
Kshatriya caste, the, 86.
Kural, 75.
Kurtz (quoted), 265.
Kurukshetra, battle of, 127.
Kuśa grass, worship of, 186.
Kusumānjali, 58.

Lakshmī (goddess), 142.
Lassen, 72.
Lecky, testimony of, to Christianity, 270.
Linga or phallus, worship of, 138.
Lorinser, Dr., theory of, on the Bh. Gītā, 79.

M (letter) in the worship of Śakti, 144.
Mādhavācharya sect, the, 151.
Mahābhārata, the, extent of, 124; subject of, 125; wars between Pāṇḍavas and Kauravas, 125; influence of, on Hindus, 130; on the Yavanas (Greeks or Greco-Bactrians), 72.
Mahārājas, worship of, 150.
Mahāśivarātri, feast of, 203.
Mahipati, 169, 171, etc.
Maine, Sir H. S. (quoted), 284.
Makar Sankrānti, feast of, 202.
Man-lion, a, Vishnu becomes, 111.
Mantra or Sanhitā, first part of a Veda, 16.
Manu, the code of, 85; date of, 85; caste, tyranny of, 87; legend of, 110.
Manwantaras, 133.
Marāṭhī literature, 168.
Marshman, Dr., 224.
Māruti, 176.
Maruts, or Storm-winds, the, worship of, 28.
Māyā, 67.
Mendicants, religious, list of, 162.
Mīmānsā, the system of, 64.
Mīmānsā, Purva, 55, 56.
Mīmānsā, Uttara, 56.
Mīrābāī (princess), 178.
Missionaries from God, 271.
Mitṛa (light of day), 30.
Mithra (in Zend) = Mitra, 30.
Moon, the, worship of, 28.
Muir, Dr. J., his opinions of Vedic theology, 21.
Mukuṇḍrāj, 177.
Mozumdar, Mr. P. C., opinions of, 241, 287.
Müller, Max (quoted), 93, 213, 279.

Nābhājī, 172.
Nāga panchamī, feast o., 205.
Nāgārjuna, 101.
Nāmadeva, writings of, 168.
Nāmbūrī Brahmans, 200.
Nānak, history of, 165.

Nanda, the herdsman, legend of, 116.
Nāralī paurnima, feast of, 205.
Pāṇḍavas, 128.
New Dispensation, the, formation of, 233; creed of, 235; ritualism of, 236; a proclamation, 236; the Flag Ceremony, 236; fire ceremony, 237; introduction of two sacraments, 237; recent language of, 240.
Nihilism, 101.
Nyāya system of philosophy, the, 58.

Olcott, Colonel, 248.
Om, meaning of the word, 136.
Ordeal, trial by, 94.

Panchagavya, 195.
Pāṇḍavas and Kauravas, the war between, 74, 125.
Paṇḍharpūr, pilgrimage to, 168.
Pāndurang, Mr. D., forms Parama hansa sabhā, 242.
Panjāb (Punjaub), 19.
Panjāb, the, Aryans in, 19.
Parker, Theodore, 228.
Parvatī (goddess), 142.
Parama hansa sabhā, formation of, 242.
Paramahansas, sect of, 161.
Paraśurāma, legend of, 88; Vishnu, incarnated as, 113.
Parāśara, code of, 284.
Pārsī mode of purification, 196.
Patanjali, 53.
Philostr‸tus, 171.
Pilgrimages, growth of, 191; places of, the Indies, 191; the Sarasvati, 191; Benares, 191; Prayāg (Allahabad), 192; Haridwār (or Har-dwār), 192; Gangā Sagar, 192; Purī, 192; Dwārakā, 192; Nāsīk, 192; Paṇḍharpūr, 192; Rāmeśvar, 192; Somnāth, 192; Omkār, 192; Badarī Kedār, 192; Tryambak, 192; Tīrthas, or holy places, 191; evils of, 194.
Pipal (*Ficus religiosa*), worship of, 185.
Pitṛi paksh, ceremony of, 180.
Pitṛis or Fathers, worship of, 33.
Plato, 51.
Prahlāda, legend of, 111.
Prajāpaṭi, 39.
Prakṛiti, doings of, 61; union of, with Purush, 61.
Prāṇa nāthīs, sect of, 167.
Prārthanā Sabhā, constitution of, 243.
Prārthanā Samāj, the, 243.
Pulayas, 202.
Purāṇas, the eighteen, description of, 13; origin of, 132; list of, 132; subjects of, 133; date of, 134; the Upa-Purāṇas, 134; religion of, 135; deities of, 136; dogma of transmigration, 138.
Purāṇa (Christian), 171.
Purush, union of, with Prakriti, 61.
Pythagoras, 52.

Rāja Nārāyaṇa Basu (Bose), views of, 56.
Rajas, principle of, 61.
Rāma with the axe, Vishṇu incarnated as, 113.
Rāma, or Rāmachandr, Vishṇu

incarnated as, 11 ; legend of, 114.
Rāma, legend of, descent of, 108.
Rāma navami, feast of, 205.
Rāmānanda sect, the, 149.
Rāmānuja sect, the, 148.
Rāmāyaṇa, epic poem, description of, 114; 123 ; contents of, 124.
Rammohun Roy, history of, 224.
Rāvaṇa, King of Ceylon, legend of, 115.
Recapitulation : pre-Vedic religion, 210 ; reverence for the Soma plant, 211 ; Vedic religion, 212 ; deities and worship, 212 ; deterioration, 213 ; the Atharva V., 213 ; ritual, 214 ; the Brāhmaṇa, 214 ; the doctrine of transmigration, 214 ; development of speculation, 215 ; teaching of the Upanishads, 215 ; dualistic system, 216 ; opposing schools of thought, 216 ; philosophy of the Darśanas, 216 ; doctrines of the two Mīmānsās, 217 ; Vedāntism, 217 ; lessons of its philosophy, 218 ; teaching of the Purāṇas, 219 ; the sects, 219 ; worship of the Sakti, 219 ; testimony of Mr. Moncure Conway as to modern Hinduism, 220.
Reforming Sects, the—
Kabīrīs, 163.
Sikhs, 165.
Dādū Panthis, 167.
Bābā Lālīs, 167.
Prāṇa nāthīs, 167.
Śīvā Nārāyaṇīs, 167.
Svāmī Nārāyanīs, 167.
Vaishṇavas of the Marāthā country, 168.
Religions of antiquity, the, extinction of, 9.
Romaka Siddhānta, the, 73.
Runjit Singh, burning of, 94.

SĀDHĀRAṆA Brāhma Samāj, formation of, 232 ; progress of, 241.
Sahuja sect, the, 154.
Śaiva Sects, the—
Daṇḍīs, 160.
Dasnāmīs, 160.
Yogīs, 160.
Jangamas, 161.
Paramahansas, 161.
Aghorīs, 161.
Urdhvabāhus, 161.
Ākāśmukhīs, 162.
Śakti, the (goddess), worship of, 142.
Śāktas, worshippers of Śakti, 143.
Śālagrāma, worship of, 186.
Sāma Veda, contents of, 17.
Sanatsujātīya, 130.
Śāṇḍilya, 155.
Sanhitā, or Mantra, first part of a Veda, 16.
Śankara Achārya, influence of, 65.
Sānkhya system, the, 60.
Sannyāsī, meaning of the word, 162.
Sanskrit works, the number of, 13.
Sarasvatī, the river, life near, 95.
Śāstras, the, description of, 13.
Satī (Suttee), the rite of, 92.
Sattva, principle of, 61.

Sauras, 147.
Seneca on the Jews, 221.
Seven rivers, country of the, 19.
Shelley (quoted), 48.
Sikhs, doctrines of, 165.
Shanars, 179.
Sin, Hindu conception of, 188; means of purification from, 191.
Sītā, wife of Rāma, legend of, 115.
Śiva, worship of, 54.
Śivājī, 169.
Śiva Nārāyaṇīs, sect of, 167.
Smṛiti, or indirect revelation, 14.
Soma of the Hindus, connected with Homa of the Iranians, 30.
Spashtadāyaka sect, the, 154.
Śraddhā, or trust in the deities, 154.
Śrāddha, or ceremonies connected with the dead, 197, etc.
Śrī (goddess), 142.
Sridharalu Naidu, history of, 244
Śruti, or direct revelation, 14.
Storm-winds, the, worship of, 28.
Śūdra caste, the, 86.
Sugrīva, the monkey-king, legend of, 115.
Sun, the, worship of, 27.
Sūtras, the, 55, 85.
Svayamvara, or tournament, 125.
Svāmī Nārāyaṇa sect, the, 153.
Syrian Christians, 79.

TAMAS, principle of, 61.
Tantras, the, authority of, 14; origin and list of, 141; divisions of, 142; teachings of, 142; worship of the Śakti, 142; right-hand and left-hand worshippers, 143; horrible rites for gaining power over evil spirits, 146.
Theosophists in India, 248.
Tīrtha, ceremony of, 180.
Tīrthankara, 157.
Tortoise, a, Vishnu becomes, 110.
Transmigration, doctrine of, in Upanishads, 51; moral characteristics of, 53; origin of, 138.
Travancore, caste tyranny in, 200.
Treta Yuga, the, 122.
Trimurtti, the, or union of the three great gods, 136, 147.
Tsokhā Melā, 172.
Tukārāma, poetry of, 168; history of, 169; quoted, 52, 145, 157, 168.
Tulasī, or holy basil, worship of, 185.

UMĀ, (goddess), 142.
Upanishads, the, age of, 17 meaning of the word, 44; text of, 46; date of, 47; guesses at truth in, 49; sorrow of, 49; pantheistic teaching of, 50; sequence of, 50; practical end of, 51; doctrine of transmigration in, 51; moral characteristics of, 53; asceticism in, 54; worship of Śiva, 54.
Upa-Purāṇas, the, 13, 134.
Urdhvabāhus, sect of, 161.
Ushas, the dawn, worship of, 27, 29.

VAIKUṆṬHA, 168.
Vairāgī (or Byragee), a, description of, 162.
Vaiśeshika philosophy, the, 59.
Vaishṇava Sects, the—
Rāmanūjas, 148.
Rāmanandas, 149.
Vallabhāchāryas, 150.
Mādhavāchāryas, 151.
Chaitanya's followers, 142.
Swāmī Nārāyan, 153.
Kartābhajas, 154.
Spashtadāyakas, 154.
Sahujas, 154.
Vaishṇavas, of the Marāthā country, 168.
Vaiśya caste, the, 86.
Vallabha Achārya, story of, 150.
Vālmīki, poetry of, 114.
Vāmana, Vishnu becomes incarnated as, 112.
Varuṇa, pre-eminence of, 22; same as Ahura, 30.
Varnasankara (mixture of classes) 77.
Vāsudeva, father of Kṛishṇa, 116.
Vāsuki, the serpent, legend of, 111.
Vāyu, the Wind, worship of, 28.
Veda Samāj, the, 244.
Vedānta philosophy, the, 65.
Vedānta Sāra, 66.
Vedas, the four, description of, 13; etymology of name, 16; written in Sanskrit, 16; parts of, 16; Sanhitā, or Mantra, 16; the Brāhmaṇa, 16; the Araṇyaka, 16; Upanishad, 17; age of different parts, 17; names of four divisions of, 17; contents of Sāma V., 17; of Yajur V., 18; of Atharva V., 18; of Rig V., 18; age of the hymns of, 18; diversity of, 18; descriptions of Aryans in, 19; hostility to, 20; invader's curse, 21; nature worship of, 21; contradictions of, 21; original faith of Aryans, 22; pre-eminence of Varuṇa, 22; etymology of, 23; character of Varuṇa, 24; Indra, conception of, 24; declension in religious belief, 26; worship of Agni, the Fire, 26; the Sun, the two Aśviṇas, and Ushas, the Dawn, 27; the Winds, the Earth, the Waters, and the Moon, 28; the homage taught in, 28; number of deities, 28; chaos in pantheon, 29; female deities, 29; triads in, 29; connection between Iranian and Hindu religions, 30; Ahura=Varuṇa Asura, 30; Mithra=Mitra, 30; connection between Soma and Homa, 30; importance of sacrificial fire, libation, and prayer, 32; degradation of gods in Avestā, 32; conflict between Iranians and Indians, 32; worship of, 33; worship of the Pitṛis, 33; contents of Atharva V., 33.
Vetāla, a devil, worship of, 179.
Vishnu, descents of, 107; becomes Buddha, 108, a fish, 110; a tortoise, 110; a boar, 111; a man-lion, 111; a Brahman dwarf, 112; Rāma with the axe, 113; Rāma,

114; Kṛishṇa, 116; popularity of, 118; evil influence of, 119; death of, 120; the Kalkī avatāra, 121.
Viśvāmitra, legend of, 87.
Viveka Sindhu, 177.
Viṭhobā, glory of, 138.
Viṭhṭhal, or Viṭhobā, worship of, 168.
Vṛitra, conflict of, with Indra, 25.
Vyāsa, a mythical personage, 65.

WATERS, the, worship of, 28.
Weber, Prof., 123, 155.
Widow-burning, 92, 224, 264.
Williams, Prof. Monier, 124.
Wilson, Prof. H. H., on Śakti worship, 144; on suttee, 93.
Winds, the, worship of, 28.
Wordsworth (quoted), 48.
Worship (forms of), 285, 287.
Worship (domestic), 211, 212.
Woman, the position of, 86; legislation regarding, 91.
Worship in Vedic times, 36; it had no temple, 36; was personal or social, 36; consisted in offerings, prayer, and praise, 37; offerings of soma, 37; sacrifice of the horse, 38; of human beings, 38; ideas connected with sacrifice, 38; necessity of the Brahman, 41; becomes more elaborate and complex, 43; reaction in, 44.

YĀJNAVALKYA, code of, date of, 94.
Yajur V., contents of, 18; on sacrificial animals, 38.
Yama, 33, 129.
Yamunā river, 41.
Yavanas, the, spoken of, 72.
Yimo, the Ruler (Jamshid), 33.
Yimo = Yama, 33.
Yoga philosophy, the, 55, 62.
Yogīs, sect of, 160.
Yudhishṭhira, a model king, 126.
Yugas, the four, 121.